MEDIUM7

EVIDENCE OF THE AFTERLIFE AND PREDICTIONS

DONNA SMITH-MONCRIEFFE

---

iUniverse, Inc.
Bloomington

MEDIUM7
EVIDENCE OF THE AFTERLIFE AND PREDICTIONS

iUniverse books may be ordered through booksellers or by contacting:

iUniverse
1663 Liberty Drive
Bloomington, IN 47403
www.iuniverse.com
1-800-Authors (1-800-288-4677)

ISBN: 978-1-4759-9033-1 (sc)
ISBN: 978-1-4759-9032-4 (hc)
ISBN: 978-1-4759-9031-7 (e)

Printed in the United States of America.

iUniverse rev. date: 6/19/2013

DEDICATION

I dedicate my research study to my mom and dad, who did everything they could to give me what I needed in life to thrive.

I dedicate this book to my children, Rachael and Brandon, and my husband Andrew. Thanks Andrew for taking care of our lives while I focused on writing this book.

CONTENTS

Author's Note   xv

Acknowledgments   xvii

Foreword   xix

Introduction   xxi

Chapter 1   **Making Sense of It All**   1

    We Are Energy, Everything Is Energy   3

    We Are Vibrational Beings   6

    The Soul Can Survive Physical Death   9

    Reincarnation   10

    The Physical World Is an Illusion   12

    How exactly can these Prerequisites help me understand the Afterlife?   13

Chapter 2   **Understanding Mediumship**   15

    Finding Gifted Mediums   16

    What Is a Medium?   18

    Who Are Mediumistic?   19

    Types of Mediumship   21

    Mental Mediumship   22

    Physical Mediumship   23

Case Study #1: Brough Perkins 26
- *History* 26
- *During the Early Years: Psychic Development* 27
- *Preparation Prior to a Reading* 29
- *How Exactly Does This Work?* 30
- *Postmortem Detailed Knowledge* 33
- *Dual Duty* 35

Case Study #2: Chris Stillar 35
- *History* 36
- *Preparation for a Reading* 38
- *Abilities* 40
- *Dependency* 42

Case Study #3: Carolyn Molnar 43
- *History* 43
- *Early Development* 46
- *Preparation for a Reading* 49
- *Abilities* 51
- *Proof of Spirit at the Church* 52
- *Teachings* 54
- *Discarnates or Guides* 54
- *Being a Responsible Medium* 55
- *Effect on the Physical Body* 55

Case Study #4: John Pothiah 56
- *History* 56
- *Preparation for a Reading* 58
- *How Exactly Does This Work?* 60
- *State-of-the-Art Medical Instruments* 63
- *Just-in-Time Prevention* 65
- *Time and Space* 66
- *Survival of Consciousness or Super- Psi?* 67
- *An Agreement with the Spirit World* 68

Case Study #5: Faith Grant 69
- *History* 69
- *Abilities* 72

Assessing the Trends 74

Chapter 3   **Is There Life after Death?**   79

Testing the Validity of Mediumship   81

Some Key Research Questions   82

Finding Test Mediums   83

Working with Sitters to Test Spirit Communication   84

Arriving at a Conclusion about the Existence of an Afterlife   87

What's in a Name?   88

Identifying the Cause of Death   94

Getting Personal   95

Rival Explanations?   101

Complementary Studies with Mediums   101

What Did We Learn?   106

Chapter 4   **Life after Death Evidence: What Do Near-Death Experiences, Past-Life Regression Therapy, and Other Areas of Study Teach Us?**   109

Near-Death Experiences   110

    • *A Blind Woman Sees during Her Near-Death Experience*   114

    • *Experiencing Life while Being Declared Clinically Dead*   116

    • *A Neurosurgeon Returns to Life*   117

Out-of-Body Experiences (OBE)   118

Past-Life Regression Therapy   119

Deathbed Visions   123

Remote Viewing   126

Putting It All Together   128

Chapter 5	**Factors that Contribute to Clear Spirit Communication**	131
	A Personal Awakening	132
	Potential for Misinterpretation	133
	Communication in the Physical World	134
	Medium: Stage of Development	136
	Medium: Symbols and Interpretation	137
	Medium: Predisposition and Personality of the Discarnate	139
	Spirit: Stage of Learning	141
	Spirit: They Have Their Own Agenda	144
	Spirit: Lessons to Be Learned	147
	Spirit: Space and Time	151
	What Role Do You Play when You Attend a Reading with a Medium?	153
	Sitter: Levels of Need	154
	Sitter: Predisposition	154
	Sitter: Post-Analysis	158
	Conclusions	160
Chapter 6	**Can Anyone Tell the Future?**	163
	Why Would Someone Want to Know the Future?	165
	Historical and Contemporary Theories of Predictions	169
	Can Mediums Predict the Future?	172
	Case Study #1: Prediction about a Future Career	173
	Case Study #2: Am I Going to Meet Somone Special?	174
	Case Study #3: Will My Mother Ever Be at Peace?	178
	Case Study #4: Meeting Someone Special	179
	Case Study #5: You Will Have Financial Freedom!	180
	The Inconsistency Problem	181
	What Do Mediums Say about Predicting the Future?	184

Chapter 7	**Predictions: What Other Factors Should We Consider?**	187
	A Grand Theory to Consider	187
	Are People Interested in Factors that Contribute to the Manifestation of Accurate Predictions?	188
	Did You Say Psychics or Physics?	189
	Is There a Role for You to Play in Predictions?	191
	Quantum Physics: How Do Our Thoughts Relate to Subatomic Particles?	192
	Three-Step Process: How Do Your Thoughts Create Reality?	194
	The Uncertainty Principle: Subatomic Particles Do Not Have a Fixed Position	195
	How Does the Observer Effect Play a Role in Predictions?	196
	Reincarnation	199
	Reincarnation: Who Were Some of the Original Thinkers?	199
	How Does Karma Play a Role in Predictions?	207
	Conclusions about Predictions	211
Chapter 8	**Challenges of Spirit Communication**	215
	Dependency	217
	The Silver Bullet Syndrome	221
	Just Give Me the Right Answer	224
	Unmet Expectations	225
	Fraud	226
	Necromancy	233
	Association with Evil	235
	Final Thoughts	248

Chapter 9	**So What?**	251
	Why Is the So What Question Significant?	252
	Connecting with Loved Ones	254
	Death Is Pain-Free	256
	They Lead Active Lives beyond the Death of their Physical Bodies	258
	Understanding Life Events: Why Do Bad Things Happen?	260
	Receiving Guidance	262
	Health	264
	Finances	267
	Career Advice	268
	Relationships	270
	The Estranged Mother and Daughter	271
	Brothers	272
	Husband and Wife	274
	So What?	277
Chapter 10	**What Have We Learned about the Nature of Reality?**	279
	What Are the Consequences of Being Unaware?	280
	Lesson #1: Dead People Still Exist, and Mediums Can Talk to Them	281
	Lesson #2: Time Is a Three-Dimensional Concept. It's Only Real for Us in the Physical Form	282
	Lesson #3: Space Is a Three-Dimensional Concept. It's Only Real for Us in the Physical Form	284
	Lesson #4: Different Planes of Existence Are Associated with Different Levels of Spiritual Attainment	285

*Lesson #5: The Concepts of Individual
Consciousness and Group Consciousness Are
Not Conflicting Concepts.*   288

Lessons #6: You Create Your Own Reality.   292

Final Note   294

Notes   297

Resources   311

About the Author   313

AUTHOR'S NOTE

Research for this book includes extensive interviews with real study participants who for personal reasons of confidentiality do not wish for their real names to be used. In these instances where study subjects wish to protect their identities and their rights to confidentiality, names have been changed; however, the content of their commentary has not been changed in any way. Five of the ten mediums participating in this research study provided consent to use their real names.

ACKNOWLEDGMENTS

I would first like to acknowledge all of the mediums who participated in the *Medium7* study. It took trust and some risk to be tested and evaluated; however, you participated in lengthy interviews, facilitated the opportunity for me to interview your clients, and in some cases were asked to review text related to the study to ensure its accuracy. We all owe a lot to the mediums that participated in this study as they have provided us with insights regarding both the limitations and possibilities of mediumship. Most importantly the information generated teaches us about the survival of consciousness, possibilities related to the afterlife, and the nature of predictions, and it increases our understanding about the power that lies within each of us.

I would like to make special mention of a gifted intuitive named Dawn Davidesco, who was the first medium to conduct a reading for me. Dawn opened my eyes to the unseen world, and with the evidence she brought forward, it launched a voracious desire to study this phenomenon more systematically.

Thank you to all of the clients/sitters who generously responded to and participated in the experiments and interviews required for this study. For some of you, I could see that recounting the details of your reading was difficult. It brought back memories of your loved ones who are now in spirit. Although some of you felt your readings were deeply personal, you shared what you could as you understood the greater importance and impact this could have on others asking questions about life after death. We are all grateful that you had the courage to participate in the study. For those of you who did share your insights and contents of your reading and do not see it reflected in the case studies or narratives in the book, your data was useful in quantifying results that were necessary to respond to the research questions, so thank you for your time and effort.

There were some research colleagues who reviewed the methodologies or participated in some of the focus groups and experiments. Thank you very much for your advice and time as this provided the necessary support to keep the research rigorous over the two-year study period.

To the editors who helped me see where areas of the manuscript needed improvement, I am sure the readers will appreciate all that you have done to make it easier to read and enjoy the material presented in the book.

Finally, I want to thank those of you in the spirit world who have been inspiring me and motivating me to continue questioning the nature of the universe. There were a few times when I wanted to take a break or perhaps give up because of time constraints and other challenges; however, I do know that your guidance and support provided me with the power to implement the research study, analyze the findings, and write this book. I cannot *see* you all, but I felt your presence throughout this journey.

FOREWORD

In an effort to learn whether our consciousness continues on after physical death, Donna Smith-Moncrieffe has been designing and conducting innovative research experiments. Results from these tests indicate that a spiritual realm exists and that some living individuals can communicate with discarnate personalities.

As a researcher Donna is unique because she strives to make her work accessible to the average person. She is well-read on mediumship research initiatives conducted by other scientists and takes their lessons into account when she is developing her protocols. There is an emotional component to psi phenomena that cannot be ignored. When parapsychologists insist on cold, sterile lab environs, they tend to see a smaller effect—a fact not lost on Donna. To address this issue, she creates hospitable test environments without sacrificing necessary controls. Results have been remarkable and—considering the large number of unique, highly specific statements made by the test mediums and controls in place—these cannot be attributed to cold-reading or fraud. Donna's information will resonate with open-minded skeptics and "left-brained" laypersons, whether they are grieving or just curious about the nature of our existence.

—Mark Ireland, Author of *Soul Shift: Finding Where the Dead Go* and *Messages from the Afterlife: A Bereaved Father's Journey in Spirit Visitations, Psychic Mediums, and Synchronicity* (to be released in the fall of 2013).

INTRODUCTION

This book is about a journey to explore and uncover truths about the nature of our universe—by this I mean understanding the environment that extends beyond the physical plane we refer to as *earth*. Is this physical plane known as earth all there really is? Are there other unseen planes of existence that we cannot see, and if these planes do indeed exist, what is our relationship to them? Obtaining answers to these questions about the true nature of reality helps bring meaning and purpose to our lives.

This journey might seem to be quite an undertaking. There are really no special tools that can help readily uncover the mysteries about space-time. I most certainly did not have access to a spaceship that could take me to various galaxies to explore and confirm the governing laws being experienced in different physical or spiritual dimensions. I am not a physicist and therefore could not use complex mathematical equations or special devices to test the behavior of tiny particles that constitute what we call *space*. You ask, "How exactly did you explore the nature of reality without the use of special tools?" Well, I failed to mention that I was able to work with ten gifted mediums with extrasensory abilities that allowed me to learn about the unseen world—a reality that without mediums might be considered to be a mythical place, one that for most would only be verifiable after they passed onto the spiritual world.

To answer questions about the nature of the unseen world, scientific methods were implemented to provide evidence about the possibility of life after death. Such results reveal answers about where we came from (prior to our birth) and where we are going after the death of the physical body. Mediums or those who have extrasensory perception and facilitate communication between the physical and spiritual world offer a legitimate method of providing answers to questions that are not accessible until you actually die. In chapter 3, more detail is provided to explain how this scientific study with ten mediums was designed to answer questions that have been asked by mankind for centuries. For now, it is useful to know that I had access to a vehicle that could help me enter into worlds beyond this world. If we are able to prove that messages from the spirit world via a medium are from discarnates (entities without a physical body) during our time in the physical world, we might be able to solve the age-old questions that seek knowledge about the source and ultimate purpose of our existence. We would not have to wait until we perished to learn the truth about who we really are.

Questioning whether there is life after death is important not only because it gives us a heads-up about the unknown, but perhaps those in the unseen world can provide us with guidance during our time on the physical plane. Such insights into the activities and spiritual laws that govern the unforeseen world might elicit guidance about how to cope with physical realities.

This book was designed mostly for people who are moderately familiar with the subject of metaphysics[1] and mediumship. With this audience in mind I make great effort to use nontechnical language, engaging stories, and even a bit of humor where applicable. Metaphysics is a philosophy concerned with defining the nature of the universe and clarifying fundamental notions by which people understand the world. Such notions include examining existence, objects and their properties, space-time, cause and effect, determinism, and free will. Even if you have advanced knowledge regarding metaphysics, you are likely to learn new theories, concepts, and findings based on a rigorous two-year study (referred to as *Medium7* throughout the book)

I conducted with mediums and eighty-eight of their clients between 2011 and 2012.

In chapter 1 I review concepts that you will need to understand before you are able to digest the discussions and findings shared in the book. Remember that if you are new to the subject of mediumship, the idea of talking to the dead can seem to be quite an anomaly, perhaps even an impossibility. Of course given our social conditioning and for some of us our Western, monotheistic religious backgrounds, we learned that no one could possibly talk to the dead. Why? Because they are dead! Certain notions, such as *the soul can survive physical death*, *we are vibrational beings*, or *we are all composed of energy*, may be concepts that need to be clarified to ensure the path is clear for you to absorb the testimonies and case studies from the research participants who received messages from a medium during the two-year study.

Once you are comfortable with the concepts, which are also referred to as the "prerequisites" throughout the book, you are now ready to meet the mediums. In chapter 2, "Understanding Mediumship," five case studies are presented that highlight various aspects of mediumship. After observing the work of mediums for the last seven years, I took note that they all worked differently and had some unique extrasensory abilities. You will learn about the early years for each of these mediums. Accounts of their early years provide responses to the following questions: Are the gifts of mediums genetic, or can they be developed? How do mediums learn they have gifts, and is there any particular event that launches their interest in embracing mediumship? The case studies also explore their preparation practices and extrasensory perceptions. Understanding how a medium prepares to conduct a reading provides insight into how changes in consciousness create shifts in reality. You will learn more about the concept of a reading—a medium's ability to use extrasensory perception to communicate with the deceased (those passed onto the spirit world also referred to as discarnates) to provide insights and messages to the sitter or client seeing the medium. Some mediums also do psychic work that allows them to access insights from their spirit guides and angels. You will also learn about how a medium shifts consciousness and enters their client's energy fields or reads the Akashic records also known as a *bank of information.*

I was inspired to write and share these case studies for two reasons. First it is important to carefully articulate how a medium is able to see, hear, smell, or feel the deceased. For example, to accept the diagnosis of a medical intuitive who is able to see inside the human body and actually taste various medical ailments, it is important to understand the mechanisms this type of medium uses to explore and diagnose medical ailments. Prior to conducting studies with mediums, I struggled with accepting the messages as a result of not having a clear understanding of the mechanics of mediumship. In my early days of exploring mediumship, after each reading I would ask the medium to describe how spirit communication worked. The responses seemed to be too general for me. It was never enough for me to hear a medium explain, "I see the presence in my mind's eye, or I feel their presence." My sense was that mediums experienced spirit communication differently and these needed to be more comprehensively described and reported to help individuals without these abilities relate to these experiences. The case studies also provide the medium's perceptions on predictions, which will provide you with more insights into how they perceive prescient information.

The second reason for highlighting gifted mediums is to provide clarity on how mediums can be useful in sharing knowledge about the unseen world. So if you were reading a book about exploring the universe that required the use of a spaceship, the author would need to devote a significant amount of time to discussing this important vehicle. For the findings to be credible, the reader would have to understand how the spaceship was able to travel between various dimensions. The point here is that to be able to answer questions about the true nature of our reality, we have to understand the primary vehicle we are using to channel this knowledge, and in this case the vehicle is the medium.

Once we have a better understanding of how mediumship works in Chapter 2, I am able to respond to one of the key research questions in my study: Is there life after death? The study was designed to determine if the soul or some form of consciousness lives beyond the death of the physical body. The question this research asks is: Does the personality, thoughts, beliefs, and perceptions of an individual live on beyond death of the physical body? If we can use rigorous methods to verify information shared by a medium to a sitter (their clients seeking a reading), then we can produce strong evidence that life exists beyond the physical death. I can recall my very conservative research colleagues who are used to my daytime research activities in criminology asking, "Why on earth are you now studying issues related to death? That seems to be a far cry from your work in crime prevention." On the one hand, examining the spirit world and death might seem like a mundane activity, especially for some who consider focusing on the *here and now* to be of greater importance. From my perspective, however, this area of study is a critical question for mankind. It would be useful to have some more insights about where we are going especially if our current lifestyle has an impact on the nature of the afterlife experience.

If you are not a research and data aficionado, you will still find the case studies of real people's testimonies in chapter 3 to be both engaging and credible. It is not only the mediums who are self-reporting the relevance of the messages they provide, it is their clients as well who share insights about the contents of their reading, enhancing the credibility of the phenomenon.

This book does not actually explore the activities of the afterlife. For example, I don't elaborate on what loved ones are doing in spirit. Nor do I elaborate on what happens when you pass into the spirit world. The nature of the afterlife is truly an important topic that has been comprehensively covered in the *Tibetan Book of the Dead.*[2] The text describes and is intended to guide one through the experiences that the consciousness has after death during the interval between death and the next life. This book does not focus on the activities that take place after death—the focus is on how mediumship can provide proof that this afterlife possibly exists. Based on the study's findings, a conclusive response to the question "Is there life after death?" is provided.

Since most of us have not died recently, even when we experience messages from a medium that demonstrate that a loved one is still present just in a different form, it is still challenging sometimes for us to grasp the possibility that the dead are still among us. We are quite fortunate in the twenty-first century, however, that the veil between the two worlds is thinning. We have several researchers and medical practitioners sharing proof of the afterlife. In chapter 4, the research and results of near-death experiences (NDEs) are presented—this area of study provides another line of evidence that proves that consciousness survives death. Who would ever believe that someone could die and return to tell us about their activities after death? Hypnotherapists practicing past-life regression therapy have also made a great contribution to this line of research. Examples of past-life regression cases are presented to illustrate how hypnotized patients reveal details of past lives that occurred in a different century and country. Scholars examining the doctrine of reincarnation[3] indicate that if past lifetimes can be verified, this can also provide proof that consciousness lives on beyond death. This examination of reincarnation pushes our view of the world as it not only suggests that our consciousness is immortal but further suggests that our soul chooses various physical bodies to experience multiple lifetimes. This particular area of study opens doors to our understanding about why our souls might benefit from experiencing multiple lifetimes. The learning is endless but of course mind-boggling at the same time. Information and research on deathbed visions and remote viewing is presented in this chapter as well. These areas of study utilize different vehicles but produce converging evidence about the afterlife. After you read chapters 3 and 4, you will have reviewed all the relevant research pertaining to the afterlife and survival of consciousness. For those of you who are healthy skeptics, while my goal is not to change your belief system, you will take note that hundreds of scholars using different vehicles and examining the afterlife all come to the same conclusion. Of course I am not going to share this conclusion just yet as it is best if you review the case studies and results beyond reading this introductory chapter to allow you to form your own conclusions.

When you make a decision to see a medium, you could be motivated to hear from a deceased loved one or to obtain guidance about present or future issues. In my case I was most interested in examining the implications of mediums being able to actually talk to the dead. I was intrigued by the implications if such phenomena were actually true. It launched numerous questions in my mind. If we are here and they are there, does that mean there is another plane of existence that we cannot see? After we perish, will we end up in one place, or do we all go to various dimensions based on our spiritual attainment while on earth? Do we play a role in the interaction with the spirit world, and if we do, what are these factors that contribute to the clarity, content, and accuracy of the messages shared during a reading with a medium? Do spirits see everything we are doing here on earth, and can they communicate that level of detail to us via a medium? After I experienced and reviewed hundreds of readings facilitated by a medium, it became clear that spirit communication was not a free flowing exchange. There were multiple factors that contributed to the clarity and accuracy of the content. Perhaps obtaining a closer examination of these factors would provide further insight into the unseen world. All of these questions are examined and answered in chapter 5.

Chapters 6 and 7 explore the area of prediction science. One of the most popular reasons for seeing a medium is for sitters to learn about what the future holds. This has been a preoccupation of mankind for centuries with most clients being interested in obtaining a sneak peek about their futures. Of course while I would agree that there might be some advantage to having prescient information, my primary reason for focusing on this area is to examine concepts, such as predetermination, free will, time and space, and general concepts that describe how the universe works.

In chapter 6, case studies of both successful and failed predictions are shared so the reader can first understand the wide range of predictions channeled by mediums. In the *Medium7* study, eighteen research participants who received detailed predictions from a medium were interviewed at several stages over an eighteen-month period. They were interviewed after their reading, and at follow-up periods up to one year (in some cases up to eighteen months) to verify the outcomes of these predictions. Findings related to accuracy rates are presented. These findings lead to another set of questions that launched further examination about the factors that need to be considered when one is receiving a prediction.

After you read chapter 7, you may be surprised to learn that you play a large role in the outcome of predictions made by a medium. To help you further understand how our universe works in relation to predictions, I take you into the world of quantum physics and highlight the relevant areas of reincarnation and karma that play a role in contributing to the outcome of predictions. Closer examinations of these areas help formulate conclusions about how our consciousness, past lives, and behaviors drive and shape our current and future experiences. Answers to the following questions are provided: If someone's future can be predicted, does that mean everything is predetermined? If certain aspects of our lives are already predetermined, how does this predetermination develop? Why does it develop and who keeps track of all of these predetermined events? Do we play a role in predictions, and if we do play some role, how do we reconcile the relationship between free will and predetermination?

The work in this book provides an objective perspective about how mediumship can be used to raise awareness about the spirit world and how it works. To ensure that I have incorporated an objective perspective, a whole chapter is devoted to discussing the past and current challenges our society faces in using mediumship to learn about the spirit world. In chapter 8 you will learn about how the silver bullet syndrome can create unrealistic expectations and limit your ability to address the challenges you hoped would be addressed via messages from a medium. In my research with mediums and their clients it was often disheartening to observe how frequently the *silver bullet syndrome* was experienced by sitters during their decision-making process. Some clients receiving readings from a medium would often become passive recipients of the information, calmly waiting for *things* to happen to them. In addition to these type of challenges, this chapter recounts the history that contributes to the existing taboo regarding the integration of mediumship into the prevailing milieu. Challenges related to the association of evil and necromancy are shared to enhance the readers' understanding of how and why talking to the dead continues to be controversial. As more of the public begins to embrace the new age movement and its related concepts, it's important that the masses gain a greater understanding of how advice and spirit communication is best used. By embarking on this discussion a number of myths about mediumship are debunked. My hope is that by demystifying myths regarding spirit communication, readers will take full responsibility for the decisions they make about their current and future lives and be more informed about how they play a role in creating their own reality. With this enhanced understanding we might be able to move forward with mediumship to open more doorways to the spirit world and subsequently discover greater truths about the true nature of our universe.

After we review the facts about our souls' immortality and the nature of reality, it is only natural that some of you would have questions about the implications of this knowledge. The *so what* question discussed in chapter 9 might sound a bit harsh, but it is an appropriate question to ask. I believe in the utility of applied research. That is research that can actually be applied by real people in their daily lives. This is not to say that pure research is not useful. It is just that after twenty years of conducting research, managing, and peer-reviewing studies using rigorous designs, I have noticed that it is often challenging to transform a study's findings into practical use for the masses. There is a deliberate attempt in this chapter to translate the findings and clarify how this knowledge can be used in your everyday life. A discussion ensues about how understanding the purpose of life can make a positive impact on our life journey. My hope is that after reading this book your outlook about the daily grind will be brighter. I share engaging and relevant case studies about how people just like you have used their knowledge about the universe and messages from mediums to enhance current relationships, make better decisions about career or financial goals, and understand the importance of inner wealth.

As shared earlier in this chapter this book is a journey to discover truths about the nature of our existence. It would be remiss of me to not summarize all of the findings produced as a result of conducting the research of *Medium7*. In this final chapter a summary is provided to highlight how working with mediums has helped us unravel the mysteries of our universe and confirmed pre-existing theories about the nature of our existence.

It is my hope that after you read this chapter you will see the universe as it truly is, and with this changed perception you may modify the way you experience reality as you move forward in your journey.

Why Me? Why This Book?

During the implementation of the research and while I was writing this book, it was always surprising when people would ask, "Why are you conducting this study about the afterlife? Why are you writing this book?" To be honest, it was quite difficult hearing these questions. To me it seemed quite obvious that everyone would want to gain greater insight regarding the mechanics and authenticity of spirit communication via a medium. It seemed obvious to me that everyone would be interested in examining any vehicle that would create greater awareness about the potential of an afterlife. Well, perhaps not *everyone* would spend years examining this, and perhaps they would not write a book about it. These questions regarding my interest in the subject area are still difficult for me to answer. For me, finding the answers and sharing them seemed to be a natural calling.

The decision to examine this area of study did not occur after a life-transforming experience. No one died. I did not have a near-death experience, and I was not instructed to take this path by anyone on the earthly plane or in the spiritual world. At a very young age though—I would almost like to say at the time of birth, but no one would believe that—I had a voracious appetite to have questions about the nature of our universe answered with concrete and credible responses. For those who know me well, even the most immaterial topic could spark my interest and an analysis that could go on ad nauseam! What made issues related to mediumship and the afterlife even more enticing was that it seemed that there were no concrete answers, limited vehicles or tools, and few opportunities to discuss these topics openly without being deemed potentially demented.

In addition to having a voracious appetite for answers, it was tiring watching people struggle with depression, illness, addictions, and hopelessness. Couldn't more people be relieved of much of these burdens if they had greater insights about our purpose for existence? In the book I provide glimpses of some of the spiritual occurrences I experienced that helped me realize that mediums provided ample opportunity to gain a greater understanding about the afterlife and our purpose for existence.

So it was a few things that launched my dedication to this area of study. My voracious appetite for answers, my perception of a growing sense of hopelessness, my personal experiences with mediums in my early years, and my professional abilities as a social science researcher—these factors culminated, and *voila*, you now know what sparked my interest in embarking on this journey.

A Few Last Notes

If you are looking for a thriller or a fear-based book, this is definitely not the book for you. I know that the mere mention of the spirit world launches visions of Halloween and the paranormal, but I make a deliberate attempt to use my scientific research to provide sound evidence about the universe—a universe that I believe is a loving one designed to teach our souls valuable lessons. My hope is that the facts and applications of this work will enhance your life and lead you to a greater understanding of how we can work with the spirit world to enhance the quality of our lives.

Even before the book was published, many people asked me about the significance of the title of the research *Medium7*. To be honest, I woke up one day with the phrase *Medium8* in my head. Once this concept was in my head, that was the day the seeds of this book were born, and from that day on the concept never left my mind. I shared the title with a medium who felt that the spiritual number of seven should be represented. Therefore, seven is not related to the number of mediums interviewed for this book. Instead it represents the spiritual light that I hope will shine on all readers who will positively transform and thrive after they read the words on every page of this book. Now we are ready to explore the research of *Medium7*.

MAKING SENSE OF IT ALL

*T*here are many concepts that will be discussed in this book that may sound questionable, controversial, and sometimes almost inconceivable. This chapter provides a description of the concepts necessary for understanding how it is possible for our consciousness to survive physical death. Such concepts provide a basis for understanding the purpose for our existence and help clarify how our consciousness contributes to our perceptions and experience. After you read this chapter, you will be better prepared to absorb the discussions involving life after death and predictions.

I often wonder why such important concepts about unseen forces, the purpose of life, and the soul were not integrated in the early school curriculum. I can certainly understand the importance of math and English, but why not even one course on the nature of our existence? We had science class, but of course the focus was on classical principles that suggested that everything surrounding us was solid matter. This classical paradigm suggested that matter was solid and was comprised of an absolute reality; this reality was outside of us rather than created from our own minds. The calculations for gravity and motion, for example, demonstrated that certain elements of the universe are predictable, further suggesting that there was one absolute reality that everyone would experience. Some of us that chose a path to seek education beyond high school may have taken courses, such as psychology, physics, philosophy, and religion to name just a few. When you combined some of the principles, concepts, and doctrines in these areas of study, you might have come across metaphysical discussions that provided an opportunity to see a different world view of the universe. Without an understanding of these concepts, referred to as the "prerequisites" throughout this chapter, it is difficult for us to make the leap from our conservative beliefs to a place where we could possibly believe that there is an invisible plane of existence that interacts and impacts our physical world.

Our social conditioning makes it easy to understand for example, that gravity is the cause of falling objects. If you are under a falling tree, experience tells you that it would be necessary to run and avoid the tree as gravity causes objects to fall. Social conditioning allows us to be comfortable with the fact that humans contribute to the development of other human beings. In fact, we think we understand the mechanics of childbirth, but outside of understanding the conception process and cellular development we really don't understand all of the "hocus-pocus" that contributes to the human conception process. The question is, what do we really know about how the universe works? We see awe-inspiring clouds in the sky but have very limited information about space in general. We can look to physicists to elaborate on the nature of space; however, despite their expertise, scholars in this field are still not sure how far space expands and can only speculate about other planets and planes of existence. In fact, quantum physics has only recently found that space is indeed material and has a functional purpose in the universe.

Over the past two decades, mankind has been questioning the validity of traditional scientific paradigms. We have an urge to solve the riddles that were once just considered miracles. We can no longer be complacent about accepting traditional ways of viewing the world. As we prepare to examine the forthcoming prerequisite concepts, I ask that you suspend your beliefs (especially ones that are consistent with the status quo) and open up to some concepts that are necessary to help provide stepping stones that will make it possible to see a new worldview. When you are reviewing these prerequisite concepts, try to relate to your own personal experiences. Have you ever experienced unexplainable spiritual encounters? For example, you may have had experiences in the dream state, felt the familiar feeling of déjà vu (having the feeling that you have already been in a very familiar circumstance), or had encounters with the unseen world. As you review the following prerequisite concepts, attempt to apply these concepts to your personal experience to enhance their meaning.

We Are Energy, Everything Is Energy

To be able to grasp many concepts about the nature of reality, we first need to grasp the fact that we are energy and everything in this world is energy. For those of you who have bought into this concept, you may find it surprising to learn that many individuals do not either believe or grasp this concept. To some the body is perceived as solid. That of course would include the bones and organs in the body. I can still recall my Kabbalah classes, where the rabbi explained, "The world is just energy—it is filled with molecules vibrating at different speeds. You can take the whole world and fit it in your hand mainly because the world is immaterial, not solid." Of course the classmates, including myself, challenged this ideology by noting for example that when we attempt to walk through a wall, we know it is solid after we incur several bruises on our forehead and experience a lingering massive headache. With such a hard concept to grasp, it's best to first review the scientific proof that everything is indeed energy.

● ● ●

"The world is just energy. It is filled with molecules vibrating at different speeds. It is immaterial, not solid."

● ● ●

Energy can be perceived in many different forms in the physical world.

The body is comprised of the same energy as a rock for example; the composition of the rock simply vibrates at different speeds, resulting in the perception that there are two different entities. We know that energy is indestructible; it changes form but can never be destroyed.

James Redfield successfully demonstrated that our bodies were really comprised of several atomic particles. His book, *The Celestine Prophecy*,[4] shares the nine great insights that mankind should consider to better understand the purpose and the cause behind the life source. I was fascinated by his demonstration of how humans compete for energy in their daily lives. This fourth insight, which he calls "the struggle," suggests that we are composed of vital energy sources that can change in relation to feelings and thoughts. Using the metaphor of a journey to Peru, he shares that when we are depressed or feeling low self-esteem or resentment, we begin to feel like we are spinning out of control. We inadvertently deny ourselves of source energy—some would prefer to call this the God force that is an empowering source of well-being and abundance. After we have created barriers that disallow us from receiving this energy, we subconsciously steal energy from others. Now I know this discussion may seem highly theoretical, but I am confident that every reader has had a practical experience at work or at home where you feel completely physically drained after you converse with a particular friend or family member. We can all relate to the feeling when your friend, Sally for example, calls you by telephone to reconnect. Sally starts off by sharing how interested she is in hearing about what's happening in your life. Before you know it you are on the phone for forty-five minutes. You are slowly starting to feel tired, anxious, and slightly depressed. Sally talks to you about the same issues she is having in her marriage and recounts the daily challenges she is experiencing with finances and career. If Sally is really feeling disconnected from her own energy sources, she may make an undermining comment about how "you need to exercise more," or even worse she may unconsciously try to upset you by letting you know about the negative rumors that have been circulating about you. During the whole telephone conversation you are barely able to say a word. By the time the phone call is complete, you are no longer motivated to continue completing what you were busy doing prior to the phone call. In general you feel like a race car without tires.

Redfield explains that this interaction takes place when one person dominates another. The dominator feels powerful by sucking vital energy from the other person. We know that wars have been fought because one faction was holding on to an irrational position for the primary purpose of stealing another country's vital energy sources. Everyone can relate to the way they feel after interactions with other individuals. In the case of Sally calling, she did not physically beat you during the phone call, but she drained vital energy that is the primary substance of the body.

In the next example, for those of you who need to see to believe, the photographs taken using Kirlian photography[5] are an effective way to demonstrate that the human body is composed solely of energy. Kirlian photography is a collection of photographic techniques used to capture the phenomenon of electrical coronal discharges. It has been the subject of mainstream scientific and parapsychology research. The camera's ability to film the true nature of living and nonliving items provides an opportunity to see what "things" are really made of. Harry Oldsfield, author of *The Invisible Universe*, has conducted experiments with Kirlian photography using humans, plants, and animal life. A simple experiment with a leaf is used to demonstrate that living items are comprised solely of energy. Oldsfield photographs a regular leaf and then compares the results with the photograph of just the leaf's stem with no leaves. You might expect the latter photograph to reflect just the stem; however, the Kirlian photo illustrates the stem with bright glowing leaves surrounding it, creating the impression that the leaves were present. This simple experiment shows that the physical leaf does not need to be photographed for one to see the full leaf because the leaf is comprised solely of energy. This same experiment was demonstrated in 1987 using PIP (polycontrast interference photography) to photograph an amputee. The Kirlian photograph illustrated the energy field of the research participant's arm even though it was amputated.

Once we understand that we are energy, it is easier to grasp for example why our souls or consciousness can continue to perceive reality even after the brain is disabled. If we are energy, we cannot be destroyed. Elements comprising the human body were present before we were born and will continue to be present beyond death. Until mankind fully grasped this concept, we believed that we were all physical beings; however, through our growing experiences with mediums/psychics, ghostly encounters, and through reading religious doctrine we are starting to realize that even during our earthly experience we are part of a larger spiritual universe. Understanding that we are comprised of energy further suggests that we are spiritual beings having a physical experience on the earth plane.

We Are Vibrational Beings

In the twenty-first century we have proof that we are energy. When we keep this in mind, we are better able to consider the concept that we are vibrational beings.

A skeptic who participated in the research of *Medium7* noted that spirit communication was made possible as a result of his ability to vibrate at a higher frequency. He asked, "Can anyone prove that we are vibrating at various frequencies?" Of course this was a reasonable question as one could not necessarily see changes in frequencies with normal sensory perception. If we understand that our vibrational frequency range controls what we see, hear, and feel, then we can easily reach the logical conclusion that entities that vibrate on different levels cannot be perceived.

In 1992 Dr. Taino invented the first frequency monitor in the world.[6] The machine indicates that the average human body vibrates at 62–68 hertz (Hz) during the daytime. A collection of measurements for various states of the human body, animals, and inanimate objects are available to the public. If we pause for a moment and reflect on the definition of a hertz (Hz), we find it is a frequency measurement equal to one cycle per second. The term frequency measurement suggests there can be varying frequencies that can be measured. The frequency monitor has identified that when a person is sick, he or she actually vibrates at a lower frequency (57–60 Hz), and death can begin at 25 Hz. After a review of hertz measures for humans and plants, it appears that higher hertz levels suggest healthier states and lower hertz levels suggest a diminished state of health. This phenomenon is demonstrated when we see that a can of processed food has 0 Hz and freshly picked fruit for example vibrates at 20–27 Hz.

The frequency monitor provides us with further proof that we are vibrational beings and inanimate objects also have varying frequencies. Metaphysicians have come to this same conclusion. The world is made of immaterial; it is simply energy vibrating at different frequencies. The human brain only utilizes 10 percent of its potential to perceive the range of frequencies in the universe, which would explain why we cannot see other planes of existences or their inhabitants using our limited sensory powers. In sections of the book where the discussion of vibrational frequencies is applied, it is best to remember a few key facts to help overcome our past social conditioning. We know that in 1876 Francis Galton invented the Galton whistle otherwise known as the dog whistle. When you blow this whistle, the human ear cannot hear it, but a dog can. The human ear perceives 18–20 Hz, yet the dog can hear ranges as

● ● ●

Humans cannot hear a dog whistle, but dogs can.

Perceptions of reality vary depending on our ability to perceive varying frequencies.

● ● ●

high as 45 Hz. This confirms that sound exists beyond our normal sensory powers. We cannot hear or see a Wi-Fi signal, but we know it exists as it provides us with the use of Internet services. These are facts that help us remember that there are many forces that have an impact on our current life and such forces are not perceivable by our five senses.

The fan example is another useful way of understanding how vibrational frequencies allow for varying degrees of human perception. When a fan is at its highest speed, the blades are turning so quickly that you cannot see anything through the blades. Even if there is a painting behind the fan, you may conclude that there isn't anything behind the fan because you are only able to see the blades swiftly moving. When the fan is turned down to a medium speed, you are able to see a bit more of the painting behind it, although not everything in the painting may be totally clear at this time. Finally, if the fan is turned to the off position, aspects of the painting are clearer as the static position of the blades create enough space to see the painting. With this example we see how an existing object (in this case, the painting) can range in visibility depending on the vibrational frequency (in this case the motion of the fan's blades).

The rate of our vibrational frequency allows us to see, hear, touch, smell, and feel other energies that are existing at similar levels of frequency. When your levels of vibrational frequencies change, you are able to perceive different realities. Once we understand this concept, we begin to be interested in using techniques that raise our vibration. Such techniques include physical exercise and meditation techniques; the latter technique is exemplified by some of the mediums in chapter 2 as many of them use this technique to align their energies with other spiritual realities. During the next few chapters that focus on the research with mediums, you can refer back to the examples of the dog whistle or the fan to make the concept of speaking to the dead more conceivable.

The Soul Can Survive Physical Death

We have covered some key prerequisite concepts, including energy and vibrational frequencies. Only by digesting these concepts can we consider the next prerequisite that will be discussed frequently throughout this book. This book will share some of the evidence that would suggest that the soul can survive physical death. This is of course a difficult concept for some to digest as it makes the assumption that the physical body is different from the soul. This assumption leads to other questions about what constitutes the soul. Is the soul a compilation of our thoughts, personalities, hopes, dreams, and memories, or are there other elements of the soul that we are not aware of as yet? If the soul is immortal, what is the purpose for its continued existence? Does the soul remain a separate soul, or does it form part of the super consciousness—a concept of a group of souls residing on another plane of existence? All of these questions about the immortality of the soul are important, and a majority of these questions will be answered throughout the book. The importance about sharing this concept at this early stage is to help you understand why it might be possible for a medium to converse with the deceased; understanding this prerequisite helps you understand that they are likely having a conversation with the soul (also referred to as spirit or consciousness throughout the book).

● ● ●

What is the soul? Is it the thoughts, memories, feelings, and ability to perceive a reality?

If it is, these are aspects of the soul that survive death.

● ● ●

The medical community has determined that an individual may be declared dead if brain death has occurred—that is, if the whole brain has ceased to function or has entered what is sometimes called a persistent vegetative state. If mankind believed that the soul died with the physical body, it would be irrational to claim that anyone could speak to the dead as it would be clear to everyone that all aspects of the human body would be dead—gone forever.

Hollywood seems to have some belief in the immortality of the soul. Such blockbuster hits include the memorable movie *Ghost* (1990) with Whoopi Goldberg and Patrick Swayze. We can all recall Patrick Swayze, who played the deceased husband whose soul was no longer able to touch and communicate with his long-lost wife after he was murdered, yet because of the survival of his consciousness, he could see her and experience an existence that was as real as it was when he was alive. Who could also forget the enticing movie *Flatliners* (1990) that engaged audiences worldwide in the 1980s? In this movie Hollywood producers were interested in exploring the concept of near-death experiences on the big screen as medical students were interested in experimenting with the afterlife. Their objective was to die for a short period of time and be resuscitated back to life to share their experiences of the afterlife.

If you are having any difficulty conceptualizing the soul and physical body as separate entities, I would ask that you attempt to be open-minded about this possibility as you review the forthcoming research study results that attempt to demonstrate survival of consciousness. The main point to understand at this stage is that your physical experience is temporary and your spiritual existence is permanent. If you have grasped the previous concept that you are *energy*, you understand that energy cannot be destroyed. It changes its consistency and may manifest differently, but it can never be destroyed.

Reincarnation

Reincarnation is the belief that mankind returns to the physical plane (also known as the earth plane) each time with a different physical body. This recycling of the body and soul between the spiritual and physical planes can continue over a number of lifetimes to allow the soul to grow and experience a variety of life perspectives and lessons. The amount of cycles for each soul varies depending on the lessons needed and the rate of the soul's growth. Buddhists believe for example that this recycling of bodies will continue until the soul reaches the level of nirvana, the state of bliss and ultimate joy. I elaborate on this concept later in the book when I explain why reincarnation needs to be considered when one is assessing the probability of making an accurate prediction.

Reincarnation is largely embraced by the Eastern religions and is accepted as a normal part of life. The Western religions, however, are slow to integrate this concept in their doctrines. In Christianity there is an acknowledgment that the soul lives beyond the body's death, but there is little guidance on their views of reincarnation or of where the soul goes. Does the soul stay in this new universe forever? Does it continue to learn more lessons? Does it have the capacity to perceive various other realities?

The concept of reincarnation is raised early in this book to help provide an explanation for some of the messages or lack thereof that comes from the spirit world. As you read the case studies in the book you will start to realize that the deceased should not and cannot always provide the information we want to hear. Skeptics often make premature conclusions about our inability to obtain comprehensive answers from the spirit world; however, it is necessary to understand the doctrine of reincarnation and soul life contracts to help place spirit communication into the appropriate context.

* * *

Experiencing a variety of physical bodies in different lifetimes allows our souls to grow spiritually.

* * *

Danielle MacKinnon,[7] who specializes in the study of soul contracts, discusses the preplanning that our souls do in the pre-embodied state (a state that we experience in the period after death and before rebirth). To put it in plain language, prior to our arrival to the earth plane, our souls create soul contracts with other souls with the goal of ensuring that particular lessons can be learned on the earth plane. For example, if your soul needs to learn patience, perhaps you are going to create contracts with a number of people and circumstances that will help you learn patience. If you were a slave trader in the seventeenth century, for you to understand the pain and injustice of your actions, you may create a soul contract in the next life to experience a life of slavery. By experiencing a slave's emotional and physical sentiments, the learning related to ethics, empathy, and human rights is achieved.

We put on a variety of bodies to help us create an existence that will allow our soul to experience different realities. If you came to earth only once and your soul experienced a life of celebrity and wealth, your soul would not have an opportunity to evolve because of its lack of understanding about poverty, ambition, fear, and other emotions that are necessary to strengthen the soul.

Soul contracts are created with the goal that all parties involved will be given an opportunity to work on the lessons that they need to learn. According to Danielle McKinnon, we have a number of primary and secondary soul contracts that ensure the necessary people and circumstances are in place to help the soul grow. With this understanding we turn to the next prerequisite concept that suggests that the physical world is an illusion.

The Physical World Is an Illusion

The physical world is an illusion. This is another statement that at first glance is difficult to believe. During my first class at the Kabbalah Centre in Toronto, within the first few minutes of the course the rabbi shared that the world was a physical illusion. He continued to explain that the world was an illusion since everything that we could see and feel was simply vibrating quickly enough for it to appear solid. Everything around us was essentially immaterial, a perception of our reality.

Understanding that the world is an illusion helps prepare you for further understanding that there is no absolute reality. The possibility of experiencing a variety of realities is based on individual perception. This means that it is possible for each person to experience different perceptions of similar objects and experiences. This is an important prerequisite concept to understanding the possibility of various planes of existences and states of consciousness. Grasping this possibility opens the door to being able to further comprehend the possibility of speaking to entities in different realities, experiencing past lives through hypnotherapy, or having out-of-body experiences—all examples of experiences that have the potential to carry you to different realities.

How exactly can these Prerequisites help me understand the Afterlife?

An overview about five key concepts has been provided to enhance your understanding of how it might be possible to perceive a reality beyond the death of the physical body. Understanding these prerequisite concepts will allow you to be more open to understanding the case studies, findings, and discussions that are presented in the following chapters. Whenever you are having difficulty absorbing an idea, it may be useful to refer to table 1. This table classifies the prerequisite concept as fact or an assumption. If the concept is a fact, it means that we currently have scientific evidence to support the concept's validity. If it is classified as an assumption, it means that there has not been enough scientific evidence to validate its existence. It may also mean that the concept is factual but the evidence does not yet meet traditional scientific standards.

Table 1 How do the prerequisite concepts help us understand life after death and our universe?

Prerequisite Concept	Fact and/or Assumption	How does this concept help me understand life after death and our universe?
We are energy.	Fact	If we are energy and energy cannot be destroyed, this suggests that our form of existence changes but never dies.
We are vibrational beings.	Fact	This explains why some individuals can perceive other dimensions. Based on your individual vibration, you will experience and perceive different realities.
The soul can survive physical death.	Assumption (with evidence to support potential fact)	Understanding this assumption helps you understand how it might be possible for a medium to communicate with discarnates (spirits without a body).
Reincarnation	Assumption	This assumption provides a rationale for why the soul dons a variety of physical bodies.
The physical world is an illusion.	Fact	Understanding this fact helps you understand that not everything you see is real and the unseen may actually exist.

Now that we have a better idea about how to use the prerequisite concepts to enhance understanding, we can now embark on beginning to understand the mechanics of mediumship.

UNDERSTANDING MEDIUMSHIP

This is the chapter that inspired me to write this book. After each meeting with a medium, I would always wonder how the medium could see, hear, or touch the deceased person in spirit. Were the deceased appearing to the medium as spirits, or did they appear as they did in the physical world? How exactly does a medium feel the pain of the sitter or the deceased? How exactly does a medium hear the deceased? By having the mediums discuss their abilities in detail, the mechanics of mediumship can be understood better. After experiencing many meetings and readings with mediums, it became clear that they all worked very differently and offered different perspectives about the nature of reality. If one medium could see dead people but another one could read blueprints of the universe through his or her mind's eye, this suggested that there were many possibilities available to learn about the nature of the universe.

In this chapter there are some definitions provided to ensure you are clear about the types of extrasensory perceptions that mediums use to share messages from spirit to the sitter. When I first began reading more about mediums, it was clear that each book made little effort to vividly describe the mechanics of mediumship. Mediums are primarily the authors of books describing mediumship. These authors have experiential knowledge and may make assumptions that most of us limited to the experience of using only the five senses will understand exactly how this phenomenon unfolds. This is evidently not the case. Mediumship is not just about defining clairvoyance, clairaudience, and clairsentience. Each medium has a specific story to tell about how the messages and information comes through to him or her. After these definitions are clear, you will read case studies of five different mediums. Each case study varies, but all of the mediums speak to the following areas:

- background and history
- early years of psychic development
- preparation prior to a reading
- type and description of their extrasensory abilities
- explanation of how the extrasensory abilities work

Finding Gifted Mediums

Some background information about my search for mediums might help you gain a better understanding of how challenging it is to find and persuade gifted mediums to participate in a scientific research study. Real mediums are not a dime a dozen. When you google the term *psychic* or *medium*, the World Wide Web makes it appear that the average human being has this rare ability. No doubt as spiritual beings we all have latent psychic powers; however, these are dormant or underdeveloped for most of us. The first challenge I encountered related to the medium's concern about being judged or evaluated. Most of the mediums who fell into this category could appreciate the importance of this type of research but for personal reasons would not consent to participate. There were a few mediums interviewed who believed that they had extrasensory gifts but were not able to demonstrate this according to the tools used in the *Medium7* study. In chapter 3, I elaborate on the criteria used to help determine if the medium was gifted enough to participate in the research for *Medium7*. Mediums who were underdeveloped, if admitted to the study, would make it difficult to make accurate conclusions about questions related to life after death and the nature of reality. The goal of this study is to further understand the nature of our universe so mediocre mediumship would create ambiguity about whether the results were related to the mediocrity or were attributable to the limitations of the universe. These mediums who were not admitted to the research study and were subsequently not included in this book were good listeners, held the qualities of a counselor or psychologist, and may have had some degree of intuition but clearly did not have extrasensory capabilities that allowed them to perceive clearly into other planes of existence. Another barrier to including a higher number of mediums in this study related to the requirements for participation in the study. Mediums were asked to do either of the following: (1) Provide a list of names and contact information of past and current clients so they could be contacted for possible interviews, or (2) after each reading, refer all of their clients for potential participation in the research. Mediums are bound by the same ethical requirements as other professionals, and some felt that this referral protocol might compromise their business relationships. Most of the mediums who consented to participate had the view that clients could make their own decisions about participating in the research.

Some of the mediums were concerned about whether the research would be designed well enough to consider their unique abilities. It is true that you can produce faulty conclusions about a program as a result of using a faulty research design. You can conclude that an intervention was not successful when it had many effective elements. In the case of mediumship the researcher's bias and inability to design the research with the appropriate controls can result in inaccurate conclusions about the capacity of mediums, the existence of survival of consciousness beyond death, and spirit communication in general. This concern is also normal given the public's misconception about a number of concepts involving the mechanics of mediumship. Some of the mediums considered for this study were concerned about being labeled abnormal and felt that the benefits of the research did not outweigh this potential social stigma.

It is for this reason that only five[8] out of the ten mediums who agreed to participate in the research offered to provide their real names. The other five offered to share their client lists or provide insights to make a contribution but were not willing to make their stories and names public. I pursued this approach to highlight the stories of real mediums as it is more credible when you can hear directly from contemporary mediums and their clients. The mediums you will read about in this chapter considered many risks and ultimately viewed the long-term benefits of the research findings to be of greater benefit than the personal risks involved in participating in the research of *Medium7*.

What Is a Medium?[9]

A medium is an individual that has the ability to hear, see, touch, feel, or taste mental impressions from the spirit world. Mediums are sensitive to the vibrations of the spirit world and therefore have the ability to communicate information from the deceased to those of us on the earth plane. Mediums receive messages or visions from discarnates (also known as entities without physical bodies) who choose to share information with individuals residing on the earth plane.

The prevailing literature on psychics and mediums always seems to indicate that you can only be one or the other. It is true that mediums can be psychics, but all psychics are not necessarily mediums; however, it is important to understand that these gifts may interact and a medium at one moment in a reading may be communicating with their guides, and angels. In the next moment, depending on the interests of the client and the nature of the enquiry, the medium may begin to do psychic work. In my observations of mediums, psychic and mediumship techniques intertwine, making the concepts interchangeable at times. Generally when mediums are not obtaining information from discarnates (those who were living agents prior to passing into the spirit world), they are engaging in psychic work. Psychic work may include clairvoyance (clear seeing beyond the use of one's eyes), telepathy (the ability to receive and understand the minds of others or send thoughts to another's mind), psychokinesis (moving matter by thoughts and the power of intention), and precognition (knowledge about events taking place into the future).

Psychic work has also been associated with the reading of auras (energy fields surrounding the body), using psychometry (using ESP to gain information from an object), dowsing (using an instrument like a pendulum to answer questions), using numerology, analyzing dreams, and using crystals for healing. The examination of mediumship in this book is skewed toward assessing the survival of consciousness and its implications for our universe. It is for this reason that I do not investigate or elaborate on these elements of psychic work.

Who Are Mediumistic?

Many persons are naturally sensitive to some extent to the influence of spirit and could therefore be considered to have the ability to tap into the spirit world. You ask, "What sets you apart from being a medium?" There are three key characteristics that set mediums apart from the rest of the population. First most mediums who have demonstrated credibility in the use of their craft had an existing physical predisposition. The physical structure of their bodies allows their cells to vibrate at a faster rate. Individuals who can vibrate at the rate of those in the spirit world are able to communicate effectively with spirits. It is interesting to note that only six of the ten mediums in this study are aware of unique physical changes in their bodies that they believe allows them to *see* spirit. The other four mediums don't deny having a possible physical predisposition but are unaware of having any physical trauma or bodily transformation that would allow them to do this type of work.

A second characteristic that a medium possesses is the ability to tune into the various changes in energy. Most of us receive signs and messages from the spirit world on a daily basis but are more tuned into the activities in the secular world. For example, when you wake up in the morning, do you write down your dreams and then reflect on them? Or do you get up and immediately attend to your daily chores? The more you pay attention to the signs from the other side or reflect on your dreams and the message they are sending, your intuition will grow, and this change leads to a heightened awareness of other planes of existence.

Finally, regular participation in activities that train the medium to refrain from using the brain during the channeling process is also important. A medium needs be able to identify whether thoughts and impressions are originating from their own brain or from the spirit world. Frequent meditation trains one to focus on the breath, allowing one to refrain from focusing on thoughts that stand in the way of communication from earth to spirit. Frequent participation in meditation allows the medium to reduce activity in the brain, which as a result enhances the flow and connection to a higher source of energy.

Swami Bhakta Vishita,[10] master of the mind and thought movement, shares his perspective on the source of mediumistic abilities in his own words below:

> It has been asserted that everyone is a medium and in a way this is true, for practically every person is more or less sensitive to spirit influence, and is capable of being developed into an efficient medium of communication with the spirit world. But it is equally true that only a certain percentage of persons possess the true spiritual

qualities requisite for the highest phases of true mediumship. That is to say, but few persons are fitted temperamentally and spiritually for the higher tasks of mediumship. We think it safe to say, however, that where a person is filled with a burning desire to become a true medium, and feels within himself or herself a craving of the soul for development along these lines, then that person may feel assured that he or she has within his or her soul the basic qualities required for true mediumship and that these may be developed by the proper methods.

(Shami Bhakta Vishita, Genuine Mediumship or the Invisible Powers, Advanced Thought Publishing, 1919, 174)

Types of Mediumship

Mental and physical mediumship are two types of mediumship. Mental phenomena cover a wide range of mediumistic phenomena, including clairvoyance, clairaudience, clairempathy, clairsentience, involuntary or automatic writing and drawing, writing by means of a Ouija board, prophetic utterances of spirits, impersonating, and inspirational control of the medium.

If this book were solely about mediumship, it would be useful to fully describe all types of mental mediumship. However, since the book attempts to unveil the mechanisms that allow us to learn more about the nature of the universe, only the types of mediumship that have been experienced by the mediums participating in this study are reviewed. The most common types of mediumship used with mediums in this study include clairvoyance, clairaudience, and clairsentience. The review of physical mediumship will be shared last as it is rarely practiced in the twenty-first century.

Mental Mediumship

Clairvoyant is the French word meaning *clear seeing*. Clairvoyants see objects, colors, symbols, people, spirits, or scenes that are not visible to the naked eye. Most mediums share that they see these visions in their mind's eye, which is also known as the third-eye chakra between their eyes in the upper middle section of their foreheads. The mediums in this study primarily spoke of two types of clairvoyance that occurred. The first type occurs when the communicating spirit implants the thoughts in the mind of the medium through a vision or symbol. This is referred to as indirect clairvoyance as the medium is not seeing the discarnate the way you and I would perceive a living person. The second type, referred to as direct clairvoyance, is where the medium is able to objectively see the spirit entities as they currently manifest in the spiritual world. Some mediums will indicate that if they do not see them fully, they will see strong shadows outlining the height and physical build. It is usually quite apparent when clairvoyants are seeing the actual discarnate as they tend to provide specific detail about the physical appearance.

Enquiring minds often want to know if clairvoyants are *always* seeing dead people. One of the first television programs to heighten awareness about mediums was Patricia Arquette's suspense thriller *Medium*. In this television series this actress who portrayed the real-life medium Alison Dubois was most frequently seeing the deceased in her dreams or at the foot of her bed. The program intimated that Arquette would see dead people at their will. This proposition is also conveyed in the very popular TV series *The Long Island Medium*. Theresa Caputo, the star of the program, is a practicing medium who conveys the notion that spirit is everywhere. Even when her very patient husband attempts to take her for a private birthday dinner, she becomes agitated as the spirits are impatiently attempting to use Caputo to share a message to other patrons at the restaurant. While it is agreed that spirit is everywhere, mediums who have participated in the *Medium7* study indicate that although spirit is always there, they have their own techniques of tuning in and out.

The medium who has clear hearing or can perceive sounds or words communicated from the spiritual realm is known as having clairaudience. Doris Stokes, also known as the Barbican, was famous for her ability to hear detailed information from the spirit world. When you watch videos of her past live performances, it is always apparent that she was solely relying on her hearing. She often had to remind spirits to use her right ear as her other ear was partially deaf because of her age. In 1980, her first written work with Linda Dearsley, *Voices in My Ear: The Autobiography of a Medium*, demonstrates the type of information she could bring forth to the physical world with clear hearing.

Clairsentience or clairempathy is another form of mental mediumship also known as clear feeling. Mediums possessing this talent will be able to perceive information by way of strong, emphatic feelings and emotions from spirit. The medium can feel the presence of spirits in the room and will communicate information based on the feelings they are receiving.

An empath is a person who can psychically tune in to the emotional experience of a person, place, or animal. Clairempathy is a type of telepathy to sense or feel within one's self, the attitude, emotion, or ailment of another person or entity. I can recall conducting a testing session with a new medium. During the meeting I had a sharp pain in my left knee that was threatening to fully distract my focus from the reading. Despite my not showing any signs of distress, the medium asked if I had a disturbing pain in my left knee. She actually showed me the location and described the exact nature of the pain. She was demonstrating clairempathy.

Physical Mediumship

Physical phenomena covers a wide range of mediumistic manifestations, among which are movements of tables, the production of raps, the manifestation of spirit lights, the passage of matter through matter, direct writing upon paper, direct voices, levitation of the medium, spirit photographs, and the production of the materialized form of the spirit. While in rare cases the spirits may manifest these forms of physical phenomena without the assistance of the medium and the participants observing in what is referred to as the *development circle*, nevertheless as a rule such phenomena are produced by the spirits only through the assistance of a medium and usually only when a developmental circle is formed. The most common types of physical mediumship in the late twentieth century included transfiguration (a mask is formed on the face of the medium, and the face is that of spirit) and apports (objects materialize and are transported to another place and rematerialize by spirit). These apports are often given to sitters during a séance or reading. During the mid-twentieth century, after the birth of the religion and philosophy Spiritualism, demonstrating this phenomenon in a concrete form was most satisfying for the public. Given the teachings of the dominant religions at that time, radical demonstrations were needed to encourage others to learn about this new religion and philosophy.

The phenomenon of physical mediumship has been rare in the twenty-first century, however, Rev. John Golsby who has been an evidential medium for more than forty years can attest to the validity of the phenomenon. His grandmother was a well-known medium in England. In addition to doing both private and public demonstrations of mediumship in the various spiritualist churches she had the ability to levitate furniture. His mother never worked privately or publicly; however, when attending circles at the Manor Road Spiritualist Church in London, England, she would often go into trance and channel a spirit entity.

In the past Rev. Golsby has demonstrated transfiguration, and can work in trance but chooses not to; this type of mediumship requires a great deal of energy and has left him feeling ill. Transfiguration mediums enter a trance state and then allow the ectoplasm (further defined in case study #3 in this chapter) to materialize. The spirit attempting to communicate through the medium can impress their face into the ectoplasm to allow the sitter to see the physical features of a passed loved one in the spirit world. John Holland, in his book, *The Spirit Whisperer: Chronicles of a Medium* indicated that those who prematurely lost loved ones in the First World War would gravitate to transfiguration séances in the hopes that they would temporarily see their loved ones again.

In addition to having demonstrated physical mediumship, Rev. Golsby has worked in England, the U.S. and Canada conveying evidence of the afterlife by identifying names, descriptions of a loved one, information about the cause of death, occupation, addresses and/or descriptions of the area where they once lived.

During an event at the Spiritualist Church in Toronto, a member of the congregation brought along his wife, Leila. She was an open-minded skeptic but really did not believe in the *afterlife*. Rev. John Golsby provided "proof of spirit" for the congregation that morning. After she received a message from the spirit world via Rev. John Golsby, Leila's skepticism quickly diminished. Rev. Golsby had asked her if her mother was now in spirit, but before he even required a response, Rev. Golsby went on to name Leila's mother, shared characteristics specific to her mother, and identified that the language she spoke was "English but did not sound like English." For Leila the level of specificity was undeniable, and the emotional revelation that her mother's spirit and consciousness survived death was life-transforming. During Leila's reading, Rev. Golsby also shared that a cat spirit was present, and he elaborated on the emotional feelings surrounding this cat. Indeed, this was additional information that transformed Leila into a believer in an instant as she felt reunited with her beloved cat, which passed away just a few months prior to the event.

This example suggests that mediums who can demonstrate physical mediumship may also be able to provide evidence of the afterlife using mental mediumship.

These definitions and classifications provide the context and clarity needed to understand mediumship. Let us turn now to the following case studies that provide additional context for how this phenomenon materializes.

Case Study #1: Brough Perkins

History

When you first begin to speak to Brough, you realize that for such a young person he has knowledge beyond his years. His thoughts are well articulated, and he is passionate about conducting readings for the public. Most apparent is his interest in metaphysics research and its potential ability to enhance our understanding of mediumship and the spiritual world. This case study is about a medium who specializes in life readings. Brough Perkins, born in Montreal, Canada, has been conducting professional readings for twelve years in the greater Toronto area but occasionally conducts readings with individuals living outside of Canada.

During his early years this young medium knew that he was different from others but was not exactly sure why. During his early teen years he found it difficult to complete basic tasks like getting up to go to school or participating in various social activities. Despite confirming mental health results from doctors that indicated that he was "normal," the depression did not seem to diminish. The feeling of hopelessness prevailed to a point where at the age of fifteen he decided that he was going to end his life. He felt at peace just knowing that the daily grind would soon be over. Right after he came to this decision, he heard a voice in his head, "Honey, honey, honey, my name is Laren." He recalls being so startled by this incident that at that moment he thought that entering the spirit world appeared more daunting than the challenges faced in the physical world. In his mind's eye he clearly saw Laren but still wondered again if these visions were being projected from his own mind. A few short weeks after a friend took a picture of him and after the film had been developed, he was surprised to see that the same face he had envisioned had also appeared in the picture. This verified that he was not crazy and that this entity was indeed around him, guiding him on his path. This picture can still be seen today in the room where Brough conducts readings for clients.

These and other paranormal incidents elicited Brough's need to read more books on metaphysics to better understand his spiritual experiences. His voracious need to read about mediumship began to grow, and with this growth a greater comfort about his gifts was also apparent.

During the Early Years: Psychic Development

In the early years Brough was just learning about his gifts. He was born with them but needed to figure out how they worked. He notes, "One area I needed to work on was knowing when to share new information. I can recall one afternoon in math class suddenly hearing, in my mind, information about my math teacher's pregnancy. I can recall bursting out in the class that the math teacher, Ms. Bernstein was pregnant and that she would be having a boy." Brough further notes, "Of course this did not go over too well as Ms. Bernstein had not shared this news with anyone and did not plan to make the announcement until a few weeks later." After he saw the astonished look on his teacher's face, he realized that psychic knowledge needed to be used with discretion.

Brough explained that during the early years he was having "random psychic episodes." He was trying to piece the puzzle together at times but felt that he needed to understand the symbols and patterns he was receiving. What did they mean? When and how should these gifts be used?

After many years of psychic development Brough began to piece together the symbols and signs and learned when, where, and how to use this information. An interesting example of this was demonstrated during our discussion about *blanks* during a reading. Going blank is somewhat of a fear many mediums have as they never know what information will come and sometimes wonder if spirit will bring the information when needed. Brough shared that blanks did happen for him on a few occasions. In the early years he was anxious about the blanks and the pauses in the readings. After years of development, he learned that there was actually information in the blanks. He can recall a reading where he had thoughts about discussing a client's potential employment opportunities, and then suddenly everything went blank. Instead of filling the blank with fluff, he went back to the thoughts prior to the blank and said to the client, "I see that you have nothing going on in the employment department right now, but there are some potential opportunities on the horizon." Understanding the symbols and how they work is a skill that is developed over a period of time. Developing psychics sometimes become apprehensive when blanks occur and automatically go into what Brough referred to as the "switchboard operator mode." A switchboard operator has a general line or comment he or she gives to every client, and an underdeveloped psychic might fall into the "switchboard operator mode" to fill the silence, inadvertently missing the meaning in the blank.

During the development phase there was a lot of effort made to interpret these symbols. He soon realized that it was not the purpose of the reading to guess all the possible interpretations of the symbols he was being given. He recalls for example getting communication from a grandfather in spirit during a reading. Soon after, the symbol presented was a flower. There was an immediate reaction to suggest that the flower was being presented by the deceased grandfather as a token of love to the client—in this case the widow. Instead of making an interpretation, he described the flower, and immediately the saddened widow's face turned to bliss as she later explained that this was the exact type of flower that she laid on her deceased husband's grave.

Preparation Prior to a Reading

• • •

"Just prior to the reading, I need to get myself out of the way." Brough makes an analogy using stars to better understand how the changes in vibrational frequencies work.

"There are always stars in the sky. Depending on the atmospheric pressure and climate conditions, you will not always see the stars, but they are always there."

• • •

A reading provides clients with guidance about their past, current, or future life events. Brough is not reading the client's mind but is preparing to remove his logical faculties from the encounter to allow the channeling of information from a higher divine source. Has anyone ever tried to make daily decisions without a brain? We have been taught that we should train our brains and rely on cerebral mass to calculate and analyze prior to making informed decisions. A medium must do the very opposite if they are to make a real connection with beloved entities on the other side. To prepare the soul for channeling, daily meditation for at least ten minutes is a part of Brough's regular routine.

Finding a quiet place and focusing only on the breath allows the spiritual body to vibrate at a higher frequency. Vibrating at a higher frequency allows the spiritual self to perceive different states of consciousness. Different states of consciousness can include seeing and hearing nonphysical entities that are vibrating on a similar frequency. Daily meditation allows Brough to easily move into a quasi-trance state during his readings.

Preparation for a reading includes ensuring the surrounding space is neat and void of unnecessary papers and items. Keeping the space neat ensures that clients will not focus on judgment about their surroundings during the reading. Judgment is a sentiment that inhibits the flow of energy required to maintain an open communication with spirit. Chapter 5 further elaborates how the vibrational energies between the client, the medium, and the spirit are interconnected.

Prior to the reading clients are asked to write down what they are looking for in a reading. This information is not seen by Brough at any time but is used to help the client focus on what they really want and helps them send a message into spirit. We always think we know what we want but until we attempt to document our needs, we realize that we may not be very clear about what we really desire.

> • • •
>
> "Spirit is like a radio. It has many channels. I can turn it down, choose a different channel, or completely turn it off."
>
> *Brough Perkins*
>
> • • •

Finally, only a first name and a phone number are required. The only purpose in receiving this information is to make contact for appointments. Brough has access to e-mails as clients make initial contact using this method; however, he does not record or use the information. Information from the client prior to or during the reading is not encouraged. Prior information about a client contributes to a challenge between deciphering whether the source of the information is from the physical plane (shared by the client) or from the nonphysical plane (shared by spirit). Clients are coming to obtain information from the spirit so it is desirable to minimize any verbal exchange.

How Exactly Does This Work?

Brough receives information from multiple sources, including clairvoyance, clairaudience, clairsentience, and clairempathy. He explains that he sees through his mind's eye, which is also known as the third eye. When the psychic phenomenon appears, it is like a big screen movie, with fragmented shots running under his eyelids. Watching this film would be like seeing snapshots of life events occurring in the past, present, and future. He describes these short films as blueprints that represent the life of the client he is reading. Only certain aspects of the movie are shown during the reading, and he does his best to share what he is seeing. These holographic concepts, which are similar to flashes of events and experiences, are normally generalized; however, during a reading the client becomes the center of the holographic concepts, which indicates to Brough that the events relate to the client.

When you listen to Brough describe the blueprint, it appears that he is tapping into the nonphysical world of the Akashic records. These records are like a bank of information containing all knowledge of human experience and the history of the cosmos. Some have likened these records to a library or universal record of every intent, experience, and outcome. Edgar Cayce, one of the world's most famous deceased mediums, acknowledged that during astral travel our souls were able to visit these records to fix past wrongdoings, assess current experiences, and glance at planned future events. Brough explained that it was difficult to respond to questions during the review of the client's blueprint as the film is moving, and he may miss important pieces of the film. This is also the reason he discourages any discussions both prior to or during the reading as all of his information is derived from a nonphysical source. If the client shares information prior to a reading, this creates another challenge known as *blocking*. The medium may have a potential inability to distinguish between the physical and nonphysical information being presented.

The clairvoyance is used for reading the blueprint but also allows Brough to see discarnates in the nonphysical world. He does not see the deceased the same way he would perceive a human body. When one sees the discarnate, there is usually a shadow or sparkles, and the face of the deceased will pop up in the third-eye region of the face.

To strengthen the clairsentience, the enhanced hearing enables Brough to communicate detail from the discarnate. This sound would emanate from the head but would be a voice emanating external to his body. With clear hearing, names, dates, times of passing, and guiding messages can be shared. For many sitters, receiving specific details provides them with proof of spirit and life after death. I can vividly recall sitting in a group séance with three clients who were meeting Brough for the first time to receive answers and potentially obtain proof of spirit. In particular one of the attendees had been grieving for a year after desperately missing her mother. She had hoped that her mother would visit in her dreams or show her a sign that she was still present, but there was still no sign that her mother's spirit prevailed. During this séance when Brough began to read Judy, both her mother and her aunt came through. While the description of the aunt was extremely accurate, when the name "Mary" was spoken, Judy became overwhelmed with excitement to hear the name of her mother mentioned. For her this was proof that her mother had safely transitioned into a new dimension. Hearing more messages about the joy her mother and aunt were having in the spirit world lifted her burden of worry.

Clairempathy is another sensation Brough recently experienced, and now he realizes that this faculty is an additional method for communicating with spirit. While he was waiting for a client to arrive for a reading, he suddenly began to feel a heavy sensation in his chest. He started to hold his throat as it became harder for him to breathe. He had contemplated heading to emergency as the discomfort in his chest was increasing and almost intolerable. This agony was soon interrupted by a knock on the door, and Brough had been prepared to apologize to the client and cancel because of this sudden illness. To his surprise as soon as the door was opened and he saw the client, the sensation diminished as quickly as it started. Within a few minutes of starting the reading the grandfather in spirit began to describe his passing, and the associated sensation quickly dissipated. Brough explained that he now understood that these impressions experienced by the medium's physical body were spirits' way of clarifying the information they wished to be conveyed to the sitter. Some spirits choose to help the medium understand the nature of a sensation by having the medium fully perceive the experience. Prior to readings, these sensations are recognized as temporary symbols to help with the forthcoming communication with the client.

All of these methods of receiving information are carried out in a trance-conscious state. Brough's eyes are usually always closed to allow him to more easily focus on the nonphysical source. There are usually varying levels of recall about information shared during a reading. In a trance-conscious state some of the reading may be recalled as the mind is still fully conscious. Full trance communication occurs where spiritual mediums are able to withdraw within and disengage from a conscious control of their mind, thus allowing them to function under the influence of a spirit communicator. When spiritual mediums are in deep trance, they are not consciously aware of the content of the communication. For the most part, most contemporary mediums no longer go into full trance as there are sometimes unintended consequences when the spirit takes full control.

Brough can also do remote readings as the information he is receiving is not from the client but from a nonphysical source.

Postmortem Detailed Knowledge

When mediums share their gifts with the public, they do it with a variety of tools and approaches. During the interview with Brough I asked him why most mediums did not channel minute details about the client's daily life. I asked this question, as skeptics often question why mediums are not able to share detailed information. I often include nonbelievers and skeptics in my research as they provide diverse views about the phenomenon of mediumship. They ask questions such as, "Why can't the medium tell me what color car I am driving or name the street that I live on? If the deceased are here with us and are around us most of the time, why can't they tell me for example what I had for breakfast this morning?" Brough's perspective on this is that a reading provides the client with the big picture from a bird's-eye view. He explains, "You don't use a helicopter to find a needle in the haystack." This means you wouldn't use spirit to tell you a minute detail about the make and color of your car. The reader is reminded here of the point that while there is infinite knowledge to be shared by spirit, clients are typically receiving information for a one hour period. The discarnates and spirit understand that they only have a limited time to communicate to their loved ones via the medium and prioritize the information to be shared accordingly. Spirit is going to use the short one-hour period to share information about what is most needed at the time and would likely not waste precious energy to share information that would not provide the greatest benefit to the client. This is not to say, however, that spirit cannot or will not decide to share minute facts when necessary. Brough and I received direct proof that this is possible during our interview. I have shared the dialogue verbatim below to illustrate this point.

Donna: "I am wondering why spirit could not demonstrate proof of survival of consciousness by sharing that someone was moving their hips back and forth during a particular date or time, for example. I feel that some people need this kind of detailed evidence to believe in the afterlife."

Brough: "Well, it's interesting that you said that. The guide that is working with you just channeled that information through you. Just yesterday I was doing some deep reflecting and was walking back and forth moving my hips back and forth. This is an activity I rarely do. Your guide used this example to demonstrate that minute details can be channeled, but in most instances it is not worthwhile to share this level of detail."

Dual Duty

Brough noted several times during his interview that his readings were multifaceted. Life readings involved reading the client's blueprint. This includes providing information about the client's past, providing guidance about current activities, and providing probability statements about potential occurrences that might become part of the client's reality. This facet of his work needs to be balanced with the ability to iteratively work with discarnates who become present during intermittent parts of the readings. This is often difficult to manage as information from discarnates and the blueprint provide different types of information with different levels of credibility. Managing how to convey these messages is a skill and a challenge all at once.

A reading from Brough Perkins involves communicating with the deceased and reading the client's blueprint. He uses a variety of extrasensory gifts to channel information that will guide the client toward their highest and greatest good.

Case Study #2: Chris Stillar

Just before conducting my first meeting with Chris, I noticed the big sign on his window openly advertising his services as a medium. It was surprising to see that Chris felt comfortable enough to openly advertise his profession as a medium. Even more surprising was that his business was directly beside a Christian church. By sharing this I am not at all suggesting that the profession of mediumship should be operating underground; however, most mediums I have met use various titles that are a bit more ambiguous. Upon greeting Chris for the first time I stated with astonishment, "That's great that your sign openly states that you are a spiritual medium." Without giving him a chance to respond I further commented, "Does anyone in the community, including the church, have difficulty with your profession being so openly publicized?"

Chris stated with nonchalance, "I do my business. They do theirs, and there have been no problems in the community." This signaled that perhaps the work of a medium was now becoming more mainstream and perhaps even socially acceptable.

When you first meet Chris, it is clear that this is someone who wants to continue to take on new opportunities and is not afraid to share his gift with the world. One of the difficulties in conducting a scientific study on mediums is that most often individuals in this profession are not always interested in publicizing their business and are not willing to contribute to research at the risk of possibly heightening recognition about their gift. This openness about Chris Stillar is important as this type of persona is what allows researchers to openly explore, discuss, and discover more about these types of abilities. You take notice that he is a grounded individual who is motivated to help people and makes his family life with his wife and children a priority.

History

Chris has been providing readings since 1997 and has made this his full-time profession conducting up to three readings a day. He has been conducting workshops, leading seminars, and using his abilities to raise funds for various charities since 2001. Mothers against Drunk Drivers (MADD in Canada) has worked with Chris to bring guidance and comfort to grieving mothers who have lost their sons and daughters to drunk drivers. He launched his new TV series (Rogers Network) called *Seeking Spirit* in 2012.

Chris explains that while he was growing up, he was not religious but would attend Sunday school with his grandmother, who was a devout Christian. He often chuckles when he ponders the irony. What would Grandma say about my work as a spiritual medium? She would have frowned on my profession and suggested that I was dancing with the devil. How ironic it is that Grandma's death actually inspired me to further explore mediumship and metaphysics in general.

Chris further reflects about his prior religious beliefs and notes that he always believed in God but was not really sure how to interpret the concept. He has always felt close to God but does not consider himself to be religious. His experiences as a medium, however, strengthened his understanding of the soul as a separate immortal entity.

As a child Chris knew he was different and recalls knowing at a young age that he was going to do something great with his life. He knew he wanted to help people and thought perhaps being a doctor was a possibility. After he took a few physiology classes, he realized that this was just not a likely possibility.

He explains that prior to having the ability to connect with the other side, there were two key events that started this life transforming process. In 1994 Chris was struggling with obesity and work-related stress. On one customary day his brain started to shut down. He couldn't remember names. Speaking was a challenge, and he couldn't recognize anyone. He was soon rushed to the hospital and fell unconscious. When he woke up in the hospital several hours later, he recalls the sense of relief after he realized he was able to regain his normal cognition. He could speak and recognize family and friends again.

Shortly after this experience he began to have severe headaches, and another similar disconcerting incident happened. He was washing his hands in the bathroom, and suddenly he felt like someone had pulled the trigger of a gun in the lower neck region. The pain in the neck region and the burning sensation that shot downward through his body made him suddenly drop to his knees. He recalls reluctantly placing his hand behind his neck, expecting to feel blood and a gunshot hole, but to his amazement his skin and neck region remained in its original form. To this day Chris is unsure about the cause of these unusual ailments.

He believes, however, that these frequent intermittent painful experiences created the physical transformation in his body that would allow him to begin channeling spirit.

The second transformational event that contributed to his abilities relates to the death of his grandmother. After the physical changes in his body occurred, in 1996 he started to have an avid interest in spiritual and new age movement topics. In August 1996 shortly after the physical changes occurred, Chris's grandmother died, and he believes this "unlocked the door" to the spiritual world. He was close to his grandmother, and the thought of death and her leaving jolted him onto a spiritual path. Shortly after his grandmother died, he can recall an entity that resembled a native Indian standing behind him. He could sense his presence and knew that he was getting thoughts from the new presence. Chris chuckles as he shares, "I thought I was going friggin' loony at the time!" The only validation that he was not crazy was that he was certain that the information coming from the native Indian he now refers to as Grey Owl was not emerging from his own mind.

In addition to having a voracious appetite to read, he began to meditate despite previously making fun of people who engaged in this activity. Initially the discipline of focusing on the breath and dismissing the endless chatter of thoughts during the process of meditation proved to be an arduous feat. He soon began to build his mediumship muscles by conducting readings for relatives and then began to realize that he could communicate with the deceased.

Preparation for a Reading

Chris shared that there were a few key principles he recommended that his potential clients should consider prior to receiving a reading. He emphasized that having an open mind, an open heart, and trust were

● ● ●

Negative energy derived from mistrust can minimize the benefit of a reading.

● ● ●

the first attitudes he would encourage be embraced to be able to open the channel to spirit. He does not demand that everyone who comes to see him believe that he can hear and see the dead. He just asks that they have open minds and hearts so they can allow spirit to communicate the necessary messages. The trust principle is important as lack of trust sets barriers of negative energy further attracting scenarios during the reading that increase the sitter's mistrust. Chris provided an example of how negative energy derived from mistrust can minimize the benefit of a reading. A mother and daughter came in for a reading. It was readily apparent that the mother was apprehensive about the session, and the barriers she put up were clearly visible. The barriers continued to rise during the greater portion of the reading as it was apparent that the expected loved one had not been channeled by Chris. Chris reminded her that the vibrations she was sending actually blocked his ability to hear and feel the messages being transmitted. During a portion of the reading a young male popped his head into Chris's mind's eye and said that he was very grateful. Chris was then shown a symbol of a stark red motorcycle with flashing ambulance lights all around. It was clear that this young male had prematurely left the physical world after a motorcycle accident. Immediately as Chris described the symbols, feelings, and sentiments of appreciation shared by the unknown discarnate, the daughter began to remember the sad and tragic accident two years ago. She shared with excitement, "Do you remember Mom when I was driving on the highway and stopped to help the young boy on his motorcycle? I called the ambulance as no one was planning to stop to help. I held this stranger in my arms until the ambulance came." She sadly recalled how this stranger died and faded into another world before the ambulance arrived. This young man coming through in the reading was just demonstrating his survival of consciousness and saying, "Thank you for being there when everyone else just kept on driving past the accident." The point here is that the mother's negative energy and determined focus on her desired connections might have severely diminished the chance of her daughter hearing this important message of appreciation. More importantly they were given life-transforming evidence of survival of consciousness.

Meditation with prayer once per day is enough to open the channels to spirit prior to his daily routine of sharing messages from spirit with his clients.

Abilities

Chris primarily has four key abilities that allow him to channel messages from the spiritual world to individuals on the earth plane. He notes, "Even though I have clear seeing, I find that the information in my head falls back into a feeling. Hearing and feeling the emotion is stronger than the clairvoyance."

When you experience a reading with Chris, he can share where the discarnate is standing in relation to the client and can feel the age, height, and relationship to the sitter. For example, he will note that he has a discarnate present who is a contemporary (same age), level above (parent, uncle, or aunt), two levels above (grandparents), or level below (children).

The enhanced hearing ability allows him to hear various voices in spirit. He can hear names, information about the sitter, and any type of information that will provide proof of the afterlife. The enhanced hearing varies depending on the spirit communicating. Given his experience with spirit communication, Chris shared, "You have to remember that we are all not great communicators on the physical plane. So if Aunt Betty was not very articulate during her time on earth, she likely has not enhanced her communication skills on the other side." He continued to explain that suicide cases are least likely to communicate effectively. They have severe guilt that inhibits them from sharing information about their causes of death and other related information. Many mediums have shared that they can often hear the accent of the discarnate; however, in Chris's case he specifically recognizes accents from Newfoundland, Ireland, and European accents in general.

In addition to the enhanced hearing and clear seeing, Chris is sometimes able to imitate the deceased entity's personality. Prior to Marla seeing a medium she was not convinced that there was anything one could say or do to convince her that her seventeen-year-old daughter, having passed suddenly of unknown causes, could still exist in some form in the spirit world. During the research she shared with the researcher, "During my visit to Canada, I went to see Chris, but I had some doubt that my deceased daughter would come through with enough evidence that she was still with us in spirit. When Chris started to behave like her, I began to cry. He began to move his mouth like her and wave his hand over his hair in the exact manner that she did. When she was living, she would also say, 'You betcha, kiddo,' and he inadvertently used this language during the reading."

Chris shared at the end of the reading that "you betcha, kiddo" was not a phrase he used normally but that he likely channeled this as further evidence of the young girl's continued existence.

Finally, clairempathy is another perception that allows the medium to feel the attitudes, pains, or emotions of the deceased. Transmitting feelings is a more precise form of communication than words. One word can have many interpretations, but when your body can feel another person's pain, this is the best means of sharing the experience. During a short preparation period prior to meeting with a client, Chris could feel the presence of a brotherly figure. This male in his sixties was trying to share his cause of death, not with words but with clairempathy. Soon after acknowledging the deceased male's presence, he began to experience the depressed mind-set of an individual about to end his life. He soon began to feel a tightening around the

* * *

I have always been clear with my clients that they need to eventually make their own connections with their children and allow appropriate time in between visits.

* * *

neck, diminished breathing, asphyxiation, and then a light floating sensation. After he was startled by this experience, Chris had to quickly recover as his client arrived. As he began to start the reading, the sensation of suicide ideation returned, and so he asked his client if she had a brother who hanged himself. The client stared in awe at Chris and said, "You're absolutely the real deal as unfortunately my brother committed suicide and died from severe asphyxiation caused by hanging."

Dependency

In chapter 8 I review some of the potential challenges associated with mediumship and psychic work. In particular I discuss the challenges related to potential dependency of bereaved parents or clients seeking prescient information. Chris spoke about the importance of informing bereaved parents that they could also learn how to make their own connections with their children in the spirit world. Understanding how to obtain power from within, raising vibrational energy with meditation, and being aware of how signs are transmitted from the spirit world, once learned, can help bereaved parents make connections with their deceased children without always having to depend on a medium.

> Chris further noted, "I have always been clear with my clients that they need to make their own connections with their children and allow appropriate time in between visits with me so that the visits ultimately end up being healthy and productive for their grief recovery. My skill set can and should aid in the grief recovery process but should never be viewed as the only means to healing."

This compassionate approach to working with the bereaved is why Chris is endorsed by the organization MADD and continues to gain the trust of his growing clientele.

Case Study #3: Carolyn Molnar

History

When you meet and speak with Carolyn, you immediately realize that you are conversing with a born teacher. In Carolyn's case she is able to understand, classify, and analyze the various types of phenomenon related to mediums and psychics and convey those ideas to her students and clients.

Carolyn was born with mediumship in her veins. She just seemed to *know* things without having a rational explanation for *how* she knew this information. She can vividly remember her first spiritual experience. At the age of eight she was very sick with a head cold. Her breathing was hindered, and she felt miserable. Intuitively she put her hands on her chest and quietly lay down, surrendering to this helpless feeling. Suddenly she heard the bedroom door open and shut twelve times. She saw a warm white light surrounding her body, and she was able to fall asleep. Upon awakening, she immediately noticed that her head cold had disappeared. She pondered, why, that was weird. I wonder what the door slamming and warm light was all about.

While this incident at age eight was her first interaction with the spirit world, Carolyn was not fully conscious of the implications of her experience. In retrospect she realizes that these spiritual events were typical in her family. Over the years she learned that her parents participated in séances, her grandfather frequently met with a medium, and her grandmother sat in development circles with a medium who read for the prime minister, William Lyon Mackenzie King. In her early thirties she began to learn more about her mother's experiences with mediumship. She recalled her mother explaining that it was really not odd to hear or see events that involved interaction with the spirit world. In retrospect the sight of ectoplasm might be unusual for some. For most of you reading this book, your first introduction to ectoplasm might have been during the movie *Ghostbusters* (1984), a comedy about three eccentric parapsychologists who start a ghost-hunting business in New York. In the movie viewers are exposed to scenes of a slimy green substance that cast members refer to as *ghost slime*. In reality ectoplasm is a substance that supposedly emerges from the medium's mouth, nose, or ears during trance mediumship. During the height of physical mediumship ectoplasm was used to aid the physical appearance of spirits in the other world. This would include being able to see the face of the deceased protruding through the ectoplasm produced by the medium. Carolyn can vividly recall her mother complaining about how the ectoplasm stained the furniture. This did not really concern Carolyn because by her early thirties she had learned a tremendous amount from her family and her mentor, Sadie Nickerson. In fact, Carolyn says she had observed the emergence of ectoplasm during a physical mediumship demonstration. She describes ectoplasm as a substance that appears to look similar to your breath on a cold day. In this particular incident the existence of this breathlike substance allowed Carolyn and other observers to see misty ectoplasm emerge from the circle leader's stomach region and then form into a hand. If there was any doubt about the existence of other discarnates, this moment completely changed that. This breathlike substance created a hand that Carolyn was able to touch.

Another telltale sign that her mediumship abilities are inter-generational is a picture of her grandparents at a gathering in Lily Dale, New York, the largest Spiritualist community in North America. Carolyn recalls hearing about her grandparents' experiences at Lily Dale, where they frequently made trips to this community to experience and learn more about mediumship and other phenomenon. When I first heard of Lily Dale, it was difficult for me to get an image of the location and purpose of the institution. This lack of awareness quickly changed after I watched the HBO movie special *No One Dies in Lily Dale*. You quickly learn that this quaint town is the center for the science, philosophy, and religion of Spiritualism. In 2013 the town will celebrate its 134th year of offering public demonstrations of mediumship and lessons about the basic truths of man. This small community of mediums welcomes anyone who is interested in exploring spirituality.

When Carolyn reflects on her family involvement, she has no judgment about their participation in development circles, physical mediumship, and other related activities. She realizes that this was just a normal way of life for her family.

Between the ages of eight and ten, there were few spiritual experiences. She can recall, however, always having an understanding about the spirit world despite not having any formal lessons at the time. During a sleepover event her friends wanted to play Mary Wentworth—a game where young children call names into a mirror, hoping to elicit a response from the spirit world. Carolyn knew intuitively that there was something about this game that was just wrong. You might think that given her inclination for psychic work, she would be excited that her friends would be interested in contacting the spirit world. This was not the case. Carolyn did not participate in this game or any type of games that encouraged interaction with the spirit world. During her interview she explained that when youth or adults call into a mirror, their intentions are to *play a game*, and the spirit world responds by doing just that—playing a game. Carolyn explains this further using her own words:

* * *

When you interact with the spirit world, your intentions are important. Always ensure you are interacting with the spirit world with positive intentions.

* * *

> When you interact with the spirit world, your intentions are very important. When you are playing a game, you intend to play and subsequently that is what the spirits will provide in return. People who are playing with spirit are also usually less knowledgeable about the spirit

world and are not aware of the importance of protecting themselves from earthbound spirits who are relatively less evolved—wayward spirits are likely to be attracted and this might result in less evolved entities impressing negative thoughts, or playing frightening or harmful tricks on the unprotected and naïve querent.

These unintended consequences may also result when playing with a Ouija board. When manufacturers mass produce these boards, it is with the intention of making money. For the naïve and unprotected user who is interested in playing and experimenting, the response is likely to be one of trickery—information that is not positive or helpful in guiding one to their highest and greatest good. I am aware, however, of people who have impressed good intentions with the Ouija board and know how to protect themselves from wayward spirits—in this case the board may be useful and positive under these conditions. Essentially, one's intention and ability to protect themselves with the appropriate prayers to the Infinite Spirit are essential.

Early Development

Carolyn's first experience at the age of twenty with a medium was quite negative. She can recall going with her sister to see a medium. There was a lot of excitement about this. This medium was sought after and was known for providing insights to the police to locate missing persons when they were not progressing with traditional investigative techniques. She recalls being led into a darkened room with candles. Within moments of the reading negative information espoused from this medium. In addition to the negative information objects began to move in the room. Carolyn asked herself, "Is this what a reading with a medium is all about? Am I supposed to feel frightened and worried about my future?" Within moments of asking herself these questions something deep inside her said, "Get out of here at once!" Indeed, Carolyn did just that. Despite feeling terribly frightened by this experience, she used her favorite pastime of retail therapy to cushion the negative feelings. During a shopping spree that took place right after this incident she was examining bed sheets in the linen department, hoping to find just the right set of double-size sheets. To her surprise, instead of saying, "I need to find a double," she was quite shocked to hear herself say, "I need to find a medium." With that statement along came a very clear vision of her father. In the days to come, Carolyn started to understand this was how psychic impressions worked. She heard herself say she needed to see a medium, and her father's face was shown in her mind's eye. This could only mean that she would need to speak with her dad about this query.

Immediately, Carolyn phoned her father; however, she was not really clear about why she would seek her father's advice and guidance about finding a medium. Carolyn was a bit surprised when she heard her father's reply after she shared her worries. He quickly responded, "This is no problem. I will introduce you to *my* medium." Carolyn thought to herself, *my* medium? Dad has his own personal medium?

Several days later Carolyn was introduced to Sadie. Within moments of meeting her there was a feeling that Carolyn knew her at a soul level. Sadie proceeded to give her a reading. This time the messages were healing, trustful, and pure. What did Carolyn take from this reading? She received two very important insights. First as a medium you have a great responsibility when sharing messages with clients. The wrong messages can cause long-term harm, so insights must be carefully shared and should only come from a source of the highest good. She was also able to resonate with this kind of message. The experience taught her the difference between a reading from a medium who did not work with the highest sources and one who worked from a loving source (Sadie). The second insight she learned was that the spirit world provided accurate and helpful information. All one needed to do was ask. Carolyn was hooked! Once these thoughts were understood, it was as though the spirit world opened up opportunities for her spiritual development.

Carolyn's early development largely revolved around weekly mentoring with Sadie, a seasoned medium who could see Carolyn's potential to utilize her psychic abilities. The weekly development mostly included a call into Sadie every Thursday night for twenty years. Sadie would say, "So read me. What can you tell me about what's happening with me?"

Carolyn can remember being hesitant about this as her confidence was limited in the early years of her psychic development. She can recall her first reading in the early days when in her mind's eye she shared information that seemed a bit bizarre: "I see a red car with snow on the fender. Interestingly, I am seeing it in a cartoon format."

Sadie quickly replied, "Oh, no, that could not be right. I just bought myself a car, and it is blue, so I am not planning to buy a new one anytime soon." Despite Sadie's emphatic disagreement about the reading, less than a month later Sadie was able to validate Carolyn's impressions. She called Carolyn with great excitement to explain that the car she currently owned had broken down and was deemed too expensive to repair, so she went to the used car dealer to look for a replacement. Her son found a car on the lot that was the right price and model—a red car with a layer of snow on the fender. That was just what Carolyn had predicted! Who would think there would be snow in May? Yet on this particular day, however, there were indeed remnants of snow.

After this incident Carolyn's ability to give readings grew as she became stronger and more confident. Sadie had encouraged her to interact more with a church upholding the tenets of

Spiritualism. "Be around like-minded people. Network more and share your teachings with the church," Sadie emphasized. These valuable teachings have stayed with Carolyn to this day. Her participation in the Church of Universal Love, a spiritualist church in Toronto, has allowed her to learn with like-minded individuals and has given her the opportunity to teach important aspects of psychic work and mediumship. The church provides an opportunity for individuals with different beliefs to explore questions about the survival of death, the purpose of being, and other aspects of metaphysics. Its services comprise singing hymns about love and peace, typically followed by an opportunity for individuals to receive a spiritual healing. Sermons of hope and motivation are followed by sessions that allow mediums to provide "proof of spirit." What is most noticeable is that different individuals referred to as *chairpersons* lead the service on a rotational basis. To the outsider this rotational principle suggests that many individuals can communicate with God. The notion of spiritual equality is evident within the church. The tenets of the church revolve around the belief in an immortal soul and encourage people to lead a life of harmony and peace by doing unto others as you would have them do unto you.

From some of the lectures I have observed in the church, speakers encourage members of the congregation to question the notions shared in Spiritualism. This kind of healthy skepticism helps the church evolve and learn more about the spirit world and the nature of its reality. Most importantly the church's philosophy is not punitive in nature—it is about learning about the nature of our universe.

Preparation for a Reading

Carolyn shared that she did not use any particular preparation techniques prior to each reading. She believes that preparation takes place on a daily basis when she makes decisions about what to read or what movies to watch. Carolyn has learned over the years that her angels and guides use the symbols in her memory to convey ideas. For example, if they want to create a concept about fear, they will use existing pictures in the medium's memory that represent the idea of fear for the medium. So watching the film *Poltergeist* would not be advisable as grisly images from that scary movie would then become part of her memory and likely would emerge during a reading. These images would not be the compassionate and peaceful symbols of reference she wants to perceive during her practice with clients. Therefore, she chooses a healthy intake of positive movies and literature, practices meditation and positive thinking, and abstains from alcohol or other substances.

Carolyn does not meditate as often as she used to because she is able to move into a *Zen* state more easily. She describes *Zen* as the following:

> Zen is about being fully present in the moment—you focus on your current thoughts, you are aware of the feelings in your body and the pictures in your mind's eye are very clear. I know when I am in a Zen-like state when I am focusing on the here and now and am operating in alternate state of consciousness. I have often started a reading with a client having a full migraine headache, however, as soon as I am in a Zen-like-state I no longer feel the pain of the migraine headaches or any other physical bodily challenges.

Prior to each reading Carolyn uses the following prayer, which she wrote, to ensure that the messages she brings are for the highest and greatest good:

> I ask only the highest and the best to come through to give me what I need to serve others. I ask that all negativity at all levels be sent back to the source

from which it came and I ask that I be surrounded by Your white light of protection as I sit here ready to receive your highest messages. I ask only my Highest Guides and Masters to come through and share messages for my greatest good.

Abilities

Carolyn uses all five extrasensory perceptions to receive messages. Specifically she sees discarnates using her third eye, which is called indirect clairvoyance. This is different than direct clairvoyance, in which some mediums actually see the discarnate in the same way we perceive each other on the earth plane. During the interview I inquired about why some mediums have abilities related to indirect clairvoyance while others have gifts of direct clairvoyance. Carolyn replied that in her case she would simply need to ask the spirit to experience direct clairvoyance although she understands that once this gift is granted, it cannot be reversed. This would mean she would be seeing discarnates more vividly on a daily basis, and this was not a condition she wanted to experience. Carolyn has found over the years that although she has extrasensory abilities when it comes to hearing, tasting, smelling, feeling, and seeing, her guides will focus and develop pre-existing strengths. Her indirect clairvoyance was her first gift to be strengthened over the years because her biology was set up to be able to see easily. She notes that with practice one can begin to confidently distinguish between symbols conveyed by discarnates compared to symbols derived from an active imagination.

While she is comfortable with clairsentience, she shares that it can be quite painful. Carolyn recalled standing in front of approximately thirty members of a Spiritualist church congregation with the purpose of providing evidential "proof of spirit" when suddenly her bottom molar became very painful. She asked, "Is anyone experiencing a pain in their mouth, in particular the bottom second last molar?" I observed this event firsthand and could clearly see Carolyn struggling with pain in her mouth despite not showing signs of being in pain prior to that moment. A woman at the back of the church put up her hand and shared that she had been experiencing great pain with that specific tooth over the past six months. Carolyn ended the message by emphasizing the need to get this tooth checked immediately. Once the message was delivered, it was noted that Carolyn resumed her message work without experiencing further tooth pain. Perhaps spirit conveying the pain via clairsentience is an accurate and fast way of communicating the message from the spirit world.

This example suggests that mediums have pre-existing strengths that can be strengthened. In addition it can be speculated that the relatively weaker senses will be strengthened in time when the other stronger senses are fully awakened.

Proof of Spirit at the Church

The Spiritualist Church often has events that allow mediums to share what they call "proof of spirit." Providing this *proof* is important for believers and newcomers to the church who have a limited understanding of the spiritual world and the nature of the soul. Marvin, a research participant in *Medium7*, attended an event at the church called the *Festival of Mediums*, where Carolyn was one of the mediums sharing messages from spirit. Marvin is the type to be open-minded about new experiences and during his interview noted that he was a voracious reader in areas related to spirituality. Any movement, religion, or philosophy that encouraged truth, hope, and peace was something he wanted to learn about. Despite learning about many religions and their views on the afterlife, Marvin had not made any final decisions on what he believed. Over the years his thirst for understanding had been assuaged by reading relevant literature, watching TV programs, such as John Edward's *Crossing Over*, and attending regular Sunday services at the Spiritualist church where visiting mediums would share messages from spirit to various members of the congregation.

At the *Festival of Medium* event when it was Carolyn's turn to provide "proof of spirit," Marvin was struck by the amount of names she provided. He observed how members in the audience verified the validity of the names and the information being shared. *Not only is communication occurring, but the evidence is remarkable*, he thought.

A short period after that experience, Marvin's co-worker Sharon shared that she was not happy in her career. She was curious about the spirit world and inquired if Marvin knew of an authentic medium. Marvin confidently referred his co-worker to see Carolyn. Sharon provided this feedback about the reading: Carolyn gave over twenty items of evidence that could not have been known by the medium. To Sharon this was proof that the information was coming from someone who at one time had lived with her in the physical form. Sharon was astonished that Carolyn was able to identify the specific illness that plagued her best friend and was able to demonstrate knowledge about a memorial service that had taken place just prior to her reading.

After he saw Carolyn give messages at the church and heard the feedback from his co-worker, Marvin decided to have a personal reading with Carolyn. As a result of a tragedy that occurred to a close acquaintance he reserved the first fifteen minutes of the reading in attempt to learn more about this tragic event on their behalf. Marvin had found it painful to watch close friends lose a teenage daughter. What was more difficult was that the cause of death was not clear, making it difficult for the parents to progress through the grieving process. Carolyn was able to convey that the death was not natural—a type of accident that was not intended. She revealed that after this death, family and friends questioned whether this was an intended suicide. She also noted that it took some time for this body to be found. When the parents heard Marvin relay these messages, they were deemed credible. Most important is that despite the deceased daughter's strained relationship with her parents, she was able to share her love and apologize for the bad relations during the few years leading up to her passing.

Marvin will never forget the outpouring of gratitude the parents felt after they learned this information. He was able to experience firsthand how guidance from a gifted medium could bring peace and hope in people's lives.

Teachings

The following is a summary of the key teaching points Carolyn shared in her interview for the research of *Medium7*.

Discarnates or Guides

Carolyn indicated that in her work as a psychic and medium it is important to distinguish the guides and angels from discarnates. The discarnates, usually your loved ones, have limited knowledge based on their own experience and spiritual levels of attainment. In the afterlife they continue to experience memory and personality from their lives on the earth plane. Carolyn can identify discarnates during a reading as they often respond with emotion and share messages that are relative to their personal perspectives. For example, one of her clients asked about how a particular loved one was experiencing the afterlife. Carolyn replied with a bit of a chuckle that *Cousin Bob* was not able to respond clearly, for he was still visiting the alcoholic bars too frequently in the afterworld. Bob's advice from the afterlife was not that useful to the sitter.

Guides and angels, however, have spiritually evolved to a higher level of existence. They have earned their titles after they have successfully learned lessons that come from experience in either the physical and/or other planes of existence. Given their levels of evolvement, their insights about current and future activities can be more seriously considered. Carolyn can distinguish the guides and angels from discarnates as the former vibrate at a much higher frequency. Their messages are derived from a higher perspective, are without emotion, and are usually clear and concise.

This teaching is important. If the medium does not clarify the source of the message, the sitter may not be able to consider the limitations of the discarnate's advice—a point that needs to be considered by practitioners assessing the validity of messages shared by mediums in general.

Being a Responsible Medium

Another key teaching point shared by Carolyn relates to the ethics and responsibility psychics and mediums must consider when they are conveying messages from spirit to clients. Mediums have to consider their clients' vulnerability, carefully share the messages, ensure there is a compassionate intention, and, most importantly, ensure that the source of the messages is derived from the highest sources of spiritual existence.

Effect on the Physical Body

Carolyn emphasized that mediums need to understand the potential effects mediumship can have on their bodies. She does not recommend that mediums conduct too many readings per day as the clarity of the messages diminish and certain areas of the body may deteriorate in the long term. During her interview for the Medium7 study she told the author that areas of the brain, including the pituitary gland, pineal gland, and hypothalamus, become overused, eventually diminishing aspects of the nervous system that runs along the spine. The amount of readings, the types of spiritual protection used, and the vehicles used to channel the messages from spirit are factors that can be modified to ensure that the challenges to the physical body are minimized.

Case Study #4: John Pothiah

History

During John Pothiah's interview it was apparent that although John was incredibly gifted with unique talents, he was extremely humble. He made sure to remind me that he was an equal to everyone else and was mostly concerned about ensuring his messages were compassionate and helpful to his clients.

When you first hear John's history about how he learned about his own psychic abilities, your initial reaction may be one of sadness and elation all at the same time. This story starts when John was just a young boy in Africa. His dad was in the navy during the war, and because of the father's status in the navy, the family had an opportunity to move to England. His spiritual gift soon became apparent once the family settled in England. John describes in his own words how he started to become aware that he had some very useful gifts,

> In the 1950s there were different educational opportunities depending on your race, so as a young boy of color I was functionally illiterate. Once I arrived in England, I was placed in a Catholic school with nuns and although I had an opportunity to become educated, I was so functionally illiterate at the age of six that I wondered if I could understand enough of the curriculum to learn at the rate of the other students. I really did not have any time to be embarrassed about my functional illiteracy. I can recall not being clear about how to approach an upcoming math test. In my dream state I would be shown the test and the approach to answering the test; it was very clear. I could see numbers: 5 + 10 = 15. In addition, once I awoke, I seemed to be able to remember all of the information illustrated

in the dreams. Here I was virtually illiterate but after writing the tests and receiving exceptionally high scores, the principal would proudly march me around the school, labeling me a genius. I was given a threepence (at the time also called a thruppenny bit in Britain) as a reward for my performance. Receiving this was highly rewarding and timely given my family's financial limitations. I continued to receive miraculous help from an unknown source. I recall for example having the confidence to open a book and read after a young girl at the school showed me how to write my name. After that, although my reading was still limited, I could somehow absorb and comprehend the contents of any book like a sponge.

Now that I look back I realize that where the formal educational system failed, the spirit world provided. My friends (entities in the spirit world) allowed me to learn skills and augment my talents through psychic means. An example of this is illustrated with my playing checkers (known as draughts in England)—after winning a game of checkers I played against a man who had advanced skills in this game. He was so impressed with my skill that he gave me his watch. It takes a few years to beat skilled checkers players, yet I, in my mind, was shown where to move the pieces and within just a few games was able to beat a skilled player—my friends were there to teach me and I was willing to learn.

Despite a long period of naiveté about psychic phenomenon John continued to benefit from spirit guides and angels, but he was not fully conscious of their presence. He thought at one point various colors around the human body were seen by everyone. What a relief, he thought, others must see these colors as well.

> It was a relief to see that others saw colors around the human body. The halos and colors around the angels in the church portraits were truly comforting. I was not different after all.

There they are … all around the heads of the angels and deities painted on the large portraits in the church and Catholic school I attended. John explained that he was temporarily elated that he felt normal for once. With all of these portraits with halos and lights emanating from these deities, this meant that perhaps mankind celebrated this natural glow that emanated around all physical bodies. This pleasant thought did not last very long. He soon learned that once again he was the only one that saw these lights and colors around everyone's bodies. This discovery coupled with the nuns' insinuations that he was abnormal culminated to a point where John simply "shut down his gifts." He thought, I have to fit in here, and so that is just what I am going to do!

After he virtually shut down his gifts during his early years, he began to recognize other talents. Writing poetry and giving advice to people seemed to be natural gifts that allowed him to channel artistic writing and guidance that would support others on their journey. The poetry and advice would allow John to fit in while he was practicing and sharing his psychic gifts. It was not really until John discovered the religion of Spiritualism at the age of twenty that he began to feel that he could be free to openly discuss his psychic abilities. As the confidence in his psychic abilities increased, he began to feel more comfortable opening up about his gifts.

Preparation for a Reading

To prepare for any type of work with the spiritual world, John meditates for as long as he can prior to a reading. He notes that it is essential to meditate between the readings to clear the energy associated with the prior reading. Using meditation to "clear the energy" ensures that he is no longer experiencing the energy from the previous client. John explained that to conduct a reading, he is actually stepping into the energy fields of the client. Although he steps into the energy field, he is still detached to a certain extent. He explains further that by stepping in the energy field, he has to change his vibrational energy to align with the client. If the client is depressed, John's vibrational range will need to be significantly lowered within a short span of time. He notes, "If I have a sitter come in for a reading who is drunk, once I step into his/her energy field, I am also going to feel drunk. I must meditate in order to ensure that I am not carrying this drunken energy into the next reading." It is important to note here that John is illustrating an example of how some mediums must align their vibrational frequency with both the client and their guides and angels simultaneously. This would mean that John would have to be detached enough from the client to ensure that he could still vibrate high enough to align and communicate with his guides and angels, who would be vibrating at a much higher frequency than humans. This ability to simultaneously vibrate at different frequencies can only be achieved with great discipline and an ability to shift consciousness swiftly. More importantly this is why John encourages only one client to attend a reading per sitting. If more than one client participates in a reading at the same time, the ability to manage the multiple communications from the spirit world and balance the varying vibrations of the client make it difficult to align and accurately communicate messages.

As John gets older it is becoming increasingly difficult for his body to withstand the effects of his clients' energy fields. John's current practice is to have his client's *friends* speak to his *friends* in the spirit world to enhance the communication to be conveyed to the sitter while he also limits any damage to his physical body.

How Exactly Does This Work?

John primarily uses clairsentience and clairvoyance to convey messages from the spirit world; however, other extrasensory gifts are used to qualify the initial symbols and feelings received. After I heard feedback from a few of John's clients, it was clear that he had the unique ability to operate like a human X-ray machine. Of course you might say, "How exactly is that possible?" John explains that after stepping into the client's energy fields with his mind shifting consciousness, he sees many colors and sparkling lights around and within the body. He explains that he does a 360-degree scan of these colors throughout the body. John eloquently explains in his own words how he is able to see within the human body to identify past, current, or future physical ailments.

> For me, seeing in the body is just like breathing. It is not a difficult task for me. When I have shifted my consciousness to be aligned with other planes of existence, it is natural for me to see colors around the human body. Of course I am not a medical doctor so it took me time to learn the significance of various colors. So when I first started out doing this work, I can remember seeing a murky color that through my knowing signified ill health. To further qualify the meaning, my friends would show me a symbol or show me the shape of a kidney. I might even receive a taste in my mouth (clairgustance) to help me understand the extent of the problem with the blood, ulcers or other medical conditions. Over the years I have grown to learn about the various colors and their significance. For example, a mercury color indicates that the client was born diabetic. The number of cells in relation to particular colors indicates cancer for

example. The number and quality of red spots in the brain indicate multiple sclerosis traits and so on. I only have so much time in a reading so spirit will help me focus on what needs to be addressed or identified for the sitter.

Over the years I have used this technique to identify both healthy and unhealthy areas of the human body. With this information I always encourage the client to check with the doctor. My insights are not offered to replace a medical doctor's advice and prescriptions. In fact, if it is in the clients highest and greatest good, I will see health issues that might not be detectable with current medical diagnostic tools. This detection of the unseen is possible as the aura extends far beyond the body allowing me to see probabilities of medical ailments as far as approximately ten years into the future. My friends will not provide me with the information if it is not in the sitter's highest and greatest good or if it will be too upsetting. For example, a mother and her daughter came in for a reading on the same day but at different times. During the scan of her body and via the communication of my friends we knew that the mother's time was coming to an end. During the reading with the mother we refrained from sharing this information as we knew she could not handle the news; however, we shared it with the daughter who we knew would be able to manage the information and would benefit from being able to mentally prepare for this possibility.

I can also recall a case where my friends did not allow me to receive the information as they knew it would affect me and would interfere with the remaining period of the client's life. I saw a man known as Ray for a reading and six months after this reading his wife, Melissa, shared that her husband, Ray, passed away recently with a terminal disease. She asked, "Why did you not see this disease or imminent death despite accurately pinpointing other ailments that Ray was experiencing?" She further explained that since the reading, Ray and his wife enjoyed six months of joy and then suddenly her husband died within a two week time span. I had two answers to Melissa's question. I shared with her that it would not have been useful for Ray to hear the information about his imminent death. There was nothing any medical doctor could do to save him. So in the absence of this daunting knowledge Ray was able to lead a normal life for six months. The second part of that answer I shared with Melissa is only something I know for myself. After several years of learning about my psychic gifts, my friends understand that I am sensitive, so they also protect me from learning information that will not be beneficial for myself and the client. So in this case I was not shown information about the imminent death. Most important is this work is not about the ego. It is about compassion and this must be the goal to be effective in this work.

Up to this point in John's interview I could not help but notice the parallels between John and the healer, known as Adam. In his book, *Dreamhealer*, Adam McLeod talks about the chakras and colors he sees in the human body after he goes into trance state. Similar to what John describes, Adam sees the lights and identifies the area of the problem. When Adam used to do one on one healings, he described how he used his mind to visualize a healthy state and was able to use his positive intention and energy to transform the ill-health to the healthy state visualized. What is consistent between John and Adam's work is that they are able to see the colors inside the human body and can identify colors and lights that are not part of the healthy states of the human body. John shared in his interviews that while he was able to identify and diagnose the state of ill-health, he did not manipulate energy with the intention to heal as described in Adam's book. John reiterated in his interview that he always reminded the client that his medical advice was only a prevention tool that should be used in conjunction with a doctor's advice and prescriptions. John shared a unique case where a woman suffering from migraines could not experience relief from anything a doctor prescribed. John suggested that almonds might work and for some unknown reason anytime this woman felt another migraine coming on, a few almonds would immediately diminish the symptoms. The medical advice provided during readings is only shared to ensure that clients take the precautionary steps to diminish the probability of a medical ailment from occurring. John emphasized that the *almond solution* worked for this woman, but it would not necessarily work for others.

State-of-the-Art Medical Instruments

John's clients have shared numerous testimonies with him about how his medical insights alerted them to problems that were not detected by traditional diagnostic instruments. It seems in many cases recounted by John that he has been able to see and diagnose illness where state-of-the-art medical instruments have not been effective. John recalls the case where during an internal scan of the chakras and colors of Helen's energy system it was clear that she had a problem in her abdominal area. John's emphasis during the reading encouraged Helen to have this area checked by her doctor immediately after the reading. The doctor checked and diagnosed the problem as a cyst that would either implode or reabsorb back into the body, suggesting that this problem did not require any type of medical intervention as the problem would resolve itself. After she reviewed John's recording of the reading and the associated warning about the stomach area, Helen went back to the doctor to have it checked again only to be told once more not to worry about this cyst. Approximately nine months after the reading, Helen was bodybuilding, and a bulge started coming out in her back, which she thought was muscle she was building. Soon after that she passed out one day at work. After friends rushed her to emergency, doctors found a twelve-pound tumor two centimeters smaller than a basketball growing and intertwining through her reproduction organs. This required a hysterectomy, and Helen was unfortunately devastated as she would not be able to bear children.

Why can a medical intuitive like John diagnose illness where medical instruments prove to be ineffective? John explains that the auras around the human body carry information about skills that the soul has mastered through many lifetimes but also carry genetic information and potential illness spanning within eight to ten years in the future. This range of time may vary depending on the age and condition of the client present. In Western society we have seen a growing integration of Eastern medical therapies that are predicated on the basis of energy systems. Therapies like acupuncture, chiropractic, and Reiki are a few therapies that are believed to work as a result of changes in the energy flow that allows the physical body to heal. John's ability to see these energy fields is quite consistent with these alternative medical therapies. Once mankind understands more about these energy systems, it will become easier to understand how a medium like John is able to see and feel these systems surrounding the physical body. State-of-the-art equipment is designed to detect three-dimensional ailments; however, a psychic medium's ability to align with other planes of existence allows him or her to connect with a fourth-dimensional reality—an existence that is not detectable by using our third dimensional medical instruments.

Just-in-Time Prevention

In chapter 9, I share a story of a woman who during her interview for this research noted that she was terrified to deal with her breast cancer until John encouraged her to have the surgery. He emphasized that he could see the location and size and given all of the other conditions in her body saw that there was a high probability that the doctors would be able to surgically remove all of the cancer. This is one of many stories. John described another case where a woman asked about her husband's health during her reading. John told her to get her husband to a doctor and have his prostate checked. He wasn't going to; however, she pushed him, and the doctors found prostate cancer in the early stages.

An example of how John's medical intuition saved a man's life involves a case of life and death. At the end of a reading while a client named Justin was leaving, John pointed out the crimson flare on Justin's upper right leg and emphasized the need to have this checked by a doctor. At the time Justin's response was that there was not any problem with that area of his body. John's clairsentience brought on a strong feeling of *knowing* that this area needed imminent medical attention, but he could not force Justin to seek immediate medical attention. Just two days after the reading a sore on his upper right leg emerged. Justin could not stop scratching the area and recalled John's warning to seek medical attention and swiftly proceeded to the emergency room at the closest hospital. Fortunately the attending general practitioner at emergency had prior experience with these types of sores and was able to immediately diagnose and treat Justin's case of flesh-eating disease—a bacterial infection that produces toxins and within short periods of time can destroy tissues like muscles, skin, and fat. In Justin's case he would have never proceeded to an emergency room to address any itchy sore; however, John's identification of the area of the body was accurate, and his insistence about seeking medical attention was too prominent to be taken lightly. Justin did indeed receive the medical attention he needed to save his life, and John's advice with the help of his friends in the spirit world provided the *just-in-time* advice.

Time and Space

John's interview elaborated on concepts about *time* and *space*. As shared in chapter 1 of this book, a primary reason for examining mediumship is to understand how mediums enlighten us about the nature of our existence. A common question posed to mediums is, can spirits experience our realities in real time? The question strives to understand if our planes of existence work on a different basis of time. The more you read the literature on quantum theory, the more you begin to understand that time is relative. The theory purports that the past, present, and future are actually occurring simultaneously in a parallel universe or alternative realities. The most important notion to consider from this theory is that *time* is not as linear as we perceive it to be here in the third dimension. With these theories it is helpful when evidence from the spirit world via a medium substantiates that it is indeed possible for the spirit world to understand and communicate using our *time zone* where necessary. John shares two cases to demonstrate that the spirit world can relay messages that are consistent in *real time.*

During a reading John paused and shared, "Someone very close to you is leaving their body right now." The man looked at his watch and made a mental note that it was 3:15 p.m. When the client arrived home, he learned that his sick brother-in-law, whom he and his wife were looking after, did indeed pass away at exactly 3:15 p.m., the same time John mentioned the passing.

In this case John learned this information from his spirit guides and angels who resided in a different plane of existence but were still able to share a precise time.

John clarified in his interview that real time is very possible when the spirit world intends to convey messages about time. If it is not in the highest and greatest good for the client, a time will not be revealed.

Survival of Consciousness or Super- Psi?

Some researchers in parapsychology have taken elaborate steps to determine whether or not information shared by a medium comes from someone who had at one time been with us on the earth plane (discarnates). The elaborate steps taken have been needed as many researchers believe that information shared from a medium may be derived from the medium's ability to read their client's thoughts or their subconscious. The following example provides evidence that mediums can indeed derive information from discarnates. This can be proven when the client learns information from a discarnate via the medium that he or she did not know.

Kelly was able to hear from her deceased father, Arthur, during a reading with John. During the reading Arthur was trying to communicate information about a square box with money. When Arthur was alive, he owned an import-export business with his son that in recent months was going into bankruptcy. There was no money in the family to help the son keep the import business operational. Arthur continued to provide John with information about the square box with money; however, Kelly could not relate to this but kept this information in the back of her mind.

A few months after the reading Kelly went to Toronto to visit her mother and explained that Arthur had come through in a reading with a medium insisting on a square box with money. While Kelly's mom was delighted to hear about Arthur coming through during the reading, she shared that she was not aware of any square box with money in the house.

When Kelly was ready to leave her mother's home that evening, she got into her van to travel home, and her van wouldn't start. She decided to stay the night with her mother, go out for dinner, and get her van checked in the morning. During her overnight stay she was following her mother into the bedroom to look for some extra night clothes and noticed the outline of something under the dresser. They both bent down underneath the dresser and pulled out a square box. Kelly and her mother were surprised to see the box as they had not noticed it before. Just as Arthur shared via John there was indeed a square box, and this box contained a wallet with twenty thousand dollars in it.

Kelly and her mother were shocked but relieved that they could help save Arthur's beloved import business. When Kelly got ready to leave the next day, she found it odd that her van started without any of the troubles experienced the night before. Was Arthur instrumental in ensuring Kelly would help find the square box? While this latter question is of interest, what is important in this case is that no one except a deceased person (Arthur in this case) knew about the box with the hidden dollars. This is proof of survival of consciousness (or life after death). Even if John had the ability to read Kelly's mind or obtain information from the person's subconscious, he would not have been able to attain this type of information from that source as no one else but Arthur knew about this *hidden treasure*.

An Agreement with the Spirit World

John has made an agreement with his *friends* to bring compassion and light to people here on the earth plane. He has agreed to share information in a special room in his home during chosen periods. When he is grocery shopping or participating in daily activities, he does not see auras, hear voices, or experience different realities. I could not help but chuckle when John shared with his strong English accent, "I will do my part, but I will certainly not be dealing with dead people all day long!" It is quite fascinating that John is able to turn his gifts off and on. Co-workers who know about John's gifts as a medium are shocked that he cannot guess anything correctly during his daytime job mostly because at that time he is just John leading a normal life until he returns to that special room where he works with the spirit world to use compassion to light the way for others on the journey of life.

Case Study #5: Faith Grant

I first met Faith in 2005 and was quite impressed with the level of mediumship she conveyed during a group reading. In 2010 during the recruitment period for this research study, I had hoped to find Faith to include her in this study but found it challenging to find her contact information. It was like she had disappeared completely. After many attempts to locate Faith, it took a few miracles before I could find her. It turns out that a few years ago someone who was displeased with her practising mediumship proceeded to start a cross burning on her lawn. Needless to say this was frightening for her family and created an everlasting fear of sharing her gift with the public. Faith is a "cover name" used to protect herself and her family. Some of the following information has been revised slightly to protect her identify.

History

Faith summed up her childhood history by stating, "Ever since I was little I was simply weird. No one could put their finger on it, but they knew something was different." She shared that her mom "clued" into these differences when Faith was at the age of seventeen. Faith explained, "I would blurt out things that no one else would know, and I would make predictions that would come true. I was not sure why I had the urge to make these statements, and I was not aware of how I could know information that was not shared via normal channels."

As a result of experiencing Faith's abilities in her early teens, her mother decided to arrange one-to-one readings with eight members of her bowling team. Faith's confidence increased immensely when the members of the league expressed their awe in Faith's accuracy and ability to know information that was not available through normal means. This launched her career conducting individual and group readings with clients.

> Mediums are sensitive to malevolent spirits.
>
> It felt like the house was constricting; it was as if the house would eventually have limited air and suffocate itself and everyone in it.

About eight years ago upon entering a home to conduct a group reading, Faith sensed malevolent spirits in the home. She had not wanted to alarm the host of the party as this would have caused unnecessary fear. Faith explained that upon entering the home, she felt like the house was constricting. It was as if the house would eventually have limited air and suffocate itself and everyone in it. She could also feel that the entity was not pleased with strangers being in the house. Faith could not explain how she knew this, but she realized that the prayer to God she always made prior to conducting a reading might not be strong enough to protect the home and the clients during the reading. Faith further explained that when she was conducting a reading, the medium and the client were opening up their energy fields. The prayer is elicited in attempts to ensure these energy fields are not intersected by malevolent spirits. However, in a case where malevolent spirits are present, it is not wise or recommended to conduct a reading.

Faith discreetly asked the host if she had experienced any unusual activity in the home. Jean, the host, apprehensively replied, "We just moved in two months ago, and we have experienced unusual sounds and objects disappearing. Most important is that the host noted that when there was no one else in the home, she always felt that there were others present. The host of the party went on to explain that she hoped these potential home issues were a figment of her imagination as this house was a dream home. Faith offered to send the malevolent entity into the light to clear the house of negative energy, and after she heard the appreciation shared by the family, Faith began to expand her services to house cleansing and eventually exorcisms. Faith began to describe her experiences with exorcisms, and while these would be extremely entertaining for the readers, I shared that this type of activity was beyond the scope of the book. Let the truth be told that the frightening aspect of this topic was the primary reason for me discouraging any further discussions on the topic. In essence the discussion of exorcism does not really add value to understanding the nature of reality. What we can take away from this aspect of Faith's interview was that she confirms that there are malevolent spirits in the spirit world. Faith continued to explain this phenomenon. She shared, "Similar to the conditions on earth, we have our share of good and evil, and this mixture is no different in the other planes of existence." There are two interesting facts Faith shared about exorcism. She notes that from her experiences she can confirm that spirits can possess another individual. She states that of the 150 exorcisms she has conducted, 60 percent are real cases of possession, and 40 percent of these are mentally ill cases where the behaviors often mimic the symptoms of possession.

As Faith continued to develop her gifts over the years she realized that she was happiest when she was using her gifts to help people. She volunteers her time providing readings in hospitals devoted to sick children. Demonstrating life after death for parents who have ailing children gives hope.

Abilities

Faith chose to explain her abilities using an experience that has transformed her life. She uses the story of Emma to elaborate on how she used her clear feeling, seeing, and hearing to share messages during her readings.

> I can recall my first experience attempting to communicate with the entity I now consider to be my spirit guide. I realized that it must have looked rather odd that I would often look over my right shoulder in attempts to both receive and share my thoughts with my spirit guide who could not be seen by myself or others. I could feel the presence and began to understand that I could relay messages about health, employment, relationships, and future predictions by hearing my guide share particular information. My guide would often communicate by popping ideas in my mind or by providing me with symbols that had associated meaning. The ideas that pop into my head from my spirit guide are more pronounced. The auditory information is different from hearing another person. Although it is registered in my mind, the voice comes from outside of my head. I would say that my hearing and feeling is strongest. Although I can see spirits, I see children more clearly and usually feel the presence of spirit entities.
>
> About five years ago I was on my way to a medium party where about seven strangers were waiting for me to demonstrate proof of life after death and to share messages from deceased loved ones. While driving to the host's party, I had a distinct

feeling that someone was sitting in the back seat of my car. I looked up into the rear mirror while backing into the parking lot and to my surprise, there was a six-year-old girl holding a stuffed bird in her hand. I quickly turned my neck 240 degrees as I knew that this was not my daughter and I needed to see if my eyes or the mirror was playing tricks. I jolted the car to a full stop and turned my body fully to be able to face the young child. Indeed, there was a young child. As I looked into her eyes, I heard the name Emma, and I immediately saw the vision of how her life passed. I could see Emma with tubes hooked up to her everywhere and could instantly feel the sensation of my body disintegrating. My bones in particular felt very weak. I could both hear and feel the sorrow of Emma's parents' pain as they watched their only daughter slowly disintegrate at the age of six.

I needed to turn my focus to the work ahead of me but still felt Emma with me as I entered the party host's home. I did four hours of readings in total for seven people but was surprised that Emma did not encourage me to connect with any one of the party members. Usually spirits present themselves long before a reading to prepare me with certain ideas or feelings. While preparing to leave, I asked the host if there was anyone here that lost a young girl named Emma. While I was describing all the details, the host's face turned several shades of red. The host spoke in shock and awe. With tears running down her eyes she said, "Emma's mother was going to come today to get a reading but at the last minute had to cancel due to limited funds. She lost her six-year-old daughter, Emma, due to lung cancer." At that moment I had sensations of shock, sadness, and excitement all at once. I was excited as I now had the possibility of connecting Emma to her mother. I made arrangements with Emma's mother free of charge to let her know that her daughter was healthy and growing in the spirit world.

Prior to Emma's passing, her parents sent her to a Brazilian medicine man with hopes of prolonging her life. During her time there the medicine man gave her an exotic parrot to take back home with her. I now realize why Emma often shows up at various readings. I love parrots and have many birds in my home. Whenever I have to face large crowds of people to give readings and am overcome with fear, I will often see a feather fall near me, and I know I am going to be fine now that Emma is with me.

Assessing the Trends

The cases shared here illustrate the most common types of psychic work and mediumship practiced in the twenty-first century. Although there are commonalities, the mediums have diverse histories, unique gifts, and perspectives about the spiritual world. It is important to embrace this diversity as it helps us gain a better understanding of how mediums interact with the spirit world. After I interviewed and analyzed the information shared in these case studies, I found a number of points worth highlighting.

During my observation of these five mediums and others outside of this study, it is clear that almost 98 percent of mediums in the twenty-first century are practicing mental mediumship. Based on the case studies in this chapter, indirect clairvoyance and clairsentience appear to be the predominant mechanisms with other extrasensory perceptions being used to support and qualify the communications of the initial transmission.

After observing hundreds of mediums over a period of nine years, I have not observed a medium perform physical mediumship during a reading. This does not seem to be the format that is used to convey proof of spirit in this century, yet physical mediumship was quite predominant in the nineteenth and twentieth century right after the birth of Spiritualism. My hypothesis is that during the advent of Spiritualism there was a great need to use techniques that would demonstrate concrete proof that the spiritual world existed. Knocking on walls, moving tables, and making objects appear and disappear might have been necessary elements of mediumship to strengthen the movement. Mental mediumship is relatively less visible and is subjective depending on who is receiving the information. From a research perspective mental mediumship is far more compelling for examinations regarding survival of consciousness. If something unseen is moving an object or rapping on your wall, you cannot be sure whether this entity was a living agent on earth at one time. This limitation hinders your ability to assess survival of consciousness. With mental mediumship as you will learn more about in the next chapter, the details brought forward allow researchers to examine the credibility of the discarnate's identity and allows further investigation into the accuracy of the information.

Another pattern with the mediums is that all of them had feelings of uncertainties about their abilities in the early years. I recall one medium jokingly stating, "It is not like I jumped out of my bed at the age of ten and said, 'Yup! I have identified my career choice. I have decided to become a medium. Communicating with the dead is all I really want to do in life!'" In fact, it seems that it was quite the opposite. We saw how some of the mediums had either attempted to shut their gift down, deny it, or even try to end their lives because of the confusion it caused. You will recall one of the mediums saying, "I felt like I was going friggin' loony!" One of the mediums interviewed in the study but not highlighted in this chapter provided this quote, "At the age of eight, I knew I was different. I felt the vibrations, yet no one else around experienced this. The vibrations felt like I was light and rising, and immediately I was in a different reality—these changes in vibrations were automatic, but I did everything I could to stop them from happening. The more I ignored my gift, the more my anxieties increased until I gave in and began to seek assistance from a mentor that allowed me to face my gifts and use them to help others who needed me to convey messages of hope." In this case we see that mediumship is somewhat of a calling. The mediums are not seeking the gift; it is seeking them.

The notion that spirit was seeking individuals to take on this work on the earth plane is further substantiated with six of the ten mediums sharing information about the physical changes that took place in their bodies prior to experiencing heightened capabilities. Four actually had back-related pain or an overall sense of distress at some point prior to experiencing heightened capabilities. Overall depression, changes in back alignment, nervous system realignments, and physical limitations in the body were some of the examples shared during their interviews. Most of the mediums felt their gifts were related to this physical change as they noticed that their mediumship capabilities grew exponentially immediately after these incidents. In addition to the enhanced capabilities, in Chris's case for example, we saw how the doctors were not able to identify a specific cause for his ailment despite his loss of memory and inability to speak when he was rushed to the emergency room. Another medium who wishes to keep his name private was told after his undiagnosed debilitating illness that his whole nervous system had been rewired. It was a rewiring that was not done by any known medical instrument developed in the twenty-first century.

It appears then that in some cases, perhaps a physical predisposition is necessary to heighten mediumship techniques.

Who or what makes these changes is not something any of the mediums could answer; however, we can conclude that in some cases a certain type of physical change in the body is necessary to do mediumship work.

The interviews with the ten mediums in this study demonstrate that during their readings with clients they do indeed move between speaking to discarnates, angels, and higher guides. Some also read blueprints, the Akashic records or use tarot cards to assist with a greater understanding of what is being communicated by discarnates, angels, or spirit guides. The extent to which mediumship or psychic techniques are used depends on the medium, the context of the reading, and the sitter.

On a final note, the case studies shared in this chapter demonstrate that these mediums went through a growth process with their gifts evolving and changing. In some cases we saw how the mediums shared that this evolution process was based on agreements they made with their spirit guides. One of the mediums in the study (one not highlighted in this chapter) used to do readings full-time, but her guides were more interested in her sharing her gifts through channeling and automatic writing. When she attempts to do one-on-one readings with clients, her gifts are minimized, and she is less fulfilled. It seems that her calling to help individuals has shifted to a spiritual calling that requires that her messages from higher spirit beings be used to bring peace on a larger scale.

We have reviewed some key concepts, learned more about mediumship, and allowed the mediums to share their stories. Now we are ready to examine the evidence regarding life after death. Is there life after death? Can mediums help us answer this question? Let's turn to chapter 3 to see if mediums can indeed help us with this answer.

3

IS THERE LIFE AFTER DEATH?

*D*uring my research with mediums, people have contacted me, requesting that I provide them with the name of a medium who was considered to be authentic and accurate. I silently protested, thinking to myself, *But I am a scientific researcher! I am not a specialist at identifying the most talented medium.* I began to resign to the possibility that perhaps people were only interested in how to obtain the best readings. Maybe they were simply interested in finding the most efficient means of connecting with their deceased loved ones or determining what their futures held. I began to wonder how interested the general populace would be in discovering the scientific methods and results that would substantiate the claims that authentic mediums made about communicating with the deceased. As a born researcher, it was somewhat disheartening to fathom that perhaps only fellow researchers would be interested in these findings. After all one of the primary reasons for writing this book was to share the results of my examination with a wider audience. These concerns persisted until I interviewed Gene.

Gene was still grieving after she had lost her husband, the love of her life. She had married at the young age of seventeen and had been in love with her high school sweetheart, Bert, for fifty years. Bert passed away suddenly of a heart attack at the age of sixty-seven. Gene was having difficulty coping with life without Bert and agreed to participate in my research study for the sole purpose of discovering whether mediums could truly communicate with the deceased. She shared that she had only one reading with a medium but was still not fully convinced. Her reading with the medium was comforting but not convincing. She shared that the medium accurately described Bert and stated his initials but could not clearly identify the cause of death. She also shared that most disturbingly the medium stated during the reading that he "missed his honey" but Bert never called her honey. In fact, he had called her Genie for the last fifty years. She pondered, why would he not tell the medium that he missed his Genie? Gene turned to me for questions about the authenticity of mediumship. This lady, who was a nurse by profession, was asking questions about the validity of the life-after-death doctrine. She questioned the status of research to date and wanted to know the verdict. She said, "Donna, is there *really* life after death? Is my Bert still with us, or is this just an unsubstantiated theory?" She was indeed interested in whether science could prove its existence and wondered whether we had the appropriate tools to measure this phenomenon accurately. She ended her interview by reminding me, "If you can prove that there is life after death, I might be able to continue to be at peace knowing that my Bert is still with us." After meeting with Gene I was reassured that while people were mostly interested in experiencing a reading with an authentic medium, many also wanted to know if the ability to communicate with the dead was real. They needed to know this to confirm that their loved ones survived their physical deaths, and they needed to know so they could prepare psychologically for their afterlife experience. This whole chapter is devoted to responding to this one question: *Is there life after death*? To examine this, we will first look at the results of a two-year study based on interviews with ten mediums and their eighty-eight clients. In honor of Gene and others who are still seeking scientific proof, the results and highlights of the methods that are used to systematically assess the authenticity of spirit communication are shared in this chapter.

Testing the Validity of Mediumship

To understand the study (to be referred to as *Medium7* research throughout the remainder of the book), there are three key elements to consider when one is attempting to validate survival of consciousness.[11] These elements are listed here:

- The researcher should not know the sitter prior to the reading.
- The medium should not know any information about the sitter prior to the reading.
- The medium obtains information directly from a discarnate residing in the spirit world.

The research needs to ensure that the investigator conducting the reading does not know the sitter (also known as the recipient of the reading provided by the medium). When the researcher is blinded, this rules out the possibility that the research participants were selected based on particular characteristics that might shape the final results of the experiments. For example, if the principal investigator of one of these research studies chooses to select only females who believe in mediumship, this may reduce the objectivity and validity of the examination.

The second element of a good experiment involves the assurance that mediums have no information about the sitter prior to the reading. The mediums in this study never had any information about the research participants who participated in controlled individual experiments or group readings set up in the *Medium7* study. Some[12] of the research participants, who were referred to the research or were identified from a list of phone numbers recorded in appointment books, did provide the medium (or their booking assistants) with first names and telephone numbers. The nature of the stringent criteria used in the *Medium7* study, and the type of information necessitating inclusion as evidence of survival of consciousness is not the type of information someone could gather from searching the Internet. To alleviate any concern about the mediums who did have access to first names and telephone numbers, in most cases the sitters usually used alternative names or used someone else to book their appointments. This is a personal strategy sitters use not because they distrust the medium but because they want to control leakage of information. This method allows the sitter to be assured that the source of information shared during a reading is coming from the spirit world.

Authentic mediums will also tell you that they prefer to know nothing about the sitter prior to a reading as prior knowledge sometimes affects their ability to make a distinction between the spirit's communication and the prior knowledge shared from other sources.

Finally, if the medium can provide accurate and relevant information to the sitter, the contents of the message are further assessed to determine if they are substantive enough to make conclusions about life after death. If all of these basic elements are considered in the scientific study, there is a possibility of obtaining valid results concerning the survival of consciousness.

Some Key Research Questions

Many people have asked why I started to conduct research using mediums. The answer is simple. I have always had a passion for philosophy, psychology, parapsychology, and metaphysics. I was curious about the true nature of our universe and mediums offered an opportunity to explore the spiritual world. I had been seeing mediums for a reading at least six times a year since 2006. I began to ask others about their experiences with mediums and found myself mentally analyzing the quality and accuracy of the messages shared by the mediums. I took great interest in how the medium's messages affected my friends and family. Sometimes I saw how people's hopes were significantly raised by messages shared by a medium, but I also saw people's disappointment when they were not able to connect with deceased loved ones or did not experience the predictions shared by mediums.

My interest in seeing mediums was largely driven by my curiosity about the spirit world. These motives helped me formulate some of the following research questions[13]:

1. Can mediums communicate with discarnates (spirits without a physical body) or spirit[14] (groups of discarnates, angels, spirit guides or highly evolved masters)?
2. Can mediums use other senses that exist beyond the realm of the normal five senses?
3. Is there life after death?

Finding Test Mediums

During the pilot phase of the study, ten mediums were interviewed in depth (in-person and by phone). Mediums were identified via the snowball technique, in which names of potential mediums were referred to me for consideration. To be admitted to the study, mediums needed to demonstrate credibility and consent to participate in the research. Participation in the research included a lengthy interview and a willingness to refer sitters to the researcher for an interview and follow-up. Only mediums with *real* talents were included in the study. This requirement would ensure that the study's results would reflect the true nature of spirit communication and would limit any impacts related to mediumship capacity. In addition to determining the medium's level of mediumship, only those who mentioned working with the white light, a source of purity with the intent to share information that is for the highest good, were admitted to the study. Of the ten mediums who were interviewed in the pilot phase, seven agreed to allow their clients to be interviewed for the research of *Medium7*.

Mediums were interviewed and asked to respond to a series of questions pertaining to the following areas:

- background/history
- preparation for a reading
- types of abilities (i.e., extrasensory perception)
- how extrasensory perceptions work (i.e., clairsentience)
- experiences using psychic abilities and mediumship
- challenges and benefits

Working with Sitters to Test Spirit Communication

A semi-structured questionnaire, one currently accessible on the *Metaphysics Research* website (www.medium7.com), was sent to the sitter prior to the interview. These questions were administered during a one-hour telephone or in-person interview to give the sitters an opportunity to respond to questions about their prior experiences with seeing a medium or psychic. They were also asked to elaborate on their religious or philosophical outlook prior to the reading. I asked questions about the sitters' religious beliefs because it was useful to examine whether prior beliefs affected their assessments of the statements the mediums shared. Sitters were also asked what made the readings more authentic. Sitters felt that mediums that remained silent prior to and during the reading enhanced the authenticity of the reading. If the medium did not encourage conversation prior to or during the reading, sitters believed that this would minimize sensory leakage. Critics have often diminished the findings of research studies with mediums as skeptics point out that mediums may communicate accurate information about the sitter as a result of accessing information about the sitter prior to and during the reading.

Sitters disclosed during the study that they believed mediums and psychics that asked probing questions and encouraged discussion during the reading might be fishing for information. The most important part of the interview involved questions about how the sitters rated the messages shared by the medium. During the research experiments in the *Medium7* study, all of the readings were recorded and subsequently transcribed. A chart with a list of statements shared by the medium was prepared and sent electronically to the research participant. The research participants were asked to review the scoring guidelines and rate the statements that would eventually be classified into high, moderate, or low levels of evidence. For research participants that had a reading without my presence, they were still admitted to the study; however, not all readings were recorded resulting in a compromising decision to include self-reported statements made by the sitter into the analysis. To address this limitation, for the research participants who had provided an account of their readings based on their own recall, the interviews required more probing to understand the context for their mediums' messages.

During the research study we used focus group meetings to obtain feedback on various aspects of the study. During one of the focus group meetings, using a diverse group of eight participants, we asked, "What type of information would you need to hear to classify messages shared by spirit via the medium as high-level evidence?" This group suggested that the medium's ability to share the full name (first, last, or nickname) of the deceased would be considered strong evidence that the medium was indeed talking to a family member or friend in the spirit world. They also noted that the medium's ability to provide a precise description of the deceased, including both physical and personality attributes, or provide details about the cause of death of the passed loved one would also be considered strong evidence that the medium was speaking with a familiar entity now in spirit. Mostly everyone agreed that information provided by the medium that could not be provided by anyone else and was very specific to the sitter would also be classified as strong evidence.

These common themes were shared by most focus group participants; however, some would add that the medium's ability to mimic the deceased and use words that were also used by the deceased when they were living could also be classified as high evidence. Based on the response from focus group participants and the eighty-eight participants completing interviews, only cases that were able to meet the criteria for high-level evidence were considered as substantive confirmation of survival of consciousness. Messages shared from the medium that were accurate but could possibly be accessed via other means and were only moderately specific were classified as moderate-level evidence. A sitter would classify messages shared from the medium as low-level evidence when the information was unclear, had not manifested in the sitter's experience, or was generalizable to others. The focus group participants had many examples to share for low levels of evidence. Statements mediums make such as, "Your mother loves you very much and sends her love" were considered too general to provide any evidence of an afterlife. They also noted that statements that fit the sitter's personality but were too general would also be classified as being low evidence. For example, a statement such as, "You are much too hard on yourself and must start believing in yourself" might be relevant to the sitter, but it is also likely to be relevant to a large percentage of the population. The Barnum effect is a psychological concept that indicates that people tend to rate general personality statements as highly accurate. This means that a statement like, "You tend to shy away from being the center of attention" could be frequently scored as relevant to the sitter when this general statement could be relevant for a majority of the population.

My favorite example was provided by a medium who was interviewed to participate in the study but was subsequently not admitted to it. This medium provided a reading for my research assistant during the medium recruitment phase of the study. The medium shared during the reading that "your mother is present and she looks just like you." Providing a statement like this without any complementary precise information is considered low-level evidence mostly because everyone has a slight resemblance to their mother. This type of information would not give anyone confidence that their mother was really present in the spirit world. Given the burden of proof required in life-after-death studies, I only assign a label of high-level of evidence when the messages fit the criteria previously described. I would argue, however, that some evidence rated as moderate has been beneficial for sitters; however, for the purpose of making valid conclusions only evidence classified in the high range has been used to respond to the inquiry about the existence of the afterlife. During the final part of the interview sitters were asked to share if they derived any benefits or experienced challenges as a result of their reading.

All statements shared by the medium would be scored using the *Medium7* assessment tool,[15] and the scored statements would be returned to the sitters for their verification. These scores form the basis for making conclusions about the mediums' abilities to communicate with discarnates in the spirit world. This conclusion is used as a proxy indicator that suggests that if mediums are capable of receiving relevant and accurate communication with discarnates in a reading, then this contributes to strong evidence that discarnates who were once on the earth plane have survived their physical deaths.

Arriving at a Conclusion about the Existence of an Afterlife

Designing a study that will accurately measure events taking place in the nonphysical world can be complex. However, when you have access to gifted mediums[16] and take the time to observe, record, and analyze the findings, the task becomes plausible. Information provided from the research participants suggests that if a medium can accurately identify a person's name (including a nickname or a specific item of relevance), cause of death, and detailed personal information under controlled conditions; this contributes to the evidence that life continues beyond death. In the *Medium7* study, it was determined that if the medium could demonstrate at least three of these criteria under controlled conditions, this would contribute to the evidence. Controlled conditions include ensuring that the medium and the researcher did not have access to any information about the sitter prior to the reading.[17] If the researcher and the medium have no information about the sitter, it can only be logically deduced that detailed information, such as a name, cause of death, and detailed personal information about the sitter must be coming from a person in the spirit world, likely a discarnate who was at one time residing in the physical world.

Let's have a closer examination of what constitutes evidence for life after death. The following case studies demonstrate evidence that there is life after death. In these cases the medium is able to provide specific information that could not be provided by anyone else other than the discarnate.

What's in a Name?

Imagine for a moment that you are a skeptic believing in events and experiences that you can only validate through your five senses. Generally your belief is that your experiences are only real and valuable if you can feel them using your hands, see them using your eyes, taste them using your mouth, smell them using your nose, and hear them using your ears. Any other type of event experienced beyond using these customary five senses is not real and likely not important. Your belief in general is that the life you experience *is* the universe and there really isn't anything beyond this. You are going through the motions of life, just focusing on typical daily challenges.

You are a male who's about twenty-four years old and at this young age you do not really have any reason to focus on what lies beyond this universe or this lifetime. On one ordinary day you hear about an odd experiment to receive a reading with a medium. The ad is interesting in that it suggests that you can get paid just for receiving a reading and participating in an interview that will be videotaped. Your first thoughts are, they say there will be refreshments and an incentive for participation. Forty dollars is not bad for one hour. You look a little closer at the requirements for the research: the male nonbeliever must *not* know the medium or researcher and be willing to participate on the date and time required. Consent to be videotaped is also a requirement. You say, "What the heck? They don't say I have to do anything." You think to yourself, I don't believe in this crap, but I can go for the entertainment.

Nonbeliever's Experiment

If you do not believe in life after death, you may be eligible for this experiment. See the criteria noted below:

I. Candidate must be willing to have a reading with a psychic medium (one hour).

II. Reading and post-reading interview will be videotaped (one hour).

III. Candidate must be a male (any age).

IV. Candidate must not know anyone involved in the research, including the psychic medium.

V. Candidate considers himself to be a nonbeliever. For example, he does not believe in life after death or other psychic phenomenon.

Note: Refreshments and a $40.00 honorarium will be provided.

Chad[18] is not the typical type to seek the advice or support from a medium. He is a young male who feels he has one life to live and will take it day by day. How does one reading with a medium change Chad's whole outlook on life? On one unsuspecting day Chad finally arrives at the "Male Nonbeliever's Experiment" and settles into a comfy couch, expecting to hear typical phrases:

You are loved by the universe. You are searching for something, but you must be patient. As he sees the medium approaching him, he wonders why this forty-something male looks so normal and questions why the symbolic crystal ball is nowhere to be seen. When will the crap begin? he wonders.

The reading begins, and the medium starts to tune into spirit and talk about various themes ranging from a deceased grandparent's alcoholism to a discussion about a miscarriage in the family. Chad has been asked not respond to anything in the reading, and his face remains neutral while the medium continues to share information. The sentiment in the room swiftly begins to change as the medium indicates that a contemporary or someone of his age can be seen lying on the ground. The medium states vehemently, "Yes, this young male who I believe is a close friend is found dead." You cannot help but notice the change in Chad's face. While he attempts to remain neutral, his skin tone transitions to red, indicating an increasing nervousness and potential dismay. The medium soon becomes quite clear that this young male recently committed suicide and shares that Chad could not have done anything to prevent this incident.

Given Chad's facial expressions, you could imagine the internal dialogue: This sounds absolutely accurate, but perhaps the medium is guessing and happened to accurately hit on the fact that my best friend committed suicide last week.

The young deceased male continues to communicate with the medium and shares the name of an item he and Chad used to frequently laugh about. The medium pauses and says, "He is now talking about donkey-dick. What is a donkey-dick?" Despite the confused expression on the medium's face, it is clear that sharing this name has hit a nerve.

Chad told the researchers at the end of the reading that the term "donkey-dick"[19] was relevant. He recalled the enjoyable times he and his friend had laughing at the first time they had set their eyes on the size of a donkey-dick. This was not a term he used with other friends, and for the first time in the reading he began to seriously consider the possibility that his invisible friend was actually alive but in spirit. The reading continued with various health, relationship, and career-related guidance.

After a short pause the mediums states, "He is getting a bit cryptic in his communication. I know this is going to sound weird, but he is showing me a jar of pickles. He is saying, 'Just say pickles.'" Chad cannot believe what he just heard. He begins to shake his head and swiftly turns to the research team to request a short respite. He quickly leaves the interview room to get a breath of fresh air. At that moment you can imagine the thoughts of this nonbeliever: Is this some type of magical trick? Perhaps this is amazing mind reading. Am I possibly on one of those reality prank shows where someone is going to jump out of the wall and say, "You just got served?" If it is one of those prank shows, perhaps a crew of people investigated all of the key facts and names and then brought them forward to the medium.

This of course would be a mind-boggling feat in itself, so Chad attempts to calm his nerves and returns to the interview room, where the researchers and the medium are anxiously hoping to complete the experiment. After the reading Chad explained to the research team that he knew without a doubt that his friend must still be present in some form. There could be no way the medium could have guessed the importance of mentioning the term pickles. Although Chad was still in a state of shock, he proceeded to explain the relevance of the term "pickles":

> My best friend loved pickles. I actually thought it was impossible to eat pickles all day long. We would eat at a Pickle Barrel restaurant frequently and I would need to buy him several jars of pickles on a daily basis but this did not seem to be enough. The name pickles means a lot, as my friend was beyond obsessed with eating pickles all the time.

What are the chances that anyone can accurately guess two

relevant names in one reading? In this particular case the term "donkey-dick" and "pickles" were names that were highly related to Chad's deceased best friend. After Chad explains the relevance of the name, "pickles," the medium channels yet another relevant name. The exact words of the medium are noted below: "So if there was one simple word that could be used to validate that this *meathead* in Alliston is picking up on something, the word would be *pickles?*"

It turns out that the medium does not normally refer to himself as a meathead but inadvertently used this name in the reading. Chad later explains that his best friend who had committed suicide just a few short weeks ago was known to his closest friends as *meathead*. The medium inadvertently channeled this name and provided further evidence that this information was coming from his deceased friend in the spirit world.

So what exactly are the chances of a medium mentioning three names in a one-hour period? We need to also consider that these names were provided under a controlled experiment. The recruitment protocol during this nonbeliever experiment was designed to blind both the researchers and the medium from learning any information about the sitters. The reading was monitored, and the sitter could only provide an explanation about a name or concept upon receiving permission from the research team observing the proceedings. To ensure that the sitter's prior beliefs did not impact the results, there was a deliberate attempt to limit a few experiments to male nonbelievers only—the group that is the least likely to validate the authenticity of messages shared by a medium.

Let's take a moment to examine the probability that someone could guess a first name correctly on the first attempt. If we can determine that this is not a likely event, this provides strong evidence that perhaps the discarnates are indeed providing this specific information via the medium. If this could be demonstrated under controlled conditions, this would contribute to the evidence that although human beings die, their memory, behaviors, beliefs, and feelings live beyond their physical deaths.

There are an estimated three thousand English first names and more than twenty thousand first names used around the world. There are at least a million first, middle, and surnames when you consider the multiple configuration of names. Let's consider the relatively conservative probability that suggests that there are at least twenty thousand first names used around the world.[20] The chances of guessing a name correctly without any other information would be one in twenty thousand. To put this in context, these odds are similar to the chances of the following:

- dying from a car accident: 1 in 18,585
- dying from any kind of fall: 1 in 20,666
- dying from being murdered: 1 in 18,000
- being injured from fireworks: 1 in 19,556

If we wanted to know the chances of someone being able to state three correct names, the result would be 1.25e-13. This is the same scientific result as 0.000000000000125 that suggests there is a one-in-trillionth probability that this event could occur by chance. When an event is likely to occur by chance, that suggests random factors contribute to its occurrence. When such an event is unlikely to be a result of chance, it is a result of a specific cause. In this case the only plausible cause would be derived from the medium's ability to learn the information from spirit or discarnates.

These odds indicate that it is quite unlikely that guessing a name occurs by chance or coincidence. It suggests that given the odds it is likely that for this event to occur it needs to occur by someone with detailed information sharing it through the medium. That would only be someone from the spirit world.

It should be noted here that some mediums actually specialize in conveying names while others do not obtain names easily. If you have a reading where the medium does not channel one relevant name of your deceased, this does not mean the medium is a charlatan. It may mean that this was not the vehicle the discarnate used to convey proof of their continued existence. With that said, there are other criteria that research participants in the *Medium7* study indicated provided strong evidence of life after death. We will examine this criterion next.

Identifying the Cause of Death

The most popular theme to be shared by discarnates in readings is cause of death. If they are not sharing their causes of death, they will likely provide information about their most salient medical conditions that prevailed just prior to their deaths or throughout their lifetimes—for example, diabetes or being paralyzed in a wheelchair. We can only assume discarnates understand that this type of information is most memorable for sitters, and therefore, sharing messages of this nature would strengthen the proof that discarnates continue to exist, just in a different form. The following example was given the highest score of three for achieving high levels of evidence for life after death. This type of example would receive the highest score of three if the medium could share precise, accurate, and highly relevant messages from spirit to the sitter.

> This is difficult for me to talk about as I am still grieving the premature loss of my husband. Over the last year I had been asking friends and family if they knew an experienced medium that could help me understand why my husband's life prematurely ended. I had been seeing a therapist for a while, but I could not expect the therapist to tell me why he had to die at the young age of forty-one.
>
> I was referred to a medium that had been able to provide accurate details for others, so I found the confidence to go for a reading. Within fifteen minutes into the reading the medium shared that he could feel

someone like a past lover or husband in the room, and he was seeing and feeling hot fire all around him. He further explained feeling the impression of driving and then suddenly feeling a collision with a lighter vehicle, more like a motorcycle. The medium shared that the discarnate communicating was showing scenes of an accident with fire surrounding a car and a motorcycle. The medium conveyed the impression that the discarnate experienced an instant death—no pain.

The medium further explained that the discarnate's lessons on earth were over. Although he died at a young age, he had learned what his soul needed to know and there was further learning that would need to take place on another place of existence.

Melissa, the sitter in this case, shared with the researcher that the police provided the same details about the fire surrounding the motorcycle and the vehicle. Melissa shared that she now had a better idea of why he died at the age of forty-one. Prior to hearing what her deceased husband shared with the medium, she had a limited understanding about souls learning lessons on earth and on other planes of existence. She admitted that she did not entirely understand the concept, but because the medium brought forth specific details about the car accident, she seriously considered the reason for his death. Finally, she shared that learning that her husband's time of death was painless was enough to help her move through the grieving process and carry on with her life.

Getting Personal

I think we all have information about ourselves or an event that no one else would know. Sometimes these very personal bits of information are never shared with anyone else for various reasons, but this type of information that we will refer to as "personal evidence" is useful when attempting to isolate whether it is possible for mediums to receive private information from friends, family members, or acquaintances who have passed on to the spirit world.

During Vicki's interview she shared that the medium provided information that only herself and her deceased husband would know. This type of evidence is given the highest score of three as it demonstrates that the messages provided during a reading must be coming from the spirit world via the medium. Vicki reluctantly described her meeting with a medium. She wanted to learn more about how her husband passed but had not known what to expect from a medium. During the reading the medium described the following details about a picture hanging in their living room:

> He is now telling me about a picture that you have hanging up in the living room. He is in this picture with some friends. They have won some type of award for their sport. He is showing me that in this picture he is holding up a *glass* of juice. To everyone else it looks like a *can* of beer, but it isn't. It's a *glass* full of juice.

Approximately three months after her reading, during Vicki's interview for the research, she explained that this picture hangs above her husband's ashes currently located in her living room. When friends visit the house, they often comment on a particular aspect of the picture. They find it odd that her husband is drinking from a can of beer in this picture. Visitors find this odd as they know that Vicki's husband never drank beer. Vicki thought this was high evidence that it was her husband communicating through the medium because only she and her husband knew that this was a glass of juice and not a can of beer. This type of information was not available anywhere else, and so Vicki came to the conclusion that her husband was still in existence just in a different form.

I have found many examples of such detail conveyed by mediums. The details provided in such examples cannot be attained on a website or from any other source of information as the nature of the statements are both personal and private. This next example is used to demonstrate how even with 1,200 people in the room such detail may only resonate with one person. I went to see John Holland, a famous medium, at the Toronto Conference Centre during a Hay House event in 2009. John's charisma and level of accuracy attracts large crowds to his group readings. On that evening I recall one particular message that fully demonstrated how detailed personal information can contribute to strong evidence of life after death. John shares the following scenario:

> I have a grandmother in spirit coming through who is quite anxious to speak with her daughter. She does not want me to bother sharing that her name is Mary as her and I both know that at least fifty people will put up their hands and say, "Yes, I am Mary." Instead John proceeds by sharing detailed information that due to the nature of the event would only resonate with one person. He says, "Who knitted the pink slippers for Grandma and put them on her while she was in the open casket so her feet would be warm while she was buried?" The crowd is silent but in awe all at the same time. After he shares this message and actually digests the information himself, he inadvertently shares what he was thinking out loud and says, "Who would knit slippers for a dead person anyway?" The audience could not help but break out in hysterical laughter, but no one in the audience could relate to the point or would take ownership of it. John had to repeat it two more times and still there was silence. John began pacing back and forth and blurted out with his Boston-tinged accent,

"Folks, she ain't leavin' until she connects with her daughter who she absolutely knows is here in this crowd tonight." To the crowd's amazement, a lady in her fifties stands up and shares in a faint voice, "Yes, my daughter, Mary's granddaughter, who is just eleven years of age knit these for her grandmother as she was concerned that her grandmother would be cold when she was buried underground in the winter." You could almost hear the awe in the minds of the crowd that evening. Knitting slippers for a dead person is a rare event, but the one person that actually knew about the occurrence could verify that the medium correctly conveyed this message. Even though Grandma was supposedly dead in her casket, she lived to share the message that she knew that her slippers were made for her to keep warm in the casket.

We have reviewed examples of evidence that demonstrate survival of consciousness. In the research that formed the basis for this book the findings indicate that out of eighty-eight readings, sixty-four (73 percent) of these readings provided at least three statements that could be categorized as high levels of evidence. Three statements in this category suggests that there is enough evidence to conclude that the event is not occurring by chance but instead is occurring because of a real causal force. This causal source is logically deduced as the discarnate (deceased person), as the medium, and the researcher were not privy to such detail prior to or during the reading. Ninety-four percent (eighty-three) of these readings demonstrated one high-level statement; however, to heighten the standards in this study, I have only incorporated cases that demonstrated at least three high-level criteria. I would confidently conclude that if 73 percent of the readings were able to provide a name, a cause of death, and provide detailed information that no one else could know, this would provide proof that the discarnate in spirit still lives on in another form. This has to be the conclusion as this type of information could not be produced by anyone other than the entity that was previously living on the earth plane.

Table 2 Percentage of high levels of evidence demonstrated by ten mediums

Number and type of high-level evidence statements per reading	Number of readings meeting the high-level evidence standard	Percentage of readings meeting the high-level evidence standard
Must include three statements that fit into any one of the following categories: 1. Providing a name 2. Providing cause of death or salient illness during lifetime 3. Providing details of personal information no one else could know	64	73 percent
Must include two statements that fit into any one of the following categories: 1. Providing a name 2. Providing cause of death or salient illness during lifetime 3. Providing details of personal information no one else could know	75	85 percent
Must include one statement that fits into any one of the following categories: 1. Providing a name 2. Providing cause of death or salient illness during lifetime 3. Providing details of personal information no one else could know	83	94 percent

For those of you who are statistical aficionados, I do want to briefly share why I used a statistical model that only focused on the medium's messages that were hits. It is possible that I could have used an alternative approach that included a ratio of hits for every miss to help determine if there was evidence for the afterlife. This model would have involved identifying the amount of high-level scores in relation to moderate and low scores. This would be a plausible model if all readings had a similar structure and if we were focusing on the quantity and not the quality of the message. Spirit determines the content, duration, and type of reading that occurs. As a result of this unpredictability, readings range in duration, content, and focus. This leads to a wide variety of statements where one reading might have few statements focusing on one area while another reading consists of up to two hundred statements that cover a wide array of topics. Given the diversity in readings, the quality and not the quantity needs to form the basis for determining success. If we were of course determining the capability of a tennis player, we would count the player's hits (balls that escape the other player) in relation to his or her losses (balls that the opponent is able to return). The latter statistical model would be more appropriate as only the *quantity* of hits would be used to determine success.

For those of you who are still pondering the impact of leaving out misses in this study, consider the following scenario: You are observing a stuntman's attempts to fly from one building to the next. The feat is usually impossible, but you indeed witness the stuntman's ability to successfully fly from one building to the next. What difference does it make if he was successful just once but missed ten or even a hundred other times?[21] The point is that he completed his stunt, it was filmed, and movie viewers were able to witness the stunt in a future movie. This is the case with examining the quality of statements provided by mediums. If these events described in this chapter are possible, whether they happen once or a hundred times, they demonstrate beyond chance that the information is coming from a source in the spiritual world.

In the *Medium7* study, the quality and type of statements are the primary criteria used to make decisions about the existence of an afterlife.

Rival Explanations?

You may be wondering if the source of information is achieved by accessing the information from the Akashic records or from the collective consciousness, also described as accumulating thoughts and memories that are accessible via telepathic means. The debate between super psi and survival of consciousness is an important one. For scholars who are interested in parapsychology, super psi is an area worthy of investigation because of the information it provides about the mind's abilities and the possibilities of a super consciousness. If mankind resigned itself to believing that mind reading was responsible for all of the information shared via a medium, theories for the afterlife would be considered defunct. When we review near-death studies, and out-of-body experiences in the next chapter, you will see how these complementary studies provide supporting evidence for the survival of consciousness theory. The mind-reading theory in these cases is diminished as a result of the numerous sightings of familiar beings that survived their physical deaths. Examples of messages conveyed by mediums are shared throughout this book, validating that the information was derived from a discarnate who at one time was indeed residing on the earth plane.

Complementary Studies with Mediums

It is always best to review other research studies in order to identify if one's study results are replicable. Although studying mediums is not a prevalent activity, there are enough research studies that can be used to build the evidence-base on validating survival of consciousness.

Dr. Gary Schwartz is a professor of psychology, medicine, psychiatry, and surgery at the University of Arizona. As an esteemed researcher in the area of energy systems, he found a way to explore the nature of energy using the talents of mediums. One would think that any type of innovative research would be considered credible, but when you receive your doctorate from Harvard and subsequently begin to conduct a study involving people who claim to talk to the dead, conservative colleagues might question the credibility of the research. In Stanley Krippner's book,[22] *Debating Psychic Experience,* he explains that the scientific community has struggled with including the subject of metaphysics, specifically the topic of psychics, in official scientific literature. The scientific community suggests that certain principles need to exist before it can be included as scientific evidence. They suggest that the ingredient that causes the phenomenon, the methods, and the results should be replicable, meaning that other scientists should be able to replicate the phenomenon under the same conditions. He notes in the book that researchers that study metaphysics are held to a higher standard, often having to demonstrate a frequency of replication that is not required in other scientific studies. In his book, *The Afterlife Experiments: Breakthrough Scientific Evidence of Life After Death,* Dr. Schwartz reports on a number of compelling experiments that demonstrate the case for life after death. In this book he also discusses the challenges of using mainstream media to share contentious findings that incite fear of the unknown. It was very interesting for me to read in his book that despite having proof of life after death, the HBO producers at the time framed the results in a way that conveyed the medium's limitations and potential inability to demonstrate strong enough evidence to support life after death. The question is why do media outlets feel that they can increase their ratings by demonstrating that mediums cannot speak to the deceased?

Why are we satisfied with hearing information that perpetuates prevailing beliefs? Why are we so afraid of telling and hearing the truth?

Table 3 illustrates one of the studies Dr. Schwartz and his team shared on the HBO special. Five different mediums conducted independent readings on a sitter named Patricia Price.[23] These mediums did not know who they would be reading and were not able to see the sitter before, during, or after the reading. This design ensured that critics would be satisfied that the mediums were not able to use verbal cues to garner information about the sitter. The design also allowed the researcher to demonstrate replicability if five mediums were able to accurately report on similar themes. The comparison method used here also offers the reader an opportunity to review the percentage of hits made by a medium compared to individuals (students studying energy systems) who have self-reported not having the capabilities of a talented medium. This is a method that can substantiate life after death if the medium's success at sharing accurate messages is significantly more prevalent than the comparison group of individuals who are limited to the use of just five senses.

Table 3 Results from mediums and students (who are not mediums)

Area of Accuracy (Example of information shared by the medium)	Percentage of Accuracy by Medium (n=5)	Percentage Accuracy by a Student (n=68)
Historical Fact: I am seeing a dead son. A son had died.	85 percent	Range in accuracy from 20 to 54 percent
Initials: I am hearing the letter M.	90 percent	
Names: He is telling me his name is Leonard.	65 percent	
Personal Description: I see a thin man, blond curly hair, and very pointy ears.	75 percent	
Temperament: This person is like an extrovert and loves to laugh and meet new people.	97 percent	
Opinion: Your son wants me to tell you that he doesn't blame you for his death.	Not scored because of the nature of the comments	
Overall Average	78 percent	36 percent

After the medium shares information about Patricia Price, each statement is scored using a tool. In general any statement from one to three demonstrates a degree of accuracy, and any score from negative one to negative three demonstrates various degrees of inaccuracy. The table above indicates that overall when five mediums attempt to read Patricia Price, they achieve 78 percent accuracy. When students who are not mediums attempt to respond to a set of questions posed by the researchers about Patricia Price, they achieve a 36 percent accuracy rate. The statistical probability of this difference occurring by chance is less than one in ten million. Put another way, it is 9.99 million times more likely that the mediums obtained the information directly from the deceased. To help put this probability in perspective, if you are flying on any of the top twenty-five airlines, there is a one in 10.46 million chance that you will die in a plane crash. So being able to obtain accurate information about the deceased based on a guess is equivalent to the likelihood of dying in a plane crash. There are five commercial airline accidents a year, but when you consider that there are on average eighteen million flights per year, five fatal accidents is relatively low. Statistically you would have to fly every day for nearly two hundred years for there to be a significant chance you would experience an accident. I hope the plane analogy demonstrates the enormous difference between the mediums and the guessed responses made by students who are not mediums. What is more compelling about this particular experiment is that the results were replicated by five different mediums, suggesting that these results would reach scientific standards.

It is a privilege to be living in a century that allows researchers the opportunity to access mediums and openly examine how mediums can demystify what lies beyond our physical death. While there *were* researchers in the nineteenth and twentieth century studying mediums, because of the contentious nature of the subject, they were not at liberty to openly conduct their studies or publish their material. In the twenty-first century there are still few researchers devoting their time to studying mediums. In addition to Dr. Schwartz's work, there is Dr. Julie Beischel,[24] who uses the most rigorous techniques possible to investigate survival of consciousness with mediums. In her article titled "Contemporary Methods used in Laboratory-Based Mediumship," the researcher, sitters, and mediums did not receive any feedback about the study until all experimental trials were completed. The study designs used eliminate fraud, cold-reading, rater bias, experimenter cuing, and even telepathy of the experimenter to limit confounding explanations that often lead to inconclusive evidence. When all of these aspects are controlled, we increase our confidence about the validity of spirit communication and its implications for mankind.

Finally, for those healthy skeptics who may still be considering rival theories of survival of consciousness, or just questioning the validity of being able to talk to the dead, it is useful to be aware of the emerging work related to scanning brain activity in mediums prior to and during their channelling. If a medium is indeed communicating with entities in other planes of existence, we should be able to see significant changes in electrical activity in the brain.

Dr. Daniel Amen is a physician, double board certified psychiatrist, and is regarded as one of the world's foremost experts on applying brain imaging science to everyday clinical practice. Amen conducted a live experiment on the Dr. Oz[25] show to identify if there were brain changes occurring during mediumship. During the experiment, Amen explained that at baseline, just prior to the medium channelling spirit, the medium's mind was in a high alpha state—very alert and active. When the medium began to channel spirit and actually demonstrate being able to provide relevant information to a sitter in the audience, her brain wave activity significantly decreased. Scientifically speaking, the brain's electrical activity in the frontal lobe decreased and the electrical waves in the temporal lobes were activated—a section of the brain known for being associated with spiritual experiences. This experiment provides physiological evidence of mediumship.

These changes in brain wave activity are very consistent with what we know about our soul's ability to transcend the physical world. When we are focussing on *activity* in this plane of existence, it is difficult to heed signs or communication from the *other side*. However, when our brain is void of thought—similar to higher states of meditation—we are able to connect with beings that exist at higher rates of vibrational frequencies.

What Did We Learn?

In this chapter I shared some of the methods and results using ten mediums, eighty-eight clients, and eight focus group participants. In this research of *Medium7* the findings indicated that 73 percent of the readings contained at least three statements shared by the medium that demonstrated strong enough evidence that life after death exists. I am able to confidently conclude that authentic mediums can indeed obtain information that would otherwise be difficult without the ability to perceive beyond the physical plane. I also conclude that given the amount of validation provided by the mediums' clients, their deceased friends, family members, and acquaintances who were among us on the earth plane at one time continue to exist in a different form on another plane of existence. This conclusion is consistent with results reported by Dr. Gary Schwartz and Dr. Julie Beischel in their respective studies.

In the next chapter we turn to continuing this discussion by reviewing other studies that use different methods of exploring the spiritual world. It is one thing to obtain proof using one method, but if other independent fields of study, including the medical community, happen upon similar experiences and conclusions, the weight of the evidence warrants considerable worldwide attention. It is for this reason that I include a review of *near-death studies, out-of-body experiences, past-life regression, remote viewing,* and *deathbed visions* in the next chapter. These studies combined with the research using mediums discussed in this chapter form the burden of proof.

LIFE AFTER DEATH EVIDENCE: WHAT DO NEAR-DEATH EXPERIENCES, PAST-LIFE REGRESSION THERAPY, AND OTHER AREAS OF STUDY TEACH US?

*T*he previous chapter shared information about how mediums can enlighten us regarding survival of consciousness. Even though the evidence using mediums is quite convincing, it is useful when we have corroborating evidence from studies that use another means of learning about life after death. In this section I will share other areas of study that assess the validity of this transitory experience that we call death[26]. These types of studies are important as they provide evidence for the afterlife, but they use a different mechanism to reach the same conclusion. The following list summarizes the converging body of evidence about the afterlife. All of these (except for studies using mediums) will be explored in this chapter.

Area of studies that provide converging lines of evidence of the afterlife include the following:

- near-death experiences (NDEs)
- out-of-body experiences

- past-life regression therapy
- deathbed visions
- remote viewing

Near-Death Experiences

A near-death experience (NDE) happens when your brain dies and the soul leaves the physical body. The term is referred to as an NDE as the soul subsequently returns to the body once the physical body is revived. If someone officially dies and can return to the physical plane to verify that during his or her *death* the person still experienced thought and perceived an existence through sight, touch, feeling, and hearing, then this is a phenomenon worth investigating.

I can recall first really thinking more seriously about NDEs after I watched the movie *Flatliners* (1990). A cast including Kiefer Sutherland, Julia Roberts, Kevin Bacon, William Baldwin, and Oliver Platt embark on a journey during their medical internship to discover what lies beyond death. In the movie each of the cast members experiences death, is resuscitated, and subsequently has various experiences, including visions about their past bullying behaviors, their immoral trysts with women, and painful memories of a parent's suicide. These behaviors eventually inspire the medical students to make amends to enhance peace in their lives. This provocative film brought the concept of NDEs to the masses.

●　●　●

During this near-death experience, I could see a figure coming toward me.

I realized it was my dad. But how can that be? Dad is dead.

●　●　●

During the research of *Medium7,* a woman named Ruth shared that a medium had validated her NDE. Before we try to understand how the medium provided validation, it is best to review Ruth's experience firsthand.

> I remember the night clearly. I felt physically and emotionally drained. I kept taking my painkillers to dull the pain, but the dose never seemed to work. Apparently I took too many and found myself drifting into an existence that was nothing like I had ever experienced. I can remember seeing a bright light and watching the shadow coming toward me. I was not afraid. I was just taking in this experience. Oddly enough I felt safe and proceeded to try to see the figure coming toward me. I could still not decipher the identity of the figure, but it spoke telepathically. I received the message, "Wait here for me. Dad wants to see you." I can recall my dad trying to comfort me and explain the cause of my pain. I don't remember his exact message, but I do recall him providing guidance about how to feel emotionally well. All the while enveloped in this warm light, I asked, "Why are you here, Dad? You're supposed to be dead!"

> Dad was encouraging me to go back to the earth plane to complete my goals and learn my lessons. I was drawn to the white light but also remembered my responsibilities and eventually found myself awake in a hospital bed with wires and nurses surrounding my bed. I had been returned to life with a different attitude and knowledge that life does indeed continue after death.

Ruth knew she had an important spiritual experience but was never quite sure if the whole experience was real. She accompanied a friend who was visiting a medium but had not expected to receive a reading that day as she was only there to provide comfort to her friend. During the reading the medium turned to Ruth and shared the following information:

> Your dad is here. He wants to validate that he was there when you died. He is telling me that it was not your time to go and that it was possible to reverse your addiction to prescription drugs. He says he is waiting to see "Lovindear." That's your mother, I believe. He is also telling me that he sends dimes to let you know that he is always there for you.

Ruth's life was transformed after she had her NDE validated by the medium. She thought to herself, how would the medium know the name Lovindear, and most importantly how would she know that my father came to meet me during my drug-induced death? Her dad was the only one that called her mother Lovindear, further validating the medium's accuracy.

Ruth also finds many dimes. Each of the dates on these dimes signifies an important date. It is quite uncanny that many of the dimes have her dad's date of passing—perhaps another way of validating his presence.

Fortunately, we have a few researchers who have published their findings on NDEs. I will highlight a few key findings from the book *Evidence of the Afterlife* authored by Dr. Jeffrey Long. A radiation oncologist by training, Dr. Long studied 1,300 individuals who experienced an NDE (to be referred to as NDErs throughout the book) and narrowed his study to 613 cases to meet the specified study criteria. Dr. Long noted that there are twelve elements of an NDE. These are listed as follows:

1. Out-of-body experiences (OBEs)
2. Heightened senses
3. Intense emotions and feelings

4. Passing into or through a tunnel
5. Encountering a mystical or brilliant light
6. Encountering other beings (deceased relatives or mystical beings)
7. A sense of alteration of time and space
8. Life review
9. Encountering unworldly realms
10. Encountering special knowledge
11. Encountering a boundary or barrier
12. Voluntary or involuntary return to the body

In addition to identifying the key elements of an NDE, Dr. Long has identified nine lines of evidence that support the existence of an afterlife. The idea here is that if many people repeatedly report similar themes during their NDE, this would potentially amount to sufficient validation to make a conclusion that the afterlife exists. Dr. Long[27] further noted that having nine lines of evidence greatly increases the probability that the afterlife exists. The lines of evidence are listed as follows:

1. Crystal clear consciousness
2. Realistic out-of-body experiences
3. Heightened senses
4. Consciousness during anesthesia
5. Perfect playback
6. Family reunions
7. Children's experiences
8. Worldwide consistency
9. Aftereffects

What is notable about these lines of evidence is that they refute competing theories that suggest that NDE phenomena are dream hallucinations, unrealistic fragments of the brain, or perceptions of reality experienced by the brain during the death of the physical body.

There have been two outstanding types of cases that demonstrate proof of an afterlife. The first type that defies any alternative explanation is that blind individuals have visions during their NDEs. The second is where the patient is able to provide information during their death that is later verified.

A Blind Woman Sees during Her Near-Death Experience

Dr. Ken Ring and Sharon Cooper[28] provide compelling stories in their research study that examine the near-death experiences of the blind. One of these case studies has been repeatedly recounted in the literature on life-after-death issues because of its ability to substantiate the evidence about consciousness residing outside of the physical body.

* * *

Death is no more than passing from one room into another. But there's a difference for me, you know. Because in that other room I shall be able to see.

Helen Keller

* * *

Vicki Umipeg, who had been blind since birth, was injured in a serious car crash in 1973 and subsequently experienced an NDE after her heart stopped for four minutes while doctors were attending to her in the hospital. Her NDE is different from Ruth's example previously described as Umipeg had never experienced being able to use her visual senses. During her interview with Ring and Cooper she shared that since birth she had been limited to relying on only using four senses to experience life. Even her dreams lacked vision as she could only interpret her dreams using the four senses she used during her waking state. An abbreviated version of Umipeg's story is recounted here:

> I began to feel myself floating away from my body, suddenly realizing that my back was on the ceiling. I could see a woman in the hospital bed

and began to realize that it was me. For the first time I could actually see the ring on my left hand. I knew that this was my ring as I had been touching it for years and as a result was able to recognize the grooves.

You would think that I would be excited to see for the first time, but this experience was so new that initially it was frightening.

From the top of the ceiling I could see that they had cut a lot of my hair. This made me mad. I could also hear the nurse say that I could be potentially deaf as a result of the blood flowing from my ear. This too made me angry. I needed to escape the hospital room and soon found myself on top of the hospital building. I felt completely liberated. As a blind woman my movements were always tentative, so the ability to freely flow above the building and see the lights and the city was extremely liberating.

We have been socially conditioned to believe that our senses are dependent on the functioning of the brain. Umipeg's case study provides us with strong evidence that sight may not be dependent on the brain and is perhaps generated by other forces outside of the brain or any other part of the physical body. So perhaps the ability to *see* is not generated from the mind at all. We need to ask ourselves, "If sight is perceivable outside of the brain, does this substantiate the existence of a nonphysical reality and life after death?"

So if during your time on earth you experienced certain colors and images associated with death, it would be logical that the brain might replay these images during the brain's expiration. Umipeg's case completely defies this possibility. She had been blind all her life, so what could explain her ability to finally experience vision during the four minutes after she was officially dead?

Umipeg's case is astounding. We often think of being limited when we are dead and thriving when we are alive. Umipeg experienced more life during her four minutes of death by being able to fly over buildings and visually perceive people and objects. Now that Umipeg is back in her physical body after she was resuscitated, she is still blind and will likely only be able to perceive reality using sight when her physical body perishes.

Experiencing Life while Being Declared Clinically Dead

This second example is an account of a woman named Pam Reynolds, who experienced an NDE during brain surgery. During part of Reynold's surgery the surgeons declared her to be clinically dead. She had no brain-wave activity and no blood flowing in her brain during a portion of the surgery. Reynolds case is important as she made several observations about the procedure that were later confirmed as being accurate by medical personnel.

Dr. Michael Sabom in his book *Light and Death* provides a clear account of this case, and there were many academic articles that provided a critique of the evidence to thwart the dualism theory that suggests the body and soul are separate, with the latter being part of a larger connected network of consciousness that resides outside of the body. First let's review the facts of this case. In 1991 Pam claimed to have an NDE during a brain operation performed in attempts to remove a brain aneurism close to the brain stem. During six minutes of this operation she had officially flatlined medically speaking, meaning that there was no blood flowing in her brain, rendering her clinically dead. The surgeons had expected this to be a risky operation as the procedure involved the lowering of the body temperature to 60 degrees Fahrenheit (16 degrees Celsius), which subsequently stopped the heartbeat and drained the blood from her head. All aspects of the surgery were monitored, and timelines recorded because of the complexity of the operation.[29]

This seven-hour surgery revealed some unique experiences. The skeptic would of course note that any patient undergoing this type of surgery would do research and perhaps would know many of the details Reynolds shared with the surgeon upon her recovery.

Let's examine some of the points that she could not have known prior to the surgery. We should take note that despite having tape over her ears she provides details about the nurse's comment regarding her small arteries. Both the doctors and Pam would not know that fact prior to the surgery, and she would not know that the size of the arteries would be relevant. She also noticed that the drill looked different from the ones the doctors were expected to use. Even under anesthesia, being able to report back on such details is not possible. In my opinion the information she overheard about her small arteries and the description of the unique drill contributed to solid evidence that she was indeed conscious during her clinical death.

NDErs who describe the light, the tunnel, and deceased beings provide an understanding of the afterlife; however, where NDErs report information that is corroborated by others during their periods of clinical death, this type of evidence produces indisputable proof that consciousness survives the physical death.

A Neurosurgeon Returns to Life

The evidence of near death experiences is fascinating. In an interesting cover article for Maclean's Magazine[30], Brian Bethune takes note of the public's rising interest in the question, *what if heaven is real?* He notes that recent polls in the United States indicate that the belief in heaven is on a steady rise. In 2010, a Canadian poll found that more than half believe in heaven with less than a third acknowledging the existence of hell. Bethune makes the important point that with the increased technologies to enhance resuscitation techniques, patients who have been clinically dead for hours can now be brought back to life.

In addition to advanced technologies, there seems to be a rising number of esteemed medical practitioners writing about how these NDE cases substantiate evidence of an afterlife. What are the chances though that a respected neurosurgeon would die and come back to share with the world that his understanding of the brain's relationship to consciousness prior to his NDE was *just wrong*? Dr. Eben Alexander[31], a Harvard University graduate and neurosurgeon experienced an NDE after contracting a rare spontaneous E. coli meningitis infection in 2008. I do not think it was a coincidence that a respected neurosurgeon would contract a rare infection—one that wiped out the neocortex—part of the brain responsible for perception and consciousness. Despite having only a 2 percent chance of survival, he was miraculously resuscitated and lived to share the important message—that despite the death of his brain, he experienced many activities in the afterlife.

I often wonder if the influx of scientific evidence, credible researchers and esteemed medical practitioners is a sign for us to take closer notice of the truth about our universe and purpose for existence.

Out-of-Body Experiences (OBE)

During the early debates about the validity of NDEs, scholars claimed that this phenomenon might be solely a result of the dying brain. This theory has been difficult to substantiate now that researchers have been able to validate the existence of out-of-body experiences (OBE). Individuals who experience an OBE have similar experiences as NDErs; however, those who experience OBEs were never launched into another reality as a result of a death or dying brain. Since individuals experiencing OBEs report similar experiences reported by NDErs, this suggests the phenomenon is not caused by a dying brain. It appears that being outside of your physical body occurs independent of the brain's functioning and these are facts that contribute to the survival of consciousness theory.

Past-Life Regression Therapy

We have yet another key to unlocking the mysteries of the afterlife. Past-life regression therapy is a technique that uses hypnosis to help the patient recover memories—memories that are from current and past lifetimes. In the twenty-first century, this technique is typically used to treat phobias and addictions or to address current life challenges. The technique usually involves a psychiatrist or trained hypnotherapist who subjects the patient to a series of questions during a hypnotic state, one that is also known as a state of deep concentration.

To better understand this concept, can you recall ever being so focused on a great book or movie that you were unable to hear or view anything else? Typically when I am focused on moving from A to B on a long drive, I often feel like I am in a hypnotic state as I don't recall the street signs or the people walking across the street, and upon arriving at my intended destination I often wonder who was driving the car as I don't recall the actual images during the commute.

Imagine for a moment that you are a psychiatrist enjoying your esteemed career in psychopharmacology. You are chairman of Mount Sinai's psychiatric department and enjoy the traditional scientific paradigm that promotes reductionism (a theory that opposes the dualism theory and the doctrine of one life and one death). One special case completely transforms your life. You are seeing a patient named Catherine, who has chronic physical ailments, nightmares, and anxiety attacks that are deteriorating her quality of life. After you have provided the appropriate suggestions to guide Catherine into a hypnotic state, you ask questions that during this state might be more readily responded to by the unconscious mind. You are amazed when you start to learn that Catherine provides information about past-life traumas that seem to occur in a different place, culture, and time zone. You begin to wonder if it is even possible that one human being can die and then live another life.

We no longer have to imagine this incident as this was Dr. Brian Weiss's experience. He shared the details of his personal discovery in his life-transforming work titled *Many Lives, Many Masters,* first published in 1988. Dr. Weiss did not believe in reincarnation at the time of his discovery, and more importantly most of his Western colleagues did not either.

I would like to digress here for a moment before we continue to examine how past-life regression supports the evidence about the afterlife. Dr. Weiss has shared in many interviews that the unexpected death of his young son allowed him to be courageous enough to share his discovery to skeptical colleagues. Throughout the book I have made reference to areas of examination into life-after-death issues where we had to be open-minded and detached from beliefs that were no longer plausible or not in mankind's greater good. If Dr. Weiss did not lose his son, he may not have embarked on a further investigation of past lives. He may not have also had the courage to openly study and report on an area of study that just did not fit the status quo. We must applaud those in the medical community (medical doctors and psychiatrists) who have come forward with their discoveries even when that meant potential career suicide and ridicule. My belief is that it is no accident that professionals who have the power to influence change are those who originate from highly respected fields of study.

> Practitioners in the medical field should be applauded for coming forward with their discoveries, especially when studying topics related to the afterlife and unseen forces were considered to be potentially career suicide.

So exactly how does past-life regression therapy contribute to knowledge on the afterlife? Since researchers have found that patients undergoing this technique have shared detailed information about past lives, this would suggest that the individual being regressed had been previously living in a different body, perhaps many bodies in a variety of lifetimes. Researchers, such as Dr. Ian Stevenson and Weiss, have regressed thousands of patients where details revealed about past lives were further corroborated by subsequent confirmatory research. The evidence for past lives is demonstrated by the practitioner's ability to link a past life trauma with a current medical ailment. In the case of Catherine and many others, after the patient was able to experience the past-life trauma that was associated with the current ailment, the therapy appears to have a curative effect on the present ailment.

Past-life regression provides evidence for the belief in reincarnation, the religious or philosophical concept that after biological death the soul continues in preparation to occupy a different physical body. There are many theories about why this occurs, but I will provide my opinion based on a review of diverse perspectives on the subject. The soul chooses a variety of physical bodies with varying potential experiences to achieve spiritual growth. If your soul needs to learn about greed, it makes sense that you might experience a life of wealth and then poverty to gain a variety of different perspectives. The soul's continuous state of reincarnation allows our universal consciousness to gain a greater understanding and achieve universal spiritual growth.

There are cases of children spontaneously sharing that they have been another person. Upon closer examination of these cases there would be no other way that the child would have access to such details, resulting in the only viable conclusion that they were recalling past-life events.

During hypnotherapy some practitioners have heard their patients begin to speak in languages that they had not learned in this lifetime. The phenomenon known as *xenoglossy* refers to the ability to speak or write a foreign language not learned during the present lifetime. Dr. Ian Stevenson assessed many cases and concluded that for an individual to fluently use another language he or she would either have to be channeling a discarnate from the spirit world or unearthing a memory from a past life. Both of these conclusions directly point to the evidence of an afterlife.

During an interview shared on *Afterlife TV* Bob Olson, the TV host, and Dr. Weiss discussed how past-life regression therapy and the afterlife were associated.[32] Olson inquired why other psychiatrists or hypnotherapists other than Ian Stevenson and a handful of others had not reported these cases of past lives. Dr. Weiss explained that traditionally psychiatrists asked closed-ended questions such as: Is your smoking related to feelings of low self-esteem? Were you hurt by the traumatic experience with the car accident? However, by asking open-ended questions, you allow the subconscious mind to take you to the cause of the problem. In Catherine's case during hypnosis she was asked an open-ended question that resulted in Catherine's consciousness accessing the period where the cause of the current ailment started. The idea of opening up the doorways to learning about past lives with the use of an open-ended question was also experienced by Edgar Cayce.

We learned about some of Cayce's extraordinary psychic gifts in the previous chapter. Cayce became famous after being able to diagnose and prescribe cures for ailments during his sleep. Prior to 1911 Cayce and the researchers investigating his gifts were only focused on eliciting information that would allow him to diagnose illness, specify treatment, and refer his patients to the appropriate medical doctor. It wasn't until an inquirer requested a horoscope reading that the public began to learn about information that substantiated evidence of patients experiencing many lives.[33] The request for the horoscope reading was an open-ended question that appealed to the greater parameters of Cayce's subconscious. Toward the end of the horoscope reading during Cayce's sleep state, he stated quite nonchalantly, "He was a monk."[34] The inquirer was never a monk in this life so the implications of this statement gave rise to the possibility that Cayce was referring to a life in the past with a different physical body.

Past-life regression therapy provides another means of understanding the afterlife. If information about past lives is accessed during hypnosis, this further suggests that the soul continues to live on and returns to the earthy plane to experience many lives.

Deathbed Visions

Deathbed visions refer to a range of experiences that happens to those who are in the process of dying. Scholars like Dr. Carla Wills-Brandon suggest that there are many cases where those attending to the dying also see spirits. This phenomenon can provide us with corroborating evidence of an afterlife if enough individuals validate their ability to see the deceased during their transitions to the other side.

The *Journal of the Society for Psychical Research*[35] reports a case study (1903) where two women watched over a young boy just prior to his death. One of the women mentioned in her account of the story was a good friend of the boy's mother, who had now passed on into the spirit world. Both of these women independently saw the spirit of the dying boy's mother but kept this information to themselves. During the sighting one of the women stood in awe and wanted to share this with the other woman and decided that it was not wise. Two days after the sighting the boy passed away, and after the official confirmation of death was made, the woman who saw the mother appear turned to her friend and started to tell her about the strange incident that occurred just two nights earlier. They both described the apparition and were able to validate each other's sighting.

The account suggests that both of these reputable women saw the mother appear. When two individual people independently have sightings, it further validates the theory that our friends and family in spirit come to the physical world to escort us back *home.*

Up until the year 2009 I had not paid much attention to the concept known as deathbed visions. I didn't need to as I was about to obtain experiential knowledge. My grandmother had just reached one hundred years on February 14, 2009. She was fully blind, confined to a wheelchair, was suffering from a great deal of pain, and was no longer experiencing any quality life[36]. My parents and I began to notice that despite her long, gloomy days in pain just prior to her passing, she would be quite excited in retelling stories about *certain friends*. Out of nowhere Grandma would say, "You know that Aunt Birdie and I had a lovely tea today? You know that Beryl was there too?" With conviction Grandma would ask, "Can you please make sure you leave out some more towels for Uncle D as there aren't enough in the bathroom?" We were so pleased about these intermittent bursts of communication that we failed to notice that all of her plans seemed to revolve around engaging with family who had passed on to the spirit world. These intermittent utterances occurred for about three months prior to her passing in March 2009. There were other signs that Grandma might be working toward transitioning to the other side. On two occasions prior to her passing she would ask my mother to look up toward the ceiling of her bedroom to share her amazing view of the white light. Grandma wondered if others could see this beautiful white light. Of course none of us saw this light, and when my mother would follow up to see if grandma was still seeing this bright light, she responded with an abrupt *no*, signifying that perhaps my mother was crazy to mention the possibility of such an occurrence.

My parents, who will rarely admit to any form of paranormal phenomenon, shared an instance just prior to her passing when Grandma's bedroom, located in my parents' home, was filled with the scent of roses. I can recall my father being stunned about the scent of roses looming in Grandma's bedroom despite the absence of any flowers that would produce such a fragrance.

The day before Grandma's passing my mother felt a presence around her all day. She could not help but feel that there was someone beside her, almost observing to make sure she was all right. Finally, just about two weeks prior to her passing I had a very lucid dream of Grandma standing at the front door of a large home. It looked like a palace with gold walls and furniture fit for a king and queen. I was left with the impression that this would be her house and that it was being prepared for her. The most important part of the dream was that Grandma was standing at the doorway entrance with her arms crossed. She was neither in her potential new home nor outside of it. The message was that Grandma was undecided about her transition to her new home in the spirit world.

All of these events leading up to her passing made me wonder whether she was actually visiting the other side, perhaps temporarily leaving the body and then returning. This would explain her making references to activities she was experiencing with people who were deceased and would most definitely provide an explanation for her commentary on the beautiful bright light. Despite being blind, perhaps Grandma was able to see this amazing white light because she was temporarily experiencing the afterlife during the final stages of her life on the physical plane. Perhaps the scented roses were sent from her friends as they were preparing to receive her in the afterlife. Perhaps the *visitor* my mother felt had come to console my mother and then escort Grandma home. My lucid dream was clear. Grandma was making a decision to transition to the other side, and her home was being prepared.

Deathbed visions are known to occur when deceased family and friends appear to the dying during their transition to the other side. The time period between the visions and the death are close in proximity. In my example with Grandma these lucid communications she was having about deceased family and friends seemed to take place over a period of about three to four weeks. I still decided to classify this example under deathbed visions as her behaviors demonstrated that she had been visualizing and perhaps interacting with her deceased friends during the period leading up to her death.

Months after Grandma's passing I received information from a medium that although my grandmother officially died in March 2009, she was *gone* long before that time. This would certainly explain the lucid conversations she was having with her deceased friends and family during the weeks prior to her passing.

Remote Viewing

Remote viewing is the ability to view and locate places with the mind. When you first hear about remote viewing, you might think that the concept seems quite impossible. It seems, however, that there was enough evidence to warrant its use for intelligence purposes. In October 1978 the Central Intelligence Agency (CIA) hired a research team and remote viewers to obtain information about countries that were a potential threat to the United States and other countries.

Joseph McMoneagle, the remote viewer for the Central Intelligence Agency in the United States, described how this worked in an interview on the Discovery Science Channel.[37] The journalists set up their own tests. They requested that McMoneagle remotely view a secret location "halfway across the world" chosen by the Discovery Science Channel staff. McMoneagle's specific task was to pinpoint a particular person somewhere in Europe. The target location was unknown to anyone other than the research staff. McMoneagle had only a picture and his psychic abilities to aid him through this task.

McMoneagle explained that the building was a state-of-the-art building made of glass with a sunroof-type ceiling. He also noted that there was a small church or chapel that was located within this larger building. Interestingly he was also able to draw a picture that resembled the target's face. He mentioned that there were many engines that were not cars. This was all correct. The target location was the London Stansted Airport, which was indeed made of glass, had a chapel, and was home to many planes that produced sounds of engines on an hourly basis. Although McMoneagle was accurately able to draw a picture of a jet engine, he failed to mention that the building was an airport surrounded by planes. The experiment was deemed inconclusive because of this miss.

In a typical experiment used to test remote-viewing abilities, the remote viewer would be left in a dark room with the use of only their extrasensory intelligence to help them locate the individual. If the remote viewer is in Australia and the target (the individual or object the remote viewer is trying to locate) is located at the other end of the world, successfully locating the target would be possible as the remote viewer is tapping into a nonlocal reality or what is also known as a collective consciousness. In the demonstration previously described, the remote viewer was asked to draw images of what he had seen surrounding the target individual or object. Since this was an experiment, the researchers were aware of the target's location and could verify if the remote viewer's images were correct.

Remote viewing raises an important issue in afterlife research. Some researchers believe that for individuals to be able to accurately view an object remotely, they would have to be either channeling the information from the deceased or obtaining it from a collective consciousness. Scholars who study the survival of consciousness like to separate discussions about discarnates from the collective consciousness. The former theory would purport that the individual's soul transitions to the other side, further suggesting that after death everything is the same except for the fact that there is no longer a physical body. Support for the theory of the collective consciousness, however, suggests that after the transition of the soul individual aspects of consciousness, including personality, feelings, and memories, merge to form a collective consciousness. Some researchers believe that parts of the consciousness, including the knowledge, feelings, personality, and memories, live on and merge with a greater consciousness.

If we adhere to the collective consciousness theory, we still must ask ourselves this question: How is it that individual pieces of information, such as names and memories, can be isolated after they are merged? How do people account for the discarnates they meet during their NDE, OBE and deathbed visions if partial aspects of the consciousness are one solid entity? My theory is that the sightings and spirit communication are sourced both from the collective consciousness and individual discarnates. The memories, thoughts, and beliefs are merged but can also be independent depending on the context and the needs of the sitter. Either way both theories support the existence of the afterlife as the soul and the consciousness survive and transform into a format that is suitable for its continued growth and the greater well-being of the universe.

Putting It All Together

This review of the key findings related to the afterlife summarizes the bulk of research that provides support for the survival of consciousness. Table 4 provides a type of cheat sheet that explains how each area of study contributes to the evidence on life after death.

Table 4 How does this contribute to the survival of consciousness theory?

Area of Study	How does this area of study contribute to evidence of life after death?
Mediumship	• Provides evidence that past loved ones and friends still exist in spirit.
Near-Death Experiences	• Provides evidence that the soul does not die with the physical death. • Provides more detailed information about the afterlife (including an understanding of the various experiences that occur after the physical death).
Out-of-Body Experiences	• Provides more detail about the afterlife (i.e., the soul has unlimited access to various places and dimensions).
Past-Life Regression Therapy	• Provides evidence of past lives (i.e., reincarnation). • Demonstrates human capacity when the mind can access the super consciousness.
Deathbed Visions	• Provides evidence that family and loved ones can appear to their loved ones on the physical plane.
Remote Viewing	• Provides evidence of the possibility of a collective consciousness that collects and records all knowledge from the past, present, and future.

Now that we have a greater understanding about the evidence related to life after death, we can take a closer examination of factors that contribute to clear spirit communication. Understanding these factors provides further insights into the nature of the universe.

FACTORS THAT CONTRIBUTE TO
CLEAR SPIRIT COMMUNICATION

*N*ow that we have heard directly from the mediums and learned about the evidence related to life after death, it is necessary to have a closer examination of spirit communication. Most people focus on the medium as the ultimate channel for spirit and have little understanding of the role the sitter and spirit play in spirit communication. Examining how the interaction of all these factors enhances spirit communication provides us with answers to the mysteries surrounding our spiritual universe. Persons interested in learning about the nature of the spiritual universe will find that the information shared in this chapter clarifies the barriers that inhibit clear spirit communication. Learning about the role sitters play in a reading will clarify how our own circumstances shape the content and accuracy of the reading. In this chapter we will examine all of the factors that contribute to clear and accurate spirit communication. Such a comprehensive assessment would require the inclusion of factors related to the medium, sitters, and various types of entities in the spirit world. All aspects of this three-way communication system will be explored in this chapter.

A Personal Awakening

I can still recall the first time a medium shared that my deceased grandmother Beryl was in the room where the spiritual reading was taking place. By the time I reached the age of thirty-eight I had only seen three astrologers and one medium. All of my experiences with the cosmos and spirit world prior to that point had been limited to information I had read in a book, learned at church, or experienced in lucid dream states. Given my limited past experiences, I was astounded first by the knowledge that this medium instantly provided the name of my deceased grandmother. I was in awe that the medium was also able to show me where her leg was amputated prior to her passing. To further explain the cause of death, the medium began to see mounds of sugar. This symbol combined with the vision of the amputated leg confirmed for me that Grandma was providing proof of her continued existence by communicating that diabetes had caused her physical death.

I knew this was not fakery. Even at the mature age of thirty-eight I knew that guessing this type of name and accurately identifying the illness that caused her physical death could not be a chance occurrence. I recall that at the time even the medium questioned the name she heard as she could not fathom why someone would be named after a *barrel*. She did indeed have the name absolutely correct as Beryl was a common name in the nineteen century in London, England.

This first experience observing a medium communicating with the deceased did not immediately launch my interest in the life-after-death issue. Instead I was most intrigued with the mechanics of spirit communication. I asked myself many questions. Were the messages from spirit always this clear? Was it a two-way communication? Could we ask anything and receive an accurate response? Did Grandma Beryl know all that there was to know, and could my communication with her be beneficial by providing insights that might help me thrive in a challenging world?

Potential for Misinterpretation

In fact, it was at this reading that Grandma Beryl apparently communicated what I considered to be a cautionary message. The medium stated, "She is telling you that you have to watch out for your close friend starting with the initial B." My mind immediately thought of my best friend, Bridgette, who broke my trust several years ago. I pondered, was my close friend Bridgette planning to do something that could potentially be harmful to me or a family member? At the time Bridgette and I were no longer residing in the same country, so I was not really concerned about being the victim of any such malevolent behavior. I did not think about the cautionary note from the medium until a group of girlfriends that included Bridgette all gathered at a vacation spot in the Cayman Islands approximately six months after the reading with the medium. Normally I would have been excited about this type of gathering, but given the medium's cautionary note and my past experience with Bridgette's breach of trust, I was reticent about the Caribbean all-female reunion. Incidentally the GOV (also known as the *girls-only vacation*) went off perfectly—just pure joy, peace, and well-being with no malevolence at all. After I saw the same medium three months after this GOV, I received another cautionary message without any solicitation on my part from the spirit about Bridgette. I was told again to watch out for my friend "Brige." At this reading the medium picked up more than the B letter but was still not pronouncing it correctly, but this time the cautionary note was qualified with this: "She needs more support, so you need to *watch out for her*. She needs you more than ever." With that clarification everything was so much clearer. I originally misinterpreted the message and used my past experience with Bridgette to incorrectly shape the intention of the reading. With this clarification I linked this new information with my knowledge of Bridgette's recent separation from her husband. I learned during the GOV that Bridgette was very concerned about losing her children in a custody battle and perhaps this would explain why the spirit (in the second reading) and Grandma Beryl (in the original reading) were encouraging me to *watch out for* Bridgette.

I had initially interpreted the message to be a warning heeding protection from Bridgette, but instead the right interpretation was that I needed to spend more time providing support. This first experience with spirit communication led me to believe that perhaps the communication system was not a clear two-way process. Perhaps there are barriers that make communication speculative. After many more years of experiencing and observing spirit communication, it is clear that various factors play a role in enhancing or diminishing the clarity of earth-to-spirit communication, and everyone, including the sitter and the discarnate, plays a vital role.

Communication in the Physical World

Before we examine the factors that play a role in spirit communication, let's take a moment to examine communication on this physical plane of existence. On the earth plane we have various forms of communication that include speaking, writing, and sign language. Determining the best way to communicate depends on the persons involved and the nature of the exchange. Under the most ideal conditions one would think that communication on the earth plane would be clear. Some factors that might enhance communication on the early plane include having a good grasp of the language being used and the proximity and comfort between the speakers. You would think that a simple discussion on the earth plane occurring under optimal conditions would produce clear communication. Do these ideal conditions guarantee clear communication? *Not really*. People use their own ideological paradigms and social conditioning, which often changes the intended meaning of the communicator.

Let's have a look at an example of communication between

two people on the earth plane who are communicating under ideal conditions but experience a major misunderstanding.

> **Matthew**: You know that I forgot to ask you how Joe at work is doing. I know that you were expressing problems with him at work. Is everything all right now?

> **Don**: Gee, I forgot to mention that Joe is no longer with us.

> **Matthew**: Well that worked out really well. It is so much better when the workplace is free of problem people. Good riddance to Joe!

> **Don**: When I said, he was no longer with us, I meant that he was hit by a train a few weeks ago and is literally no longer with us.

In this example we see how erroneous communication can lead to misinterpretation and potentially harmful comments. All of us have experienced miscommunication and misunderstandings with communication on the earth plane. In fact, it can take quite a bit of energy to ensure we are being clear both orally and in writing. Once we agree that communication between human beings on the earth plane is imperfect, it is easier to relate to the challenges we encounter between our world known as the earth plane and the spirit world. For the purposes of this chapter the term "earth-to-spirit communication" is used.

It is not entirely accurate to conceptualize the spirit world as one place that is separate and apart from the earth plane. Some hypothesize that the spirit world is right here on earth; the only thing separating the two worlds are the laws that govern its existence. Using the term "two worlds" may also be inaccurate as depending on the belief system, there can be a number of different planes of existence. It is beyond the scope of this chapter to examine the composition of the spirit world; however, if we can agree at least that the spirit communication referred to in this chapter is between the earth plane and other planes of existence that use different forms of communication, we can go forward in taking a closer look at what is really going on when a medium mediates between the spirits and sitters who exist on the earth plane.

Medium: Stage of Development

In this section of the chapter the medium's role in spirit communication is examined. Hudson Tuttle[38] was one of America's seers during the launch of Spiritualism. In his book, *Mediumship and Its Laws*, he emphasizes the importance of recognizing the medium's levels of development when assessing the accuracy of spirit communication. The level of development is an important factor. Most mediums are born with their gifts but enhance their sensitivity to the spirit world through various levels of development. When Tuttle speaks of a set of levels to experience, this does not mean that all mediums at the same level will experience the same abilities. For example, two very experienced mediums may be at a full stage of development where one has the gift of clearly sharing names while the other rarely hears names but sees the physical characteristics of the discarnate clearly. Others may not have the strength of clairvoyance or clairaudience, but picking up the emotions and the personalities is a specialty. The medium's level of development should be taken into consideration when one is assessing the accuracy of the guiding messages shared. Achieving the desired levels of development includes mastering many aspects of mediumship. In Bhakta Vishita's book, *Genuine Mediumship*, he describes the importance of achieving discipline and the appropriate levels of mental condition. I have taken a brief extract from Vishita's book to illustrate how a medium's mental condition can affect the outcome of a reading. I have paraphrased some areas to enhance reading efficiency.[39]

The young medium, however, should beware against striving too hard to be the instrument of the phenomena of spirit impersonation. An intense anxiety, and desire to please sitters, frequently tends to produce a cloudy mental state in which the ideas in the mind of the medium blend with the spirit communication, and thus produces a most unsatisfactory result, and one which is apt to confuse the minds of the sitters and sometimes may arouse suspicion that the medium is trying to practice deception. For this reason the young medium should not seek the attendance of persons desiring a test séance; at least, such should be his course until he has learned not to be carried away with his desire to satisfy such persons attending his circles. He should endeavor to cultivate a mental condition of calmness, and a determination not to influence or to interfere with the spirit communications in any way whatsoever, but, instead, to allow himself to become a passive instrument for the communication. The medium should remember that he is not a dealer in merchandise warranted to please, but is, instead, a medium of communication between the spirit and those still in earth-life.

A medium's level of development and ability to be a passive instrument for spirit communication will enhance the clarity and flow of spirit communication.

Medium: Symbols and Interpretation

You will recall reading in chapter 2 about how some of the mediums use symbols to help communicate messages from spirit. Experienced mediums will share that when they receive information, even when the symbols and impressions are clear, they are not responsible for the interpretation of the symbols. For example, you will hear John Edwards, a famous medium, share that swirling air with the two people in question will mean a "whirlwind marriage." This symbol and its associated meaning may only be appropriate for Edwards. Swirling air may mean different things to different mediums. I have heard many mediums indicate that their spirit guides (also known as controls during the early years of mediumship) aid with spirit communication by impressing symbols into their minds. The guides impress symbols that elicit meaning that only the mediums would know.

Experienced mediums know that it is important to only share the meaning related to the symbol and to avoid the temptation to further interpret how the symbol and its meaning can be applied to the sitter. Spirit communication can become confused when the medium attempts to explain how the symbol applies to the sitter's life. Most successful mediums will describe what they see and ask the sitter to relate this information to their current experience. For example, when the medium says, "I have a grandmother K here with me, and she is showing me a beautiful home with flowers growing—the field of blooming flowers is infinite." The sitter responds, "That is my grandmother Katie, and she is likely confirming that my many dreams are now starting to come true. I have felt her presence around me when I am gardening, and in the last six months I feel like all the seeds I have sewn are starting to materialize. I am fulfilling my dreams both at work and at home." If the medium used their own physical mind to interpret these symbols, many possible interpretations could have been conceived. The medium may have interpreted that the sitter was going to be moving into a beautiful new home with a garden, that the sitter recently planted new flowers, or that the sitter recently acquired a large property. The interpretation issue has plagued mediums and psychics mostly because society's misguided notions of spirit communication create pressure for the medium to provide *all* the information. The attitude from society and some skeptical researchers is that if the medium knows some information, he or she must know all of it. Any attempt on the medium's part to encourage the sitter to provide information (such as explaining how the symbol applies) is considered by some to be an indication of the fishing techniques used by individuals who do not possess mediumistic abilities.

When mediums conduct several readings a day, those relying on symbols to communicate messages might be fatigued after they have had to translate symbols into meaningful information. This aspect of spirit communication became clear after I interviewed Sharon, a psychic medium who found the constant barrage of symbols challenging after she had conducted six readings a day for twenty years.

Spirit communication can be enhanced when the medium derives meaning from the symbol but allows the sitter to use the meaning to apply to his or her current life and experience. A medium's attempt to do otherwise may confuse the sitter, reduce credibility, and inhibit the discarnate's efforts to convey the message.

Medium: Predisposition and Personality of the Discarnate

Finally, another factor that may contribute to clear earth-to-spirit communication relates to the compatibility between the medium and the discarnate. It may be hard to believe, but the medium, who of course is human, has opinions and a personality that may be more compatible with certain discarnates and not others. While most mediums have a code of ethics, they are not infallible and may take a disliking to the discarnate who was a child molester, or they may even be dismissive of the discarnate who comes across as having no ambition. The discarnate picks up this dismissive energy, and the communication may be affected by the dynamics. We need to remember that there are relatively few gifted mediums, and millions of discarnates who are always attempting to share their messages. Discarnates have few options and must work with the medium their loved ones choose to visit. It is always remarkable to hear when a discarnate makes sarcastic or disparaging remarks toward the medium. Who would think that the discarnate would make a sarcastic comment about the medium's clothes or character or even say, "Hurry up, Blondie. I have to get back to my work here in the spirit world?" During one of Lisa Williams's readings on her show, *Life among the Dead*,[40] she tries to convey messages from the spirit world to grieving family members. Imagine how the communication was affected when Lisa Williams was feeling harassed by a spirit who was flirting with her while she was giving a reading! It was apparent that despite her efforts to carry forward the pertinent messages she was somewhat startled and distracted by the spirit's flirtatious behavior.

During the preparation of one of my experiments with a medium and a group of four sitters, the medium shared some insights that helped me see how a discarnate's personality might have a potential effect on the outcome of a reading. In this experiment the sitters were unknown to the medium, and I planned to record and later assess the medium's ability to provide messages that resonated with the sitters. Just prior to our arrival the medium shared with us that he had a very bossy grandmother in spirit waiting for the séance to begin. Apparently she hit him on the head to let him know that we were coming up the stairs. The medium heard her say, "Hurry up. My daughter is here, and I have been waiting for a while to talk to her." In this particular case the *bossy* grandmother in spirit did indeed turn out to be the mother of one of the sitters who was coming up the stairs at the same time the medium was patted on the head. It turns out that the hit the medium received was more like a friendly pat, and there did not seem to be any personality conflicts that affected the reading. I share this case not because the medium and this demanding grandmother in spirit had any personality conflicts that affected the reading. I share it to illustrate that those in spirit continue to have many of the traits that they had on the earth plane. These characteristics may not always work well with the medium, further limiting the transmission or clarity of potential messages. We need to remember that while spirit and our deceased loved ones have the potential to enhance our understanding, our loved ones still have similar personalities and predispositions—these peculiarities are present during spirit communication.

We see here from these points shared that the clarity, accuracy, and content of spirit communication depends on the medium's level of development, the extent to which he or she interprets the symbols he or she receives, and the dynamics between the discarnate and the medium.

While most of the public place the responsibility of spirit communication solely with the medium, in this chapter it is emphasized that the sitter and spirit play equally important roles in spirit communication. To understand this concept, I compare a musical instrument and a medium. If you have proof that the tenor sax you are playing is working and demonstrates the capacity to play well-tuned music, then you can be satisfied that you have a functional instrument that performs as intended. If under various circumstances this instrument does not play well or the audience is not hearing the notes as intended, one might conclude that other factors beyond the instrument itself might be responsible for performance levels. This is also the case with mediums. Like the tenor sax, the medium may perform differently depending on the sitter and discarnate present.

We turn now to exploring the role of the discarnate in spirit communication.

Spirit: Stage of Learning

In this section of the chapter a reference to both spirit and discarnate is made. During a reading a medium may not convey if he or she is communicating with a discarnate or spirit. During a reading, depending on the nature of the message, it is most useful if the medium can clarify the source as a discarnate (the soul of someone who once lived on the physical plane) or *spirit*, an umbrella term that includes angels, spirit guides, or other highly evolved masters. Discarnates and spirit play an important role in the accuracy, content, and clarity of the messages being shared in earth-to-spirit communication.

I have always wondered why discarnates could not *always* share their names or provide details about their activities in the spirit world during spirit communication. It was perplexing why in one instance they could convey detailed names and then in other instances only be able to provide loving but general statements such as, "I am still around you and love you all very much." While the latter type of message might be very healing for clients, it has not always been compelling enough for sitters to accurately identify the discarnate. It certainly is not a statement that can be used to demonstrate proof that humans survive their physical death.

I have found the following literature to be useful in explaining why the spirit's stage of development can contribute to their ability to communicate effectively.

In Jane Roberts's book, *Seth Speaks: The Eternal Validity of the Soul* (1963),[41] Seth, a spiritual entity, channels information about spirit life to the author Roberts. Seth explains that in the post-death period discarnates need to adapt to the atmosphere, which includes movement, communication, and general functioning. Some discarnates may adapt to their new environment faster than others depending on their states of consciousness and perspectives held on the earth plane. Recall for a moment the first time you learned how to eat solid food, drink from a cup, walk without support, ride a bike, and speak your mother tongue. These types of activities were necessary for you to be able to function in the physical world. For example, some of us learned to walk faster than others, which suggests that these abilities evolved differently for each child. Seth's explanation of the mechanics in the spirit world is consistent with our experience in the physical world. Some discarnates don't adapt quickly and often need helpers to remain with them until they are fully reacquainted with the spirit world.

Hudson Tuttle further validates the theory that some discarnates need to adjust to their new environments. In his book, *Mediumship and Its Laws: Conditions and Cultivations*, he shares a story about his experience waiting to hear from a friend who promised to provide proof of the afterlife once he transitioned to the other side.

In his book he explains that Captain D. B. Edwards, who was a friend and distant relative living in one of the eastern extremities of Long Island, was a sea captain until nearly seventy years of age and one of the most unselfish, sympathetic, and spiritual men he had ever met. Tuttle explains that Edwards became an ardent Spiritualist and agreed that upon his passing he would communicate with Tuttle to confirm the existence of an afterlife.

Nearly six months passed after Edwards's death and Tuttle had still not heard from Edwards. This was unusual as Tuttle was a gifted medium and was experienced with sensing the presence of spirits in the nonphysical form. During the night after Christmas, Tuttle was finally conscious of Edwards's presence. Edward used telepathy and various forms of ESP to communicate with Tuttle. He explained that he had waited anxiously to confirm the afterlife; however, it took him a long period of time to awake to the reality that he was indeed dead. Edward also explains that after he had lived a life full of pain, he was enjoying the sense of peace. Most important was that he did not wish to awake from this pain-free state of bliss in fear that he would somehow be returned to the physical form.

He further explains that he tried to come but just did not know how. It appears that Edward attempted to communicate with Tuttle on many occasions but did not have the ability.[42]

* * *

Time and time again I wanted to let you know that I was "alive in spirit." I did not know how to approach.

* * *

He noted that *others* could have assisted him by conveying his message to Tuttle on his behalf, but he was determined to wait until he learned to speak directly.

Edwards was able to explain to Tuttle that he could not come to him to validate his survival after his passing because of two main reasons. Firstly he was engulfed in a peaceful existence, and after he had experienced so much pain, he did not want to do anything to disrupt this feeling of bliss. Secondly he had not learned the mechanism required to communicate with earthly spirits. You will recall the discussions in the first chapter about vibrational frequency. Spirits are vibrating at a much faster frequency than those experiencing the reality referred to as the earth plane. The ability to vibrate at a lower frequency requires skill and training. Tuttle and Edwards's experience is important. It demonstrates that discarnates need time to adjust to their new surroundings after they transition from the physical to nonphysical realities and this adjustment period may contribute to lack of communication. Miscommunication or potential confusion may arise when the discarnate intending to communicate requires assistance from other spirits. Any expansion of the simple three-way telephone call may become broken telephone because of the higher potential for miscommunication.

Spirit: They Have Their Own Agenda

One of the most important factors in spirit communication relates to the fact that discarnates and spirits decide who will speak and what they will speak about. During the research for *Medium7* it was often surprising to learn that most participants thought that the medium had the power to encourage the desired spirit to communicate. I probably should not have been surprised as I too had made similar assumptions during my first few meetings with mediums. My assumption was that I could send out silent prayers to my deceased friends and relatives and this would signal my interest in hearing from them via the medium. The second assumption I had was that once contact was made with loved ones they would answer all of my questions as I was certain that they had an interest in my well-being. The third assumption I had was that once contact was made with a deceased loved one, it would be a free-flowing, two-way communication similar to our system of communication on earth. It took many years and an examination of several case studies to realize that my earthly assumptions were quite flawed. Every good medium will explain that they do not have control over what spirits decide to communicate during a reading. They also note that loved ones in the spirit world have their own agenda. They may wish to speak about priority areas that you may consider irrelevant or menial relative to your priorities.

For example, you are a sitter that is interested in determining the best career path and hope to receive guidance from loved ones in the spirit world. You are on a path where the corner office is considered successful, and you are interested in how to achieve the CEO status you so desire. Your current career path is fast-paced, competitive, and financially rewarding. However, despite the status and financial rewards, you suffer from lethargy, frequent depression, and lack of fulfillment. You are aware of another potential career path where you can still use your skills. The rewards of this alternative path are inner wealth and greater well-being as a result of helping others, but you feel that this path is unrecognized. During the few readings you have experienced over the past year it has been frustrating for you that spirit has not directly responded to questions about your current career and instead made references to finding inner peace and provided advice that seemed quite unrelated to your current career. In this type of scenario it may be that spirit has its own agenda that might include encouragement to seek another path that eventually provides greater fulfillment.

On the earth plane if we initiate communication and the intended audience responds by introducing an entirely different topic, it may appear rude; however, during spirit communication when the responses are not directly related to the inquirer's question, this should not be construed as miscommunication or erroneous. Instead the sitter should understand that the discarnate or spirit is identifying a priority that they feel is in your highest and greatest good.

Another useful example of spirit having their own agenda was demonstrated on the show, *Exposed: Psychic in Suburbia*. During an episode in this show, the gifted medium Maureen Hancock had an initial sitting with Joleen, a young woman who wanted to know if her deceased mother approved of her fiancé, Kevin. When Maureen does actually bring the deceased Mother through during the reading and obtains confirmation about a number of issues, Joleen expresses excitement about being able to indirectly communicate with her mother. Excitement quickly turns to a calamity when Joleen asks the medium to determine if her mother supports the upcoming marriage to her future husband. The distress and ambiguity occurs as Maureen shares that her mother does not provide a response to this question and retreats, meaning that her energy fades and communication has significantly diminished. Maureen thinks that this is the end of the reading and it is business as usual. To Maureen's surprise, however, the fiancé storms into the medium's office on the day after the reading demanding an explanation as to why having a reading with a medium could prompt the swift break up and the respite of their wedding. Maureen tries to explain how mediumship works and offers to bring the deceased Mother through with both of them present.

Another reading with Joleen is scheduled with her fiancé present to see if the unintended break up could be resolved. To everyone's surprise, once again the deceased Mother does come through in the reading, but again does not want to discuss the upcoming marriage. Instead, she shares signs that lead Joleen and Kevin to find a forgotten fur coat in the basement where they later find an unclaimed life insurance policy. This vignette ends with exultant tears as Joleen has more money to fulfill her dreams.

This episode demonstrates that spirit does not work on demand. The spirit world decides who will communicate and if and when they do decide to communicate with us in the physical world, it will be about an issue that *they* feel is important. In this case, Joleen was focusing on her wedding while her deceased Mother was focused on revealing the unclaimed life insurance policy.

Spirit: Lessons to Be Learned

Many research experiments used to test the validity of survival of consciousness are based on the assumption that spirit works on demand. There is an assumption that if there is indeed life beyond death, we earthlings can obtain any type of information from the deceased, which can be subsequently used to make conclusions about the afterlife or lack thereof. Some of the tests journalists and laypersons use to test mediums demonstrate their lack of understanding about the nature of spirit communication. In this section of the chapter I would like to explain why spirits cannot work on demand all the time. What I learned from my own research was that not all desired information could be revealed at the time of a reading. This limitation was rarely the result of resistance or lack of understanding between the medium and spirit. The lack of information was often the spirit's way of ensuring the sitter's soul lessons would not be inhibited. As referred to briefly in chapter 1 and more intently in chapter 7, when one is attempting to assess the accuracy of spirit communication, one has to consider the lessons we have committed to learning during our time on the earth plane. The term "soul contracts" refers to the idea of souls in the pre-embodied state making contracts and agreements to benefit each other during their time on the earth plane. For example, learning the lesson about loving one another or understanding that we all come from the same source may be two primary lessons that are to be addressed during one person's lifetime. To learn these two lessons, perhaps we would agree to soul contracts that involve being born into a race that is either racist or suffers from extreme racial oppression. By experiencing both sides of this issue in different lifetimes, the soul can experience various perspectives and gain a better understanding of why individuals behave and react under certain circumstances. Why are people racist and feel it necessary to don frightening clothing and burn churches and homes? By experiencing the soul contracts, we might learn that the origin of violent racist behavior is fear and insecurity or a lack of personal esteem. Understanding this may reduce hatred and encourage forgiveness. This global attempt to learn life lessons would theoretically create a sense of peace and understanding, perhaps leading us to the biggest lesson that we are all one.

How exactly does this effort to raise soul awareness relate to clearer spirit communication? It relates because all information cannot be shared at all times. Premature sharing of information with sitters could hinder their ability to learn their lessons in a manner necessary for their souls' progressions.

I found evidence of this in my study. During a reading between Lilly and a medium, I was permitted to record and use the data for further analysis. During the question-and-answer portion of this reading Lilly shared with the medium that she hoped to be married with children in the near future. She and her boyfriend were having some challenges, and the medical community was not able to guarantee a future pregnancy. My notes taken during the reading noted that the medium kept reporting on the fact that she would indeed be married to her current boyfriend but that the medium was not getting any symbols or spiritual response in regards to the pregnancies. The young lady left the reading without getting an answer about the pregnancies. After Lilly left the room, the medium explained that she was not getting any symbols or information related to the pregnancies and indicated that when this usually happened, she would directly share that she was just not receiving any information. After the medium conducted all of her readings for the day, to provide qualification to the data recorded, she shared that once Lilly left the building, the information about her pregnancies freely flowed to her. She noted that Lilly would indeed have two, possibly three children but would suffer a lengthy barren period prior to these pregnancies. The first pregnancy would be difficult and would unfortunately result in a miscarriage. I took note of this information and asked the medium why she thought that the information did not come through during the reading. She noted that she was not 100 percent certain but speculated that spirit did not want this knowledge to be shared with the sitter. The medium further suggested that sometimes the information was never revealed for the greater good. In this instance, because the medium learned this information after Lilly left, she surmised that Lilly would need to experience this aspect of her journey on her own without any foreknowledge. Perhaps learning that she would have to wait much longer and then suffer a miscarriage would demotivate her from continuing to seek the medical advice she was currently pursuing. Mediums who have positive intentions to help mankind, ask that the information from spirit come forward for the sitter's highest and greatest good. In this case it was in Lilly's highest and greatest good that she not learn any information about her future pregnancies.

Another useful case involves Roger and his wife, Kelly, who had been having marital problems for years. Kelly felt that Roger did not listen or take responsibility for his family's lives. Roger felt that Kelly was demanding and did not allow him to lead his own life. These differences resulted in Roger and Kelly living separate lives while living in the same home. Roger had been seeing the same medium for twenty years. He often enjoyed the guidance and comforting words she provided over the years. As a result of the level of confidence and trust Roger placed in this medium, he listened attentively to the guidance from spirit who suggested that he and Kelly should travel to Italy together. The medium shared that this trip would be offered to them and would allow them to be together with other family members over a six-week period. Indeed, four months after the reading this trip did present itself. Roger was astonished and skeptical about the thought of placing himself in this scenario with his estranged wife, but after he had a few awkward conversations and received some impressions based on strong intuition, Roger decided to join Kelly and other family members on this trip to Italy. He noted that he learned a few important lessons on this trip with Kelly. He realized that many of the nagging points that Kelly used to share with him were really only intended to help the family. It seems that the new scenery, fresh air in Italy, and the focus on meeting new family changed his perception of her motives. Kelly also shared that during the vacation she realized that Roger showed responsibility in different ways. He may not have managed the house or the finances, but he always made sure the family was protected, and his presence was comforting for the family over the years. Only a few weeks after the trip Kelly had an unexpected stroke and never recovered from the surgery. Just three short weeks after they returned from Italy Kelly was gone. She had passed on to the spirit world.

A few months after Kelly's death Roger revisited the medium. Roger wanted answers about why the medium saw the family vacation but did not see Kelly's imminent death. The medium told him that she did not receive any information about Kelly's death. She did recall spirit emphasizing the importance of them vacationing together. She also explained that spirit only revealed information that would be in a sitter's highest and greatest good. She further surmised that if information about an impending illness was shared, Roger and Kelly may have postponed the trip and never had the opportunity to gain a better understanding of each other's intentions. The vacation offered Roger and Kelly an opportunity to learn their intended lessons and to advance their souls. Providing information to inhibit this would have been inappropriate.

In this case Roger did not receive a comprehensive message from spirit via the medium, but he received enough to help ensure that he had an opportunity to address this important aspect of his soul contract.

With this understanding we can take note of this important aspect of spirit communication. Too much knowledge can inhibit the sitter's spiritual growth, and therefore, spirit communication cannot be assessed based on the medium's ability to share comprehensive information in all circumstances.

Spirit: Space and Time

Given the amount of factors to consider with earth-to-spirit communication, it is a wonder that we even receive worthwhile messages at all—different galaxies, dead people talking to living people, spiritual laws to consider, varying vibrational frequencies, and potential misinterpretation—and it seems that the list goes on. One of the factors that has plagued mediums and researchers for years relates to the interpretation of time. When a medium states a date or provides any type of message that involves the use of time, there are often questions about the validity of the information. Is the discarnate's perception of time similar to the sitter's?

Physicists like Albert Einstein, through discoveries, supported the view that space and time were based on mankind's perceptions of our reality. Einstein taught us that light always traveled at the same speed of 670,616,629 miles per hour yet time and space changed according to human perception. This lesson taught us that there were no absolute measures of space and time and these concepts were relative. Understanding this theory of relativity provides some insight into how we might have similar experiences yet have multiple perceptions of reality. This is an important concept and its examination in mediumship provides us with insights into the mechanics of the universe. Many mediums will say that the issue of time between the spirit worlds creates a mystery and often generates confusion about the timing of the information being shared. Therefore, understanding the nature of space and time is an important factor in understanding spirit communication. To illustrate this example, let's examine the case of Vivian. Vivian shared an interesting account of her reading where the medium was clearly gifted and accurate on many accounts. She explained that the medium knew that she had been divorced. He described details about her former husband, explaining that he had been abusive, an adulterer, and fairly unambitious. Vivian was quite amazed that the medium had the correct initial physical description and personality of her ex-husband. The confusion on Vivian's part started when the medium began to discuss the future husband. The medium spoke of a new husband to come in two years. He noted that the man would be loving. He provided the initial of the second husband and described the husband-to-be as a dream come true. He noted specifically, "He will be attracted to your hair." Vivian explained that despite such accuracy on many levels there was one key problem. During the reading when this message was shared the medium indicated that Vivian would meet her husband-to-be in about two years, yet Vivian was already married to husband number two. Husband number two fit the medium's prediction perfectly. He was loving. The first initial was correct. The personality was all Vivian could ever desire, and he always reminded her about how much he liked her hair.

Vivian's case demonstrates how messages from spirit can be accurate but misaligned in the timing. Why did the medium suggest husband number two would be arriving in two years when he was already part of Vivian's life? Should we conclude that the medium was accurately reading the time but still needed to have this translated into earth time? One of the mediums in this research indicated that the time issue related to the predetermined birth date of the sitter. If the predetermined date was altered due to various factors, the timeline would be off throughout his or her lifetime. Others suggest that sharing the specific timing of an event was futile as there is no concept of time in the spirit world. The latter notion is based on the theory that there is no present, past, or future as reality is taking place all at once within multiple realities. The mystery about time is perplexing as achieving accurate communication about the timing of events via a message from spirit is inconsistent.

After I reviewed many cases where the timing shared by discarnates via the medium was misaligned, I was inclined to conclude that communicating the accurate time between the spirit and earth plane was not possible. This perspective abruptly changed during my own personal reading. Incidentally I have noticed that anytime I was about to finalize a section of this book I would be guided to view another perspective. During a reading I received with Helen, a medium I was testing to determine her eligibility for the *Medium7* study, another perspective regarding the issue of space-time emerged. At the start of the reading the medium vehemently declared, "September 22, 2012, is going to be a really powerful day for you." She then proceeded to say, "*Saturday* September 22." She quickly got up from the table and headed toward the calendar hanging in the kitchen. She stopped and looked over her shoulder and noted, "I love it when spirit is so precise. I want to see if September 22, 2012 actually falls on a Saturday." She returned to the reading area with a complacent grin and placed the calendar on the table. She clapped her hands and proclaimed, "Yes indeed, September 22 in 2012 is a Saturday!" Both the medium and I had been thrilled, not because I was supposed to have a great day but because it was evidence that spirit can indeed communicate precise timing right down to the year, month, and day of the week. I adjusted my conclusions on this subject and now realize that the context, purpose, and factors related to the sitter determine the specificity of time shared by spirit via a medium.

What Role Do You Play when You Attend a Reading with a Medium?

The sitter plays an important role in spirit communication, although you may have thought that the medium and discarnates were doing all the work. You thought you could just sit back, relax, and miraculously obtain information that would provide instant cures and answers. This is far from the truth. The sitter's level of need, predisposition toward interacting with spirit, and the effort to reflect and analyze messages conveyed by a medium during the post-reading phase can enhance the accuracy and clarity of spirit communication.

Sitter: Levels of Need

I recall sitting at the Toronto Conference Centre, enjoying an event showcasing three mediums: John Holland, Lisa Williams, and Collette Barron-Reid. During Lisa's session she was engaged in a reading involving a desperate mother and her deceased son in spirit. The deceased son in spirit was anxiously attempting to provide the medium with information to perhaps ensure details surrounding his murder could finally be shared with his mother in the audience. He provided details about two other victims involved, described the warehouse where he was murdered, and clarified that his death was indeed a homicide and not an accident. The audience sat still during this riveting twenty-minute exchange. In this scenario it was clear that the mother was desperate to learn this information, and so the deceased son in spirit was given the opportunity to access the medium and retain her for the greater portion of her session. My observation after I viewed several group events with mediums is that discarnates and spirit, in general, always provide messages to those most in need. These needs might include information about a premature loss of a loved one, healing information, or messages that have the power to transform lives. Needs derived from greed or selfishness receive less attention as spirit's purpose is to provide support and motivation to those in great need.

Sitter: Predisposition

In addition to need the predisposition of the sitter plays a part in spirit communication. Predisposition in this context refers to the sitter's level of openness, negativity, and anxiety both prior to and during the reading with a medium.

We need to remember that we are spiritual beings with varying levels of vibration. As discussed in earlier sections of this book the spirits need to lower their vibrational energy, and we need to increase our vibrational energy to create clarity in the communication channel. Imagine that you are closed and full of negative energy while you are read by a medium. Immediately your energy fields are blocked, disallowing a signal to the spirit world. Even if loved ones on the other side wish to communicate, it makes it more difficult to create a clear channel when your negative energy is blocking these pathways. I have encountered nonbelievers who transmit signals during a reading that could inhibit communication; however, the results suggest that clear communication can still prevail under these conditions. Other factors like need may have outweighed the sitter's predisposition, providing enough of a purpose to create an open channel. Researchers who don't take need and openness of the sitter into consideration when they are assessing messages from spirits may erroneously conclude that either the medium is not well developed or that earth-to-spirit communication is not viable.

A sitter's level of negativity might include feeling depressed, angry, or resentful. Any type of fear-based emotion emanating from the sitter creates a misalignment of vibrational energy between the medium and the sitter.

We know from Abraham's teachings shared by Esther and Jerry Hicks in their book, *The Astonishing Power of Emotions*,[43] that negative thoughts and emotions attract people and scenarios with a similar vibrational frequency. The negative frequencies block the sitter's ability to allow positive messages, people, or scenarios to become parts of the sitter's reality. A medium participating in the *Medium7* study shared that from his perspective he often noticed that when sitters were closed, discarnates would fade, disallowing the medium to share any messages from the discarnates who had initially come forward.

Being closed creates a potential misalignment of vibrational frequencies, resulting in unintended signals to discarnates that they are not welcome.

The analogy of the ship floating into shore has always been helpful in gaining a better understanding of why our desires are delayed or expedited by our feelings. I am sharing it here to help readers understand how our own thoughts and feelings contribute to living our dreams.

> Your thoughts and feelings are like the water in the sea. Your dreams are like the ship navigating the seas. When you are anxious, sad, or fearful, your internal waters become rough. As a result, your dreams are like a ship on a stormy sea. Your dreams and desires become delayed as a result of the ship not being able to sail directly to the shore.

> When you are content, loving, and full of appreciation, your internal waters become calm; a ship on a calm sea is able to navigate effectively. Your dreams and desires are easily achieved as the ship floats to the shore—a place of well-being and fulfillment.[44]

This ship-on-a-stormy-sea analogy highlights how this spiritual law operates. Our thoughts and emotions affect our ability to create the reality we desire. I have observed how messages derived from readings with mediums are affected by this same spiritual law. From my observations of readings with mediums and sitters, the querent who is calm and allows the medium to freely share messages from spirit is more likely to receive relevant and accurate information. The ability of the sitter to listen and wait seemed to allow spirit a greater opportunity to provide clarity and meaningful content. On the contrary when sitters anxiously interrupted the flow of messages with questions, the responses did not seem to be as relevant or comprehensive from a sitter's perspective.

Let's review an example of how anxiety can affect clear communication in a reading. Roger and Dana were dating for several years, and as a result of unfortunate personal circumstances, they needed to break up. Roger and Dana were very much in love but were not able to share this love openly because of the secret nature of their affair. They were not able to speak to one another for several months during their separation period. Roger had found success with a medium over a year ago (2011) when he was seeking closure about his father's death; however, his sole purpose for seeing a medium in 2012 was to find out how Dana felt about him and whether the circumstances would change to allow them to be together in the future. Roger sent out this request in a silent prayer prior to the reading, hoping someone in the spirit world would respond to this prayer via the medium. During the reading almost the whole hour had passed, and there was still no acknowledgment from spirit about his sorrow regarding Dana. In fact, he was growing more anxious and more frustrated as a result of hearing messages about his co-worker's upcoming pregnancy, his mother's need to check on her thyroid gland, and his need to exercise more. Sadly he seemed to only be learning about suggested career opportunities and other people in his life that were relatively insignificant. Why nothing about Dana? After all he sent out prayers, and that is all he needed to know. Finally, at the end of the reading the medium asks if Roger has any questions. He of course asks if spirit can share whether Dana misses him and enquires if they will be together again. He thinks to himself that he wishes that he never had to voice his wish as any subsequent response is less convincing. The medium replies, "Your time alone right now is necessary for healing and reflection. You will know the right steps to take when the time is right." The medium states that this is all that she can share at this time. Roger is of course frustrated and disappointed in this general response and is disheartened with this reading.

Six months after that reading Roger revisits the same medium to seek guidance on a different matter. During this reading Roger recalls that he was visiting the medium with no real agenda. He was calm and more curious about how the medium could enlighten him about the nature of reality. He was calm and open to whatever spirit wanted to share. To Roger's surprise, within ten minutes of the reading and without any prior prayers or solicitation, the medium asks, "Who is Dana?"

He replies calmly, "A past friend."

The medium shares, "Spirit wants you to know that Dana misses you terribly. She is doing her best to move on but is finding it difficult. She has deep love for you but knows that a life together is not possible, so she maintains her distance." Roger recalls feeling a few teardrops slowly fall from both eyes. He was overwhelmed with excitement and a sense of closure all at the same time. This unexpected message was long-awaited and finally came.

The case of Roger and Dana signifies the importance of allowing spirit to provide messages in their own time. Roger's initial anxiety and heightened expectation produced limited information, but his state of calm in the second reading facilitated an environment that provided him with vital information and hope to help him continue on his journey.

Sitter: Post-Analysis

Finally, the sitter plays a part in spirit communication by closely reviewing the material he or she has heard during the reading. What you hear during a reading cannot be digested readily and needs reviewing for a few hours to a few days after the information is shared. There are a lot of thoughts going through your head when a medium is sharing about one hour's worth of information. Digesting the information and carefully reviewing names and circumstances, which might not come readily by overthinking, is needed. For example, during a reading you may have the medium ask you if you know an "F." She or he will explain that this person took care of you in your younger years and wants to share that you are doing a good job with your kids. You focus and overthink about who this F could be. In fact, during the reading you think that this is not a good validation of spirit and perhaps they have the wrong person. Overthinking during the current reading is futile. Let's digress for a moment and reflect on what happens when you obsess about remembering a name or finding something you are searching for. The medium shared that a male contemporary with the letter "F" is sharing a message. You attempt to recount every scenario where you might know "F" and may not be successful. After you have surrendered attempting to identify "F" and have moved onto another mental thought, suddenly you have a flash of the name and the scenario you were attempting to remember. Everyone can likely relate to this phenomenon when you have suddenly misplaced your favorite pen you were using. You spend twenty minutes frantically searching for it and then give up. After you give up the search for your favorite pen, you locate another less preferable pen and begin to work. Probably not more than five seconds after you begin working with the new pen, you effortlessly find the pen you were initially looking for.

It is also important to remember that querents do not know all of the deceased who are sharing messages during a reading. James, a participant in the research for *Medium7*, was astonished to learn that a medium could provide factual information that was contrary to his understanding. In James's example the medium shared that she could clearly hear the name *George* and received a strong impression that George was James's grandfather, who had died prior to ever meeting his grandson. As a result of James's reticence to acknowledge the connection, the medium noted that the grandfather's presence diminished. James had only heard his mother refer to her father as Papa Aitken so the name *George* did not resonate with him. During the post-reading period James was surprised to learn from his mother that although she referred to him as Papa Aitken, everyone called him George. James of course would not know this because George had passed away thirty years before he had been born. We see in this case how uncertainty about the identity of the discarnate can diminish earth-to-spirit communication. Sometimes the post-analysis period provides an opportunity to assign meaning and relevance to the messages shared.

These examples demonstrate the importance of using quiet time during the post-analysis phase to further comprehend earth-to-spirit communication. Not all the information shared during a reading will resonate with inquirers, further suggesting that the post-reading analysis is important for enhancing the efficacy of earth-to-spirit communication.

Conclusions

Earth-to-spirit communication does not always provide the best way to share information between the physical (earth) and nonphysical realities (spiritual planes of existence). In fact, other researchers might propose an even more complex system where other spirits not related to the discarnate are involved in the communication. For now if we focus on this simple three-way paradigm, we need to at least take into consideration that the sitter, the medium, and spirit play a role in the communication.

If you are on a journey seeking enlightenment and are curious about the validity of this phenomenon, the factors shared in this chapter need to be taken into consideration before you prematurely rush to any type of judgment about the validity of spirit communication. Scientists also need to understand these factors and incorporate them into research designs that attempt to produce evidence-based knowledge about survival of consciousness and the existence of the paranormal in general.

Scientists critiquing the research designs that attempt to obtain evidence-based knowledge in the field of metaphysics and the paranormal continue to insist on the importance of utilizing traditional evaluation research designs and standards prior to making informed recommendations on the validity of spiritual phenomenon. To be open to researching spirit communication, however, we need to understand the universal laws that help cultivate or inhibit useful spirit communication. The traditional scientific concepts, such as certainty, replication, and causation, cannot necessarily be applied when one is examining the universal laws that underlie the conditions of earth to spirit communication. Table 5 summarizes all of the factors that contribute to clear spirit communication. Understanding these factors will allow you to gain insight into the *real* nature of our universe.

Table 5 Factors to consider when examining earth to spirit communication.

Who plays a role in spirit communication?	Factors that contribute to clear spirit communication
Medium	• Stage of development • The extent to which the medium applies his or her own interpretation • Dynamics between the medium and discarnate (including predisposition and personality)
Spirit/discarnate	• Stage of development/soul evolvement • Spirit/discarnate's choice to communicate • Consideration of the sitter's spiritual growth (lessons to be learned) • Space-time differences
Sitter/client	• Levels of need for a specific message • Levels of openness to allow spirit to share a message • Levels of negative energy: depression, resentment, anger, or anxiety • Levels of post-analysis

Up to this point in the book there has been a focus on addressing questions related to the mechanics of mediumship, the survival of consciousness, and earth-to-spirit communication. To have a comprehensive understanding of the nature of our universe, it is useful to also review the nature of predictions and determine whether anyone can predict the future in a consistent manner. We are ready to review this topic in the next few chapters.

CAN ANYONE TELL THE FUTURE?

Singin': "Don't worry about a thing,
Cause every little thing gonna be all right!"

Bob Marley, Three Little Birds, 1977

I can remember thinking as a young child, is everything that will happen to me predetermined? Perhaps if everything is already written, I could sleep in, watch my favorite TV shows all day, and simply not worry about my future as something or someone had already created the blueprint, and I would simply follow.

I can recall thinking, I might not have to worry about paying for university tuition, and I could avoid any future terrifying blind dates that are often necessary to meet Mr. Right. The thought of the doctrine of determinism brought me some solace. I can also recall pondering the catastrophic consequences of believing in this potentially faulty philosophy. What if I had spent all my time enjoying recreational activities and delayed planning my future only to learn that I needed to be an active agent in my life. I contemplated the possibility that I might actually have to do some work to be productive and reach my potential.

This deliberation carried on for several years until I finally realized that perhaps the concepts of determinism and free will were interrelated. I came to the conclusion that it might be possible that some aspects of our lives are destined and others are mapped out with various probabilities. The actor needs to make decisions that will either augment or diminish these probabilities, and these choices and actions known as free will create the destiny.

My thinking at that time was molded solely by anecdotal evidence and life experience. I can recall the day this thinking was complemented by academic knowledge. It was first-year sociology. I was nineteen years of age and seriously intimidated by the professor and the other thousand students gathering into a lecture hall at the University of Toronto. The professor invited the class to discuss the nature/nurture debate in relation to mental illness. For example, there is evidence to show that schizophrenia is an illness that is genetic (nature); however, there are also studies that demonstrate that the individual's surrounding environment can either augment or diminish the unfavorable symptoms of this disease (nurture). I recall realizing at that moment that nothing is fully predetermined. There were other factors that might contribute to a variety of outcomes.

Understanding and being open to the relationship between destiny and free will is the first step in understanding the nature of prophecy. One of the objectives of the research for *Medium7* was to answer the questions about whether a medium or psychic could accurately predict the future. The study also sought to answer questions about the consistency of prophetic statements and the factors that contributed to a medium's ability to predict the future. This is an important question not only because it reveals information about how our universe works but because it also gives us further insight into how much investment we make in seeking individuals to tell us about our future. By definition mediums are known for their ability to see and hear the deceased; however, they are also known for claiming to predict the future. Scientifically studying this possibility provides us with answers about mankind, the universe, and the truth in general.

This chapter will share case studies of both successful and failed predictions. *Medium7* study results pertaining to the accuracy rates of predictions will also be presented.

Why Would Someone Want to Know the Future?

Recent polls taken in the United States indicate that at least 70 percent of the adult population has visited psychics or mediums at least once in their lifetime.[45] The vast majority of individuals who visit a medium are hoping to make contact with friends or loved ones who have departed the physical plane. Although most mediums focus primarily on contacting the deceased, some also make predictions. Predictions made are typically about future relationships, careers, finances, and health. During the research for *Medium7*, a focus group met to provide feedback on the findings generated from the scientific study. During this focus group the participants were asked their thoughts about why predictions seem to be of interest to the public.

Of course there are a few reasons why people are interested in predictions. The most common theme revolves around the notion of hope. In this century we have seen staggering employment problems, world catastrophes, ill health, and rising divorce rates. If someone could accurately tell you that everything was going to be all right, this might raise your hope and reduce your worry. We all know the song written by Bob Marley about the three little birds telling us not to worry about a thing because everything would be all right. These lyrics discourage worry for a good reason. There is medical evidence that shows that reducing worry and raising hope can actually contribute to increased recovery rates and pain reduction. A hopeful person benefits from a positive outlook because his or her body is less likely to produce the chemicals that prolong illness and are associated with a negative outlook. To explain how hopelessness can prolong an illness, Dr. Jerome Groopman[46] looks to the effects of substance P and cholecystokinin also known as CKK. These chemicals, when released in the central nervous system, have the opposite effect of endorphins and enkephalins. CKK helps send the messages of pain to the brain, thus increasing ones hopelessness and suffering. Groopman argues that these two chemicals are produced when a person is constantly reminded of an illness and the grave circumstances of their infirmity.

Medical studies also show that raising hope and decreasing worry can decrease the likelihood of heart disease. Scientists believe that the human body's natural reaction to stress is to release hormones, such as adrenaline and cortisol, into the bloodstream. When the body carries too many of these hormones in the bloodstream, the heart rate increases, and the blood thickens. In some cases this chronic condition precedes a stroke or heart attack. Worry, stress, and anxiety can weaken the immune system and make one prone to infections and illness. When your body releases stress hormones, your immune system reacts by sending out white blood cells. This compromises your immune system and leaves other parts of your body open to attack by viruses and bacteria.

Esther and Hicks, who wrote *Ask and It Is Given* (2008),[47] spoke about the importance of raising hope while attempting to manifest joy in one's life. They believe that a stream of positive energy (from God or source energy) is always coming toward us to increase abundance, but negative energy, such as hopelessness, actually blocks positive energy. This type of negative energy is said to prevent mankind from creating a positive reality.

While the research for *Medium7* shows that searching for hope and attempting to alleviate worry were the two most common reasons for seeing a psychic or medium, members of the focus group also noted that knowing one's future might help prevent a negative occurrence. Perhaps it might increase awareness that would result in the prevention of a future illness or an unnecessary altercation.

During the research phase we had the opportunity to hear at least four significant cases of mediums sharing information that contributed to the prevention or reduction of a fatal illness. One of these cases related to Claira, who learned from her doctor in 2010 that there were small signs of potential cancer in her left breast. She was told to deal with this promptly to ensure the problem would not escalate. She was also told that the cells were likely benign, so future surgery would not necessarily be required. Unfortunately Claira was paralyzed by this information and refused to follow up with the relevant medical professionals. At the time Claira indicated that her state of mind was unfortunately pessimistic. She stated, "If I am going to die, there's not much that I can do about it, and if I am not going to die, then the cells were benign all along." About two months after this news from her doctor Claira was asked to join a friend who was getting a rare opportunity to see a medium. Joyce called Claira with excitement. She had been waiting two years to see this gifted medium and had booked two spots. Her husband changed his mind about attending, and the other space needed to be filled. Claira was curious about seeing a medium and figured that it would at least be an entertaining experience. During the reading Claira was astounded by the medium's ability to identify her medical condition. He shared that there was a malignant tumor in her left breast and that it needed to be removed immediately. He also told her that if she proceeded with the surgery, she would be fine. Shortly after this meeting with the medium Claira found the courage to meet with the doctor. Indeed, she learned that she did have a malignant tumor in the left breast.

During Claira's interview for the present study she told the research team that the medium was accurate about the location, stage, and type of cancer. After she heard this prediction, Claira was able to complete her follow-up visit with her doctor and gathered the courage to face the necessary surgery. Claira indicated that prior to seeing the medium she had been paralyzed by fear, but by receiving what she believed to be divine guiding messages, she found the motivation to have the surgery that prevented the spread of the malignant tumor.

Finally, focus group participants noted that predictions could be helpful if they provided confirmation of being on the right path. Meredith's case demonstrates how a medium's predictions can aid with validation of a career path. Meredith recalls the day she went to see a medium. While she was visiting her sister in New Jersey, she was excited to learn that her sister's friend could not make a previously scheduled appointment with a medium. She saw this as an opportunity to learn more about the spirit world, although she did not really believe that our souls were infinite or that certain people had paranormal powers. She was pleased, however, to find out that the appointments had been made by a complete stranger, further assuring her that the medium could not possibly have had any personal information about her prior to the reading. At the reading the medium told her several bits of information, some relevant and others still to be verified. Close to the end of the reading the medium said, "They (members in the spirit world) tell me that your heart is in filmmaking with a special interest in filming, editing, creating, and changing the way images are produced. You will be successful with this and recognized for your filmmaking talents one day. This type of work is your destiny."

After the reading and during the ride home Meredith shared some of the information and messages with her sister. She emphasized how shocked and excited she was that a perfect stranger was able to validate her career goals. Filmmaking was currently a passion of hers, and in her heart she knew she was gifted; however, she needed validation and confirmation from what she considered to be a divine source. If entities in the spirit world predicted this as her destiny, then perhaps there really was a chance that this could materialize. This confirmation was exciting and increased Meredith's motivation to pursue her dreams.

Before further exploring cases of both accurate and failed predictions, it would be useful to review the scientific theories that provide a foundation for the conclusions made about making accurate predictions.

Historical and Contemporary Theories of Predictions

Most of us live from day to day working to pay the bills, trying to earn enough for a much-needed vacation, and we hope to find more time to be with the friends and family. It is hard to imagine that there are some of us who spend time focusing on subatomic particles and their behaviors. Most people simply live their lives and never question the principles of gravity, atoms, or the nature of space and time. Since most of us are not physicists, we would not think that our interest in learning about our future is linked to physics, but indeed, an understanding of the universe and the nature of reality can give us great clarity on this matter.

The following is a review of the key physicists and theories that provide scientific explanation for both the possibility and the limitations of mankind's ability to make accurate predictions. This review will provide a solid understanding of why the nature of our universe does not allow anyone to make accurate predictions on a consistent basis.

We should probably look to early pioneers to further understand the origin of these ideas. Why might we think that individuals with divine gifts would be able to make accurate predictions about the future? It might be because our early pioneers in the seventeenth century provided some very convincing evidence of determinism that led to an increased belief in the possibility of prescient abilities. Experiments conducted by astronomers like Kepler and Galileo in the early 1600s provided a foundation for the belief that it was even possible to make predictions. The discovery of predictable motions of astral objects through space was seen as paradigms for successful forecasting. It was not only astronomers who supported this deterministic theory. Scientists like Newton and Marx also believed in determinism. They believed in the philosophical doctrine that every human event, act, and decision was the inevitable consequence of prior fixed events. Essentially they believed that these were parts of a natural law and individual free will could not intervene to change the originally intended path or event. Specifically Newton's principles of time and space provide us with concrete definitions. Absolute space assumes that all distances seem the same to all observers. Absolute time implies that each second passes in the same manner for everyone. These notions of space and time mean that mankind can use concrete measures to chart future behavior whenever the current conditions are known and can be measured.

The church also supported this theory of determinism. It was beneficial for the church to promulgate that sin would lead to a set of absolute consequences as this belief system increased social control and acquiesced the masses. Some religious sects supported determinism as it was linked with the theory of divine intervention. For example, Calvinism and certain Protestant creeds proclaimed that humans had lost their free will in the act of original sin and could only regain it through salvation. In this context God foreordains who will be blessed and who will be damned.

By the early twentieth century we had a solid foundation from various areas of study supporting determinism. In the latter part of the twentieth century, however, we started to see new evidence that questioned deterministic laws. The French mathematician Jules Henri Poincaré (1903)[48] noticed that small differences in initial conditions could produce significant changes in the final phenomena, and as a result of this knowledge determinism and prediction started to become less plausible. One could say that Poincaré was the predecessor for Lorenz's chaos theory, which suggested that a small difference in an initial condition created widely diverging effects, rendering long-term prediction impossible.

In addition to these discoveries, two relativity theorists confirmed Einstein's theories. The more mass in a given region, the more distortion of space and time. They soon discovered that space-time could morph itself into a myriad of possible shapes with some even defying the laws of cause and effect. The concept that space-time was malleable began to diminish the ability to concretely distinguish between the past, present, and future. If space-time could morph into various possibilities, then that also supported the notion that outcomes were based on a set of varying probabilities. At the turn of the twentieth century, the study of subatomic theory and quantum theory began to grow creating an even greater discredit to the earlier evidence of deterministic principles.

One of the most important findings in quantum theory is that when we attempt to observe and measure an effect, this actually changes the outcome. In 1927 Heisenberg discovered the "uncertainty principle."[49] If the outcome can be changed by just the simple act of observing, this defies the theory that the outcomes had one absolute determined outcome. This is an important discovery as earlier deterministic theories had implied that a medium's prediction would be the absolute result. Yet the notion of the uncertainty principle intimates that the observer (each individual) plays a critical role in the outcome of his or her own events.

Edgar Cayce (1877–1945)[50], one of the most influential and gifted psychic mediums of his time, made many notes on the possibility of prediction. His hypotheses take both determinism and the more modern theories of uncertainty into consideration. As we learned in an earlier chapter a soul's purpose to learn various lessons is predetermined, but the path to learning such lessons are malleable. This view suggests that both determinism and free will must be considered in the predictions equation.

* * *

Determinism or free will?

The only thing that is predetermined is the lessons we came to the physical plane to learn. So if you came to learn patience, confidence, or trust, those will never change. How you learn these is malleable, and that is where free will plays a part in determining the nature and timing of these outcomes.

**Edgar Cayce
(1877–1945)**

* * *

He concludes, however, that every prediction has a degree of probability where only the actor can enhance or reduce this probability.

By the beginning of the early twentieth century as we moved through our journey of further understanding the nature of our universe, our limited understanding of physical laws had created the perception that everything was predetermined, thus allowing prediction by mediums to be possible. By the end of the twentieth century, however, we learned that any calculation of prediction needed to take the observer into account. Let's turn now to answering these questions: Can gifted mediums (via paranormal means) predict outcomes with accuracy? Can they consistently make accurate predictions? I make the conclusion that gifted mediums absolutely can accurately predict outcomes; however, there are specific factors that contribute to and increase the likelihood of producing accurate predictions on a consistent basis.

Can Mediums Predict the Future?

We have examined why humanity has had a prolonged interest in predictions and have reviewed the relevant historical theories. It is useful now to answer a key question: Can mediums predict the future, and if they can, is the accuracy rate consistent enough for society to fully invest in these predictions?

One of the mediums in the research study wondered why this question would even be posed. She noted that while psychics are typically associated with making predictions, mediums are known for communicating with the deceased. Although this is indeed a typical classification, in the present study every medium made some predictions during the readings they provided, rendering this a relevant question for the *Medium7* study. Based on anecdotal evidence beyond the current research, it also seems that mediums are not limited to just communicating with the deceased; they often make predictive statements during their readings with clients. Mediums tend to make predictions at a lower rate than psychics with predictions occurring at a rate of 5 to 15 percent. It is useful to know the accuracy rates regarding predictions prior to making emotional investments in such prophecies especially since seeing psychics or mediums is increasing in popularity.

In a majority of cases with a medium, the source of the prediction is coming from the deceased person (discarnate) or higher evolved entities, such as guides and angels. So we must ask, "Can discarnates and other spirit entities predict the future? Do they have a greater perspective from their plane of existence?"

Eighty-eight research participants provided case studies that either validated or enhanced doubt about a medium's ability to make accurate predictions about the future. Of the eighty-eight individuals who were interviewed in the *Medium7* study, eighteen participants had precise enough predictions that could be followed up and measured. An example of a precise prediction would be this: "Your family will be buying a new house somewhere between August and October next year. I am feeling the region of Tucson, Arizona. This change is related to your husband's career. This will be a positive change for the whole family." The following case studies demonstrate examples of where the mediums' predictions were validated or not validated.

Case Study #1: Prediction about a Future Career

In October 2010 Diana had been looking for a promotion or a new career path. Diana fortuitously ended up seeing a medium. At the last minute an acquaintance asked her if she wanted to see a medium as she had other commitments and could not make her scheduled appointment. This was Diana's first reading, so she was eager to learn about what would occur during this one-hour, one-on-one meeting with a medium. In addition to many other pieces of information she learned Diana heard some very specific prediction-type information about a future job. Diana learned that a position with a new organization would present itself in about four months. She was told that this would be the *one*. The medium was certain it was a new position, and she noted that the new surroundings were different from her current job environment. During the reading it was also shared that there would be a lot of travel by plane and leadership opportunities, and the medium described in some detail the type of people (specifically one named Paul) who would create challenges at the workplace. In this new position there would be many spiritual tests to pass, including patience, love, and forgiveness. Four months after the reading Diana saw an advertisement for a new position and got the job. By February 2011 and at the time of her final follow-up with the research team, Diana was able to confirm that she did feel that this new position was the *one* especially because it created a number of enjoyable new work experiences. To date she had more leadership and travel opportunities when compared to her previous job. The people, including the one named Paul, who the medium predicted would be problematic, had already presented themselves, but the guidance provided helped her understand that she could overcome these challenges. At the time of the final follow-up (six months after the initial reading), Diana could see that this position tested her patience and ability to forgive; however, the spiritual tests related to love were yet to be seen.

We can see that almost all of the work-related predictions that were made did actually happen for Diana. Given the specificity of some of the predictions, including the name and the types of work activities predicted, this case demonstrates that the medium providing this reading was able to accurately make predictions about Diana's future career path.

Case Study #2: Am I Going to Meet Somone Special?

The next case is considered a retrospective case study. In this instance the sitter had been seeing the medium for ten years and had written down every detail from every reading. This method provides a researcher with the rare opportunity to examine and validate events that might take place many years after a reading is completed. In a laboratory or academic study setting researchers would typically be limited to a one-year follow-up period after each reading. This is not ideal, as the outcome of a prediction can manifest several years after a prediction is made. A more accurate examination of the prediction rate was possible as a result of the detailed journal notes produced by this client over the ten-year period. This case study focuses on a prediction about relationships, which is a popular area of uncertainty for sitters.

Like many young women, Sarah is hoping to meet someone. She sees the same medium over a period of approximately ten years. We know from the Medium7 study that along with queries about career and financial stability, seeing a medium for guidance about relationships is quite popular. For the purpose of highlighting how predictions might work in regard to relationships, I have selected some key points from Sarah's case to share here.

● ● ●

Branden

"You will meet a guy named Branden in the next few months. He is the skater-type. I believe he is involved in skateboarding. He is tall with brown shaggy hair."

● ● ●

In 2002 Sarah hears from the medium that the boyfriend she is currently seeing will likely cheat on her during the relationship. This medium in particular is always reluctant to share news of this nature; however, if there is some possibility that the news can change the sitter's course of action, a judgment is made, and the information is revealed. Upon hearing this information Sarah knows in her heart that it is very likely to be true as she had already seen signs of potential cheating. Despite having these concerns Sarah remained in that relationship with Rob for four years. It turned out that Sarah obtained validation about the cheating three years later.

In November 2006 the medium shares that she will soon

meet a young gentleman named Branden. Sarah shares, during the interview for the research of Medium7, that "while I was hopeful that I would meet a Branden, I went back for a reading two months later, and the medium saw that I would meet a Stephen and actually be in a relationship with Stephen." He specifically states that the name is spelled with a "ph" and describes various compatibilities and notes specifically that the number seven and a band will be associated with this meeting. He adds that one of her friends already actually knows Stephen.

Sarah pondered about this and questioned, "What about Branden? I thought you said I would meet a Branden."

The medium replied, "I do indeed still see a Branden, but perhaps Branden will come into your life later. I am not exactly sure why I see Branden in the relationship department."

Sarah actually did meet Stephen a few months after the reading at Club 77 located in Hamilton, Ontario. In fact, he was in a band, and one of her classmates did know him. Stephen and Sarah dated for four years, and as far as she could tell he was faithful to her during their relationship. The physical description offered by the medium was remarkably similar. Sarah showed the author Stephen's photo where he posed with his band members.

● ● ●

Stephen

"You will meet a Steven in March … spelled Stephen. He is cute with long black hair, and you are both sexually compatible. He plays in a band.

The number seven is associated with this meeting, and one of your friends knows him. This one will not cheat on you"

● ● ●

During her relationship with Stephen, Sarah went to Sweden to visit her parents, and it was during this trip that she eventually met Branden. All of the physical characteristics shared by the medium were very accurate. What is interesting about this prediction is that while the information was accurate the medium shared at a subsequent reading that he did not feel that this Branden was the right Branden. As time went on Sarah felt ambivalent about her feelings about Branden. She felt that perhaps Branden was that special one, especially since the medium had predicted the meeting, and that even though she did not have strong feelings for him, perhaps she would need to give it more time to determine if this was really love. Sarah continued to remain friends with Branden but was conflicted about her feelings for him.

During the interview Sarah shared, "I did not pursue anything with Branden, but interestingly I was interested in Branden, developed a liking toward him but never acted on it. So essentially the medium was right that Branden did belong to the *love relationship* department in my life. It's just that he was not someone I would be in an actual relationship with." She paused and further noted, "There was a lesson to be learned from encountering Branden, and it was associated with the relationship realm of my life, even though I did not become intimately involved."

This case shows that mediums can predict the future by providing details that actually do manifest. Secondly, the case of the cheating boyfriend provides us with insight about how such information can be used to help the sitter make informed choices. Together this collection of information provided by the medium allows the sitter to make an informed decision rather than hastily make reactive decisions based solely on messages shared from spirit via the medium. The lesson learned here is that sitters are always encouraged to use free will and to consider all sources of information, including guiding messages shared by the medium prior to making final decisions.

In the case of Branden, the medium stated that she would be meeting someone named Branden. The sitter can interpret this in many ways. When a medium shares this type of information sitters believe that it likely signifies a romantic relationship or a relationship of some importance. When the relationship does not work out or is not romantic in nature, the sitter might suggest that the medium's message was inaccurate. We can see in this reading that the meeting of Branden had a purpose but was not necessarily for a romantic relationship. Nonetheless, the prediction that Sarah would meet Branden was accurate.

Finally in the case of Stephen, we also see that a medium can predict details. In this case the medium had the correct spelling of the name, the meeting area (Club 77), physical characteristics, and other important facts.

I illustrate this case of love as this is a common reason why individuals visit mediums. They either want to obtain insights about when they will meet someone, or they wish to know about the fate and quality of their current relationships.

Case Study #3: Will My Mother Ever Be at Peace?

Paula would not normally visit a medium. She had heard from a friend that perhaps seeing a gifted medium might put an end to her worry about her mother. Paula's mother had been suffering from meningitis for several years, and Paula had been requesting that her doctors strongly consider euthanasia (otherwise known as mercy killing) to put an end to her mother's pain. Paula loved her mother and wanted to have her with her for as long as she could, but she could also not imagine the pain her mother was enduring. After Paula directly asked the question about when her mother would pass, the medium indicated confidently that she would pass by the end of the summer. At the six-month follow-up period (four months after the summer ended), Paula's mother was still alive and still suffering with meningitis. This was clearly a failed prediction.

● ● ●

Paula

"I love my mother dearly. She has had meningitis for several years and has been suffering. I don't want her to go but she is in such pain, and her quality of life has severely diminished. She has asked me to help the doctors perform euthanasia."

● ● ●

Why did this gifted medium offer a message that was so

inaccurate? The next chapter explores how factors, such as free will or predetermined contracts, can further explain why predictions are not possible in all cases.

Case Study #4: Meeting Someone Special

Joe had been looking for someone special in his life and wondered if he would ever settle down and be married. Joe had not had anyone special in his life for a long time and wondered if it was meant to be. During his research interview he indicated that he felt that hearing a message from a gifted medium might bring some hope to a gloomy situation. The medium provided the initials of a potential mate and suggested that within the year he would meet someone and be in a close relationship. Joe was somewhat excited about this prospect and took note of the initials and description.

During his follow-up research interview a year later, Joe mentioned that he still had not met that special someone. In fact, he said that over the past year his romantic experiences were limited to two very disappointing blind dates. Joe also hesitantly shared the fact that he had gone out of his way to interact with a neighbor whom he liked and who more importantly had the initials and physical description that the medium had shared with him at his earlier reading. After Joe tentatively attempted to intermingle with his neighbor, he soon learned that his potential romantic prospect was not interested in males, and so the possibility of this quiescent love match based on the medium's prediction quickly diminished.

Joe was puzzled at this outcome and frequently referred back to his notes. At the initial reading the medium also shared that during the year he would travel to a new country for business. He was also provided with the three letters "Bel," and although the medium knew the name was longer, because of the unfamiliar country name, the medium only felt comfortable sharing the term "Bel." Joe actually found out four months after the reading that he would be traveling to Belarus on business. Joe pondered, with such an accurate prediction about business travel, shouldn't the prediction about romance surely manifest? In fact, at the one-year follow-up session Joe was still single, and the prophetic romantic message had not manifested.

In this particular case one could conclude that the medium was either not gifted, that he or she was not performing well that day, or that predictions about love are just not possible. In this particular case we know the medium had some ability to predict detailed information as he was able to predict a business trip to Belarus, an unusual business travel location for Joe. In the next chapter we explore the various factors that contribute to consistent, accurate readings applying Joe's case study.

Case Study #5: You Will Have Financial Freedom!

In this case study not one but two different mediums shared with Cindy that she would have more than enough money to retire easily and even have money left over for her grandchildren. Each medium who shared this information had provided other information to Cindy that validated the medium's abilities. The mediums were able to obtain the first names of Cindy's deceased relatives and were able to describe details about past events quite accurately. Each medium predicted the same financial outcome. After an eighteen month follow-up Cindy is now three years past her preretirement age and continues to struggle with her finances. She does not see any sign of her situation improving and has lost all hope that this prediction will ever come true. This is considered to be a failed prediction as both mediums clearly stated that she would be wealthy by preretirement age and this has not materialized. This chapter highlights the fact that although mediums have the capacity to predict information, they may not be able to *consistently* make accurate predictions. To understand more about this, it is important to take a closer look at the factors that contribute to accurate predictions. Determinism, free will, karma, interpretation and challenges related to communication between different planes of existence can help us understand why individuals, even those with paranormal faculties, cannot always accurately predict the future.

The Inconsistency Problem

One-fifth (20 percent) of the research participants allowed us to follow up with them right after their reading, at six months, at one year, and at eighteen months after the prediction was made. No other study other than the present study (*Medium7* 2011-2012) has conducted follow-up measures with clients of psychics or mediums to determine prediction accuracy rates.

This aspect of the research is the most interesting yet the most puzzling. We have just reviewed a few cases where accurate predictions were made by gifted mediums. There were also cases where similarly gifted mediums made predictions that were inaccurate. If we have established that the medium is gifted, then there may be other factors that contribute to the accuracy of a reading. First let us examine the results found in the present study I conducted in 2011. Of the eighty-eight participants, approximately 20 percent or eighteen participants actually had specific predictions that met the criteria for follow-ups. These eighteen individuals were followed up at six months post-reading and then at one year post-reading. Participants who could respond comprehensively to all the predictions at the six-month and twelve- month periods were not contacted at the eighteen month measurement phase. The results below indicate that when these predictions were followed up, one third were found to be *accurately* predicted. Another 28 percent showed *partial accuracy.* One such example of a prediction resulting in *partial accuracy* occurred when a participant indicated that the medium predicted she would have a permanent teaching position in the upcoming school year. The medium said that the teacher she would be replacing would be having twins. This was partially accurate as the sitter did get the permanent position in the month of September following the reading, but the teacher she replaced was not pregnant and was not having twins as predicted. Another 22 percent of the sitters fell into the *unmeasurable* category as they had not actually experienced the prediction by the eighteen month follow-up date. For cases to fall into the *unmeasurable* category the dates during the reading were ambiguous, or not initially provided, making it difficult to use a specified time period to assess the level of accuracy.[51] We cannot count these as fully inaccurate as we know from the retrospective case studies that a prediction made by a medium could actually manifest several years after the prediction.

Finally 17 percent of predictions are actually *inaccurate*. When the sitters were contacted during the follow-up phase, three sitters indicated that the information shared was inaccurate. An example of this can be seen in the case of Francesca, who was told that her daughter would be pregnant with a girl by the fall. The daughter did not become pregnant at all and still had not been pregnant one year after the reading. These results indicate that even when the medium is gifted and has been able to demonstrate being able to accurately predict the future or successfully contact the deceased, this does not mean that all of his or her predictions will manifest as described during the reading or in some cases may even be inaccurate. This suggests that there is inconsistency in being able to make accurate predictions.

This leads to some new questions. Are there factors that need to be present to increase the accuracy rate? What role does time and space play in making accurate predictions? Does the sitter play a role in the accuracy of the prediction?

A review of the rates of predictions provides a context for the case studies previously shared.

Table 6 Summary of Predictions Rate in *Medium7* Study

Level of Accuracy	Percentage and number of participants	Explanation
Accurate	33 percent n=6	The prediction was validated after the reading by the sitter either at the six-, twelve-, or eighteen-month phase. All aspects of the prediction mirrored the medium's information shared during the reading.
Partially Accurate	28 percent n=5	Some of the prediction was validated after the reading by the sitter. Not all aspects of the prediction mirrored the medium's information shared during the reading.
Inaccurate	17 percent n=3	None of the information predicted by the medium occurred in the time frame specified or the information predicted did not manifest.
Not Measurable	22 percent n=4	The information never manifested; however, it is possible that the information could manifest after eighteen months. It would not be appropriate to score these events as inaccurate, as it is possible that the event could still occur after the study period.

Note: Of eighty-eight research participants, eighteen individuals had very specific predictions that could be monitored at six-, twelve-, and eighteen-month intervals. The percentages in table 6 are related to eighteen participants taken from a random group of participants who participated in a reading with at least one medium in the present study. n= number of participants

What Do Mediums Say about Predicting the Future?

In following up with the mediums regarding the findings of this research there were varied responses; however, a majority of the mediums affirm that their predictions constitute information with varying levels of probability. Here are some quotes from mediums,

> The predictions I see and share relate to a possible future. I encourage my clients to take this information and consider it with all other sources of information and take full responsibility for making final decisions.

> When I make a prediction, I see different size beads on a necklace. Some are small, moderate, and large beads. Large beads tell me that this event is very likely to happen. When this event appears to make a strong impression, it usually means that the event is near. When it is a small bead, this tells me that there is some likelihood that this event may occur but it is not in the near future, and many possible factors, including a change in focus on the part of the sitter, can create a different outcome. I try to qualify my predictions by letting my clients know whether the predictions are small, moderate, and large beads.

> This may sound funny, but I remind my clients that I am here to connect with the deceased. If Aunt Mary provides a prediction about my client's future, I always say, "Would you have taken Aunt Mary's advice about financial matters

when she was living?" My main point here is that the deceased have a greater perspective on life relative to the physical world, but they should not be considered experts on all matters. My second point is that while some spirits have a greater perspective than my clients about their future, they do not have control over my client's free will. When I connect with the deceased, I am compelled to share their messages, although I always remind the client that it is their responsibility to make their own life decisions.

I provide a prediction if that is the message I am getting. Clients are always told, however, that the medium and the deceased are not responsible for making decisions about the client's life and their future. A client is responsible for making their own decisions and must use the guiding messages as one source of information to consider among many others.

Spirit guides and angels have greater knowledge about the probability of events than discarnates. It is important in a reading to refer to spirit guides and angels for prescient information rather than invest in precognition type information provided by discarnates. In the end, the predications I provide from either source have varying levels of probability; my clients have the free will to alter these varying levels of probabilities. In the end my clients have the power to alter the outcomes of the predictions I share in a reading.

These quotes indicate that mediums are also aware of

limitations in regards to their predictions shared from the spirit world. So it seems that mediums would agree that there are some limitations in making accurate predictions consistently. It is evident that the general public does not have a clear understanding about the circumstances and factors that contribute to an accurate reading. This ambiguity has prompted a further investigation and identification of the factors that contribute to an accurate prediction; we will turn to this examination in the next chapter.

PREDICTIONS: WHAT OTHER FACTORS SHOULD WE CONSIDER?

*I*n the previous chapter we explored the outcomes of various types of predictions and identified a rate of accuracy based on eighteen research participants. For this chapter we are focusing on what factors beyond the medium contribute to the manifestation of predictions. In this study there was an operating assumption that in the *Medium7* study we were working with authentic mediums who have gifts as demonstrated in the chapters "Understanding Mediumship" and "Is There Life after Death?" If the mediums are gifted and the predictions do not manifest as demonstrated in the post-reading period, perhaps there are other factors that explain the nature of predictions.

A Grand Theory to Consider

If we can identify and examine other factors contributing to predictions that go beyond the medium's capabilities, perhaps we will have an opportunity to learn more about the true nature of this universe. Three pre-existing notions, including (1) quantum theory (uncertainty principle and observer effect), (2) reincarnation, and (3) karma are examined in this chapter to identify how they contribute to the outcome of a prediction.

A grand theory that emerged during the research of *Medium7* suggests that the uncertainty principle (a quantum physics concept that will be explained further in the chapter), the observer effect (another quantum physics concept that will be explained further in the chapter), reincarnation (the soul's recurrent entrance into different physical bodies), and karma (what ye reap, ye sow) interconnect and contribute to the probability of an event manifesting. Each of these three areas[52] of study equally contributes to the accuracy of the prediction, and having a closer look at these will help us better understand the true nature of our existence.

To effectively apply these concepts, we will revisit one of the failed predictions in chapter 6 intermittently throughout this chapter to apply these theoretical concepts to a real case study.

Are People Interested in Factors that Contribute to the Manifestation of Accurate Predictions?

A general question raised during the focus group discussions in this study was: If mediums can accurately predict the future, why is this not consistent? How can a medium accurately predict one event but not the other? Are there other factors beyond the medium's capabilities that contribute to the manifestation of a prediction? What can this analysis teach us about the nature of reality?

The debate about predictions launched my interest in conducting focus group sessions to help me further understand the public's perception about predictions made by mediums. One of the focus group participants shared the following:

> I have been told by two mediums that I would have a new career opportunity within a year. I have been waiting for this new job to manifest; however, after eighteen months I am surprised that I am still in my current job. I am even more

> surprised because both of the mediums who shared this prediction are authentic and quite gifted. I have received accurate predictions from both of these mediums in previous readings, so I am wondering why this particular prediction has not manifested.

I asked the eight focus group participants if they would be interested in further understanding factors to be considered when one was assessing the probability of predictions manifesting. I was surprised to hear that a majority were interested mostly because oftentimes people seemed more eager to receive predictions rather than analyze the factors that contributed to their manifestation. I have always been intrigued by the nature of predictions, and after years of being a recipient of many predictions made by mediums I have been curious why some predictions manifested but others did not. Do we play a role in the prediction manifesting in our physical world? If we play a role, how does that work exactly? If a medium can predict an event with success, perhaps this suggests that the event was predetermined. If the claim that our souls have experienced many past lives is valid, do our past lives play a role in the timeliness of these predictions manifesting?

As a result of the focus group findings, it appeared that others were interested in further examining the nature of predictions. Of course I had to answer the call.

Did You Say Psychics or Physics?

I can recall the first Kabbalah (Qabbālâ) class I took at the age of nineteen. This was just a hobby at the time as I was also taking a few optional philosophy and religion courses formally at the University of Toronto. Kabbalah, considered to be a school of thought, primarily seeks to clarify the nature of the universe and respond to various questions related to the nature and purpose of existence. Its goal is to help humankind reach a greater understanding of spirituality. I had been intrigued with Kabbalah's acceptance of such concepts, including reincarnation, karma, and the spirit world. Most importantly I was impressed with the doctrine's willingness to demystify the nature of reality. I was surprised when the rabbi introduced the course by explaining that the next few classes would be all about physics. I started to get a sinking feeling in my stomach. Was I in the wrong class? Should I run out the back door now before I thoroughly embarrass myself? Perhaps he said *psychics* and not *physics.* Indeed, the rabbi did say physics. He explained that it was necessary to study both physics and metaphysics to really understand the universe beyond our understanding of the three-dimensional physical plane of existence. Every time he said the word physics, my mind immediately went back to math class in high school, where except for the few Einsteins in the class, most students would struggle to work out complicated math equations. By the second and third Kabbalah class he began to talk about a branch of physics that I

* * *

We can take all the solid objects in the world and contain it in one hand.

* * *

was able to resonate with at a deeper level. I was no longer fearful of the potentially complicated equations. The rabbi shared information about quantum physics (also known as quantum theory), a branch of physics dealing with physical phenomena at microscopic scales, namely atomic and subatomic levels. In simple terms this branch of physics looks at how, why, and what constitutes the universe. The focus is on both the seen and unseen aspects of the universe. This branch of study recognizes that to fully understand the nature of the universe, humankind would need to study the behaviors of the tiniest particles that comprise the atom.

To this day I will not forget the demonstration the rabbi made. He was trying to show us why everything we perceive is just an illusion. The rabbi explained that although everything appeared solid, it was *not* solid. He clarified, "We can actually take all the solid material of the universe and fit it into one hand." This teachable moment made me realize that everything I had learned before about the nature of reality might not be true. From that moment on I confidently put on my physics hat and suspended belief systems previously held.

With that being said I will need to touch on some physics in this early part of the chapter, so I do hope that you will do what I did in my Kabbalah class. Put on your physics hat, suspend all fear of technical physics equations and concepts, and then be open-minded. When the concepts in this chapter become a bit challenging to absorb, I encourage you to refer back to chapter 1, where I define some of the concepts that form the basis for the theories to be discussed.

Is There a Role for You to Play in Predictions?

Most of the focus group participants in the research of *Medium7* felt that a prediction made by a medium indicated that it was likely to manifest as the event was somehow predetermined. However, humans are agents with the ability to think and make choices, so might the client play a role in their prediction manifesting? We would need to examine the theory of free will in relation to predetermination theories to answer this question.

Free will is the ability of agents to make choices free from certain constraints, including physical laws and moral certitudes. Within this definition there is an inherent suggestion that the agent has some choice and freedom to attain various goals as he or she journeys on his or her chosen path. Essentially the philosophy and science about how thoughts create reality is an important part of free will. If science could demonstrate beyond doubt that we create our reality through our thoughts, then we could also conclude that thought is made up of the smallest particles that comprise the atom, which are also known as subatomic particles.

People will often question the viability of free will as they feel there are restrictions on the physical plane that reduce the number of paths they can pursue. Understanding the mechanisms that underlie free will provides a greater understanding of how this is possible. Once we have mastered this part, we can examine how free will and other related concepts explained by quantum physics provide a partial explanation for Joe's inability to experience the prediction conveyed by the medium.

Quantum Physics: How Do Our Thoughts Relate to Subatomic Particles?

Before we can go any further into really understanding how our free will interacts with predictions, we need to have a good understanding of exactly how our own thoughts relate to the tiniest particles that comprise matter (also known as subatomic particles).

To understand this we need to start with Newtonian physics—a theory based on the late-seventeenth-century belief that the universe was made up of what was believed at the time to be solid objects (atoms), which were attracted toward each other by gravity. This theory was extended in the nineteenth century to include the structures of atoms as being the fundamental building blocks of nature. Of course it is logical for us to have believed that atoms were essentially solid as humans have never been able to walk or see through solid objects like walls.

Albert Einstein found that these atoms could be broken down and analyzed further and that the subatomic particles that collectively formed the atoms were pure energy. At that time Einstein believed that this energy he had discovered was in the form of particles. In other words they had an *appearance* of being solid.

Researchers have identified that the tiniest form of matter in the universe is a subatomic particle and not an atom as taught by Newtonian physics for many years.[53] If you wanted to examine the composition of the universe, you would have to analyze the properties of the tiniest particles. The only problem is that if you cannot detect, see, or feel them with state-of-the-art instruments, you would have to create an innovation that would allow you to validate their existence. In the 1930s science evolved to a point where validating the existence of subatomic particles could be measured. Measurement was made possible with the invention of the first practical particle accelerators. These early machines made beams of protons that created collisions within the atoms that resulted in the discovery of quarks and leptons—subatomic particles that comprise the structure of the atom.

These subatomic particles exist as a *field of probabilities*. When you focus on these leptons and quarks, they are activated, and their probability distribution changes, which suggests that thoughts and observations contribute to changes in their transformation and activity in general.

Although Einstein's theory enlightened mankind about the composition and true nature of the atom, there seemed to be some disagreement about the true foundational properties of an atom. *Was it a tiny particle or a wave form*? Einstein and Niels Bohr, another physicist, debated over this question for years until Bohr made an important discovery that the basis of the atom (the foundation of the universe) could exist both as a wave form *and* a particle. The relevant part of this discussion is that, through a series of discoveries, scientists found that wave forms composed the foundation of the universe prior to it being observed. That would suggest that without our contributing thoughts and observations the universe would exist as a field of probabilities. When we produce a thought and observe these waves, they collapse, and a particle or matter is formed. This transformation of the wave form to a particle forms the basis of what we eventually experience as *reality*. At first this concept of particles, wave forms, probabilities, and a physical reality might be mind-boggling at best. So to simplify the meaning and purpose of this discussion I have created the following three-step process for you to refer to throughout this chapter. This three-step process demonstrates a simple explanation of how our thoughts create reality. We can be grateful to Einstein, Bohr, and other physicists who made this theory clear via their various scientific discoveries.

Three-Step Process: How Do Your Thoughts Create Reality?

Step 1: The basic nature of the universe is comprised of *wave forms* or what is also known as an infinite field of probabilities.

Step 2: Observations form thoughts. These are produced by humankind and other living entities.

Step 3: Original *wave forms* collapse and creates a tiny *particle*, also known as matter. These tiny particles create your reality.

Depending on the feeling behind the thought, material objects form with different shapes, densities, and sizes. In other words prior to any thoughts elicited by mankind there was a field of probabilities. For example, a desire to play hockey would ignite a reaction in the wave form, potentially transforming it to a tiny particle and subsequently increasing the probability that the desire to play hockey may be realized.

The link between thoughts, tiny particles, and their resulting structure is demonstrated by Dr. Masaru Emoto,[54] who published his experiments in 1999. These experiments involve exposing samples of water to different words, pictures, or music and then freezing and examining the aesthetics of the resulting crystals with microscopic photography. Emoto claims that different water sources, created from exposure to a variety of thoughts, produce different crystalline structures when frozen. For example, water exposed to positive words like *love, passion*, and *happiness* would produce a beautiful complex snowflake structure. Water exposed to feelings related to *sadness* and *hatred* would transform into less complex, dreary pictures.

When you sit back and absorb the mechanics behind Emoto's experiment, you will realize that this idea is really not that far-fetched. Mankind has been gathering in groups and praying for health and peace with the hope of positively transforming lives. This type of activity has been initiated without having scientific proof that prayers have potent healing powers. Sending peaceful thoughts and prayers to others has been a common practice prior to mankind having knowledge regarding the underlying mechanisms of quantum physics.

The Uncertainty Principle: Subatomic Particles Do Not Have a Fixed Position

We now understand the link between our thoughts and the external world around us, which as a result brings us one step closer to understanding how our thoughts and their related intensity contribute to the outcomes of predictions shared by a medium. The next step is to understand some of the key behaviors of these subatomic particles.

Fortunately for us we have quantum physicists who studied the behavior of the tiniest subatomic particles. In 1927 Werner Heisenberg used mathematical equations to try to measure the exact location of an electron orbiting around the nucleus of an atom. Understanding this would provide more information about the properties of matter. He eventually concluded that it was impossible to know the momentum of the electron, as the more you learned about one aspect, the less certain you were about another. Specifically in his concept of the uncertainty principle he concluded that the better you know the position of a particle, the less you know the momentum, and the more you know about the momentum, the less you know about the position of the particle. He also concluded that the particles did not have specific positions at any given time. In fact, all he could conclude was that there was a probability that these subatomic particles were at a point in each "cloud."

Given these facts, we can return to our prediction case and assess the implications. These thoughts communicated from the discarnate about Joe's potential new love are received by Joe, who in turn creates new thoughts about the information received. According to Heisenberg's theory, this would suggest that the underlying behavior of these thoughts is not fully predictable as the particles don't have a specific position at any time. It seems that if one cannot measure the position and time of the thought, one cannot accurately predict its future behavior. This discovery suggests that the probability that the prediction will or will not occur is partially based on the intensity and nature (i.e., sad or excited) of Joe's thoughts. This principle known as the uncertainty principle explains why predictions may be inconsistent as the content, and time of manifestation lies within a field of probabilities.

• • •

The better you know the position of a particle, the less you know the momentum, and the more you know about the momentum, the less you know about the position of the particle.

Werner Heisenberg

• • •

How Does the Observer Effect Play a Role in Predictions?

In addition to the mathematical equations conducted by pioneers in the field, scientists have used actual experiments to further understand the nature of subatomic particles. If we can understand the behaviors of these particles, we can understand the nature and potential behavior of the universe. In quantum physics the term *observer effect* refers to changes that the act of observation will make on the event being observed. Fortunately, the double-slit experiment designed by Thomas Young in the early 1800s demonstrates how this phenomenon works. The double-slit experiment involves the use of light and water waves being projected through one and then two slits to observe changes in the behavior of subatomic particles. After he independently projected the water and light waves through each slit, first Young and then other scientists observed the patterns, recorded measurements, made assessments of the patterns, and made conclusions about specific patterns of behavior. After his team was confused about the inconsistency of patterns, they used a measurement device (similar to a mechanical eye) to actually see which slit the particles were moving through. This device was designed to actually observe the particles as they passed through the slits. Through the use of this monitoring device, they learned that the outcome of one experiment changed when it was observed. What is most intriguing about this experiment is that the phenomenon being observed would change specifically when data points about the observations were recorded. This discovery was inconsistent with classical experiments where a particular cause could be predictable if certain conditions were present. This was not the case in the double-slit experiment.

Let's apply this finding to our prediction example. Joe receives the information from the medium about this potential new love and begins to focus on it. He thinks about it on a daily basis, dreams about who this new partner might be, and surmises about where he might meet her. He also emits some negative emotions and thoughts as he worries about being alone for an extended period up until meeting a compatible partner. As Joe begins to increase his thinking about this potential new partner, more particles are launched, creating and shaping the circumstances surrounding this potential new partner. The interesting part about this creative process is that negative emotions and thoughts increase the probability of an event occurring but may indeed manifest realities that are not consistent with the intended desire. Joe's thoughts elicit his motivations and subsequent action to make choices related to meeting a new partner. These thoughts and choices create various possibilities that lead to potentially different outcomes. If Joe does not focus on the issue and does nothing to nourish the thought, it is possible that the thought will remain a small probability and indeed may not manifest into Joe's physical existence. So Joe's observations of the prediction are very much like the observation device used to observe the particles moving through the slits in the double-slit experiment previously described. The patterns and final destinations of the particles (Joe's thoughts) changed the outcomes (Joe's potential reality with or without a partner) when they were observed.

Based on the scientific evidence produced from the double-slit experiment, I can confidently conclude that we each play a role in the manifestation of predictions conveyed by a medium. Given the nature of subatomic particles and its powerful transformative properties, perhaps one could argue that quantum physics could provide a full explanation for why a prediction did or did not manifest. Quantum physics provides us with an understanding that we cannot predict the space and time of the subatomic particles. Given the particles' relationship to thoughts, we cannot predict exactly when the thoughts will eventually manifest. This uncertainty coupled with the notion that Joe has free will to produce various thoughts suggests that the outcome of Joe's prediction is partially controlled by him.

I note that the uncertainty principle and the observer effect provides a *partial* explanation for Joe's prediction. I emphasize *partial explanation* as I have reviewed some case studies where research participants like Joe conveyed that they were producing positive thoughts about potential events that still did not manifest. If Joe constantly focused his thoughts on his prediction, visualized his new love, talked about this new love, and actually made attempts to meet this new partner, it would be difficult to solely use the observer effect to explain why the prediction did not occur. In this case, all of the thoughts should accumulate at some point to create his desired reality.

It is apparent that there are additional factors that need to be considered when one is examining the nature of predictions. It is for this reason that we turn to examining the role of past lives and their potential impact on the manifestation of predicted outcomes.

Reincarnation

At the beginning of this chapter I indicated that in addition to the other factors being discussed, reincarnation should be considered to gain a more comprehensive understanding regarding contributing factors that have a potential effect on prescient information. Now that we have a better idea about how the quantum physics concepts were applied to the prediction about Joe's potential new love, we need to understand how reincarnation contributes to this same prediction.

Reincarnation is the repeated incarnation of the soul or immaterial part of man's nature. At the time of death, it is the passage of the soul as an immortal essence into another living body. People often confuse reincarnation and transmigration. The latter is different from reincarnation in that transmigration is the belief that humans sometimes passed into the bodies of the *lower animals* as a punishment for sins committed during past lives. For the purposes of this chapter we are only referring to reincarnation—the belief that upon the physical death of the body the soul *eventually* enters a new body. The area of reincarnation has been systematically studied, producing evidence to support the existence of the doctrine.

Reincarnation: Who Were Some of the Original Thinkers?

Before we can apply the doctrine of reincarnation to Joe's prediction, we should first review some of the history and the original thinkers in this area. The doctrine of reincarnation can explain some of the mysteries regarding the purpose of mankind's existence. A doctrine like this would have to have a substantive history for its tenets to continue into the twenty-first century. The Egyptians are the first who propounded the theory that the human soul is imperishable and that when the body dies, it enters into some other body that may be ready to receive it after a period of existence in the discarnate state. The idea is that the soul continues to cycle between the material and nonphysical states, wearing different physical *coats*, each time learning new lessons to enhance spiritual growth. The idea is that these different *coats*—living as a different gender and race with different types of status and belief systems—would allow the soul to experience lessons that would eventually bring the soul to a state of purity. According to researchers, incarnations can range from forty years to three thousand years, depending on the time it takes for the soul to identify the life environment that would best enhance its learning.

Virtually all religions and philosophies believe or integrate some aspect of reincarnation.[55] Among the Chinese there was an esoteric teaching concerning reincarnation. Lao-Tze, whose classic work, the *Tao Teh King*, taught reincarnation to his inner circle of students that there existed a fundamental principle called *Tao*, which is held to have been identical with the *primordial reason*, a manifestation of which was the *Teh*, the creative activity of the universe. The union and action of the *Tao* and the *Teh* preceded the universe, including the human soul, which he taught was composed of several parts, among them being the *huen*, the spiritual principle, and the *phi*, the semi-material vital principle, which together animate the body. Lao-Tze said,

> To be ignorant that the true self is immortal, is to remain in a grievous state of error, and to experience many calamities by reason thereof.

> Know ye, that there is a part of man which is subtle and spiritual, and which is the heaven-bound portion of himself; that which has to do with flesh, bones, and body, belongs to the earth; earthly to earth—heavenly to heaven. Such is the Law.

Some have held that Lao-Tze taught the immediate return of the *huen* to the *tao* after death, but from the writings of his early followers it may be seen that he really taught that the *huen* persisted in individual existence throughout repeated incarnations, returning to the *tao* only when it had completed its round of life experience. For instance, in the *Si Haei* it is said, "The vital essence is dispersed after death together with the body, bones and flesh; but the soul, or knowing principle of the self, is preserved and does not perish. There is no immediate absorption of the individuality into the Tao, for individuality persists, and manifests itself according to the Law." Chuang-Tze said, "Death is but the commencement of a new life." Other Chinese teachers taught that the soul consists of three parts, the first being the *kuei*, which had its seat in the belly and which perished with the body; the second being the *ling*, which had its seat in the heart or chest and persisted for some time after death but which eventually disintegrated; and the third, *huen*, which had its seat in the brain and survived the disintegration of its companions and then passed on to other existences.

Pythagoras was the great occult teacher of Greece, and his school and followers accepted and taught the doctrine of reincarnation. Much of his teaching was reserved for the initiates of the mystic orders founded by himself and his followers, but still much of the doctrine was made public. Both Orpheus and Pythagoras, although several centuries separated them, were students at the fount of knowledge in Egypt, having traveled to that country in order to be initiated in the mystic orders of the ancient land, and they taught the doctrine of rebirth (another term used to describe reincarnation). The Pythagorean teaching resembles that of the Hindus and Egyptians insofar as it is concerned with the nature of man—his several bodies or sheaths—and the survival of the higher part of his nature, while the lower part perishes. It was taught that after death this higher part of the soul passed on to a region of bliss where it received knowledge and felt the beneficial influence of developed and advanced souls, thus becoming equipped for a new life. The idea was that these souls had not reached the desired stage of development, which would entitle them to dwell in the blissful regions for all eternity.

An abbreviated review of the early teachings of reincarnation suggests that there are some variances in the doctrine depending on the religion and philosopher responsible for sharing the tenets. Most important is that there are some common beliefs that are shared amongst all of the teachings of reincarnation. The first recurring principle regarding reincarnation is the soul is immortal. It exists before birth and continues to exist after death. Another recurring theme is that the soul learns lessons by living in a variety of physical bodies that would attract the necessary teachings to advance spiritually.

For the purposes of this chapter it is more appropriate to focus on the incarnation phase prior to birth. Reincarnation can include the life review phase occurring after the physical death of the body, the spiritual development that may continue in the spirit world, and the preparation for the future incarnation phase; however, it is the latter phase that is most relevant to the discussion about predictions.

In chapter 5, I touched on the preparation phase during the discussion of soul contracts. The information shared suggested that just prior to incarnating into new physical bodies, soul contracts are created with individuals and inanimate objects. Such contracts would provide the necessary circumstances to expose and teach the souls the required lessons to enhance spiritual growth. These soul contracts are a pertinent factor to consider when one is assessing the probability of events manifesting in our lives.

In her interview with Bob Olson on *AfterlifeTV,* Danielle MacKinnon explained that an individual soul could incarnate with a plan to address many lessons and may therefore create several soul contracts with many other souls. For example, it may take fifty soul contracts with other persons in one lifetime to learn the lesson of forgiveness. It is also possible that despite an individual's soul contract to achieve the lesson of forgiveness, they need other lifetimes to learn the lesson. To demonstrate that you have learned forgiveness, you might be tested several times in one lifetime. You might be placed in adverse circumstances that require you to forgive your enemies.

It is theorized that tedious planning and sometimes thousands of years pass before a soul is ready to incarnate into a new physical body. During the *AfterlifeTV* interview, MacKinnon explained that because of the number of soul contracts required in each lifetime, oftentimes the entry into the physical body is delayed to ensure the appropriate souls (also known as the soul group system)[56] simultaneously return to the earth plane.

Now that we have a better understanding of the concept of reincarnation and the role of soul contracts, let's return to the prediction about Joe's potential new love. Mediums can indeed identify the nature and content of the soul contracts created prior to the soul's return to the earth plane. During the research of *Medium7* we identified several instances where mediums conveyed the key lessons that were to be learned in the sitter's lifetime. Here are the relevant excerpts for Joe's case where three different mediums identify soul contracts and lessons that Joe is destined to learn in this lifetime. The consistency of these messages suggests that the soul lessons are commitments that are predetermined.

> **Medium (#1):** You have made several pacts with a number of people to learn lessons of patience and selflessness. You will be surrounded by circumstances that continue to test your patience (2008).

Medium (#2): The skill of learning how to give generously to others in a selfless way will continue to be tested in this lifetime. You will be tested with co-workers and be given an opportunity to give unconditional love in two long-term relationships; these partnerships may or may not be within the bonds of marriage (2010).

Medium (#3): Spirit tells me that you prematurely ended a relationship. You were doing all of the giving but did not feel that there was the appropriate reciprocity. You may have left this relationship but will continue to experience the same scenario in other relationships until you learn that reciprocity is not always a necessary requirement for a solid relationship. Sometimes you will do all of the giving, and other times you might be the beneficiary (2011).

The excerpts previously noted suggest that during three independent readings three different mediums identified selflessness and patience as Joe's key lessons to be achieved as per his soul contracts. What is clear from these excerpts is that mediums can indeed identify and predict the life lessons that are to be achieved in an individual's life. These seem to be predetermined. The soul contracts put in place prior to the spirit's re-entry into another physical body seem to be guaranteed to ensure the soul learns the intended lessons. In 2010, one of the mediums told Joe that he would have the opportunity to give unconditional love in two long-term relationships during this lifetime. Giving unconditional love means that at times you will have to keep giving and possibly forgiving even when your partner is not behaving in a loving manner. Unconditional love is also related to patience. When you are giving without your partner's loving reciprocity, your patience is continuously tested as you wait for the day when you will experience being a recipient of your partner's love. By applying the reincarnation principle to Joe's example, we see how his soul contracts of patience and selflessness are currently being tested. During the research interview Joe admits to prematurely leaving his first long-term partner as he perceived her lack of reciprocity to be an unfair exchange. Perhaps the delay in meeting his new partner is necessary to ensure that Joe is partnered with Ms. Right, who will teach him selflessness and help him learn how to cope with patience.

In the final follow-up interview with Joe approximately twelve months after the prediction was made by the medium, Joe was still hoping to meet his new partner but was still single. He indicated that he was running out of patience but felt that he was being provided with a number of opportunities to address one of his life lessons of selflessness. He also felt that he constantly had to face experiences where he would need to cope with his director's lack of reciprocity in the workplace. He described the anger and frustration he felt after he was not recognized for his leadership at work. He shared another example where his CEO publicly reported that the successful advertisement campaign that he led was a great accomplishment. He was nearly crushed, however, when his CEO publicly named another person as the reason for the campaign's success.

Joe explained that after the medium clarified the nature and content of his intended life lessons, he began to be more tolerant of the challenges he experienced as it was clearer how these circumstances were strengthening his character. Joe further explained that he was finally learning how to gracefully experience selflessness. Although he was not publicly awarded for his achievements, he started to understand the benefits of having increased confidence and a sense of accomplishment as a result of making beneficial and innovative products.

● ● ●

Soul lessons are predetermined; however, *how* you learn the lessons is your choice.

● ● ●

In his book, *No Soul Left Behind: The Words and Wisdom of Edgar Cayce*, Robert Smith notes that lessons to be learned (soul contracts) *are* predictable as they are predetermined prior to birth. However, once born into the physical world, the individual can use free will to determine the timing and path that will help him/her learn his soul lessons. Understanding this raises some other questions. If these aspects of the individual's life are predetermined, does that mean that the medium has a greater likelihood of *seeing* them during the reading? If these life lessons are predetermined, does that mean they must always be addressed in one lifetime? Is it possible that it takes more than one lifetime to learn the lessons? If life lessons can be learned in multiple lifetimes, then perhaps only the intended life lesson is predictable, but the actual outcome is not.

Although this topic raises many questions, it appears that the intended soul lesson can be identified by the medium; however, predictions about the timing and other details about how the individual will address the lesson during their lifetimes are not predetermined and as a result are less predictable.

At this point we have examined how the uncertainty of subatomic particle placement can affect the predicted outcome in Joe's life. We reviewed how his focus or lack thereof could change the probability of the event manifesting in his life. We concluded that Joe's free will could significantly shape the outcome of predicted events. We also reviewed the concept of reincarnation, where we learned that soul contracts were predetermined and could clearly be predicted by the medium. Understanding the soul contract could contribute to a greater understanding of why Joe's new partner had not yet manifested. As shared at the beginning of the chapter it was noted that the laws of karma also needed to be considered when one was assessing the probability of a prediction.

Quantum physics and reincarnation contribute a great deal to solving the riddle of predictions, but the important spiritual laws underlying karma need to be considered to have a comprehensive understanding of the nature of predictions.

How Does Karma Play a Role in Predictions?

Karma is the law of cause and effect as applied to the life of the soul. It is a law whereby the soul reaps the results of its own sowing or suffers the reaction from its own action. The concept suggests that past behavior contributes to a present outcome. We are all familiar with the following phrase: "As ye sow, so shall ye reap." This suggests that if you have been giving selflessly to your favorite charity, the law of karma conveys that you will receive the comparable benefits that the recipient of your charity received. The underlying mechanism suggests that reaping the reward of your good deeds or paying the debt for negative actions can be received at any time. It could be received immediately after the act, or it could occur thousands of years later in another lifetime.

One view of karma[57] is that the law of cause and effect works within a reward-and-punishment paradigm. This perspective theorizes that karma provides rewards for good deeds and discharges punishment for evil acts. This concept carried to its logical conclusion would insert that every bit of pain and unhappiness in this life is the result of some bad deed done either in the present life or in the past and that every bit of happiness, joy, or pleasure is the result of some *good* action performed either in the present or past life. Although this philosophy and ideology is not as integrated into the Western culture, you hear Americans frequently using phrases such as, "What goes around comes around," or, "What did I do in my past lifetime to deserve this?" The occasional use of these phrases suggests that the concept of karma has been absorbed at some level in the Western consciousness.

Another less punitive perspective proposes that the karmic law must not be confused with ordinary reward and punishment for "good or bad deeds" but that the law acts just as does any other law of nature. The reaping that we sow is to help us become individuals who are ready to enhance knowledge, minimize mistakes, and move closer to perfection. This less punitive paradigm suggests that when we make mistakes, we reap consequences that help put us back on a path that will enable us to reach our highest and greatest good. Some would argue that it would be difficult to learn the lesson if the consequences were meted out in a subsequent lifetime. One might be less likely to learn from mistakes when the effect takes place several years after the cause is activated. It would be difficult for the agent to link the cause and consequence, making it difficult to learn exactly how the cause created the consequence.

The proponents of karma suggest that what is most important is mankind follows the golden rule that suggests that you should "do onto others as you would have them do unto you." Understanding this rule allows mankind to reflect on past behavior with a view to improving future actions.

Why would we need to consider karma when we are examining predictions? Well, if after Joe receives the prediction from the medium and has been thinking positively about meeting a new partner, his actions have been in alignment with the prediction to date. If his soul contract to learn selflessness could be achieved by meeting another partner, this would also be in alignment with the prediction. If these aspects of the theory previously discussed still cannot fully explain the outcome of the prediction, perhaps karma might explain why Joe's prediction did not materialize.

Of the eighty-eight readings conducted in the research of *Medium7,* twenty readings had at least thirty-two statements in total that mentioned past lifetimes. Mediums often share relevant information about past lifetimes if it will enhance the understanding of the current issue the sitter is experiencing. Studies using hypnotherapists who focus on learning about past lifetimes would certainly generate more statements from their clients related to past-life issues as the use of hypnosis would allow the client to relax and access relevant memories.

In Joe's three readings with a medium there was no

information about how Joe's past lifetimes related to his current situation. However, judging from some of the examples provided in related literature, it is possible that past deeds are contributing to current circumstances. In her book, *Many Mansions: The Edgar Cayce Story on Reincarnation*,[58] Dr. Gina Cerminara shared a number of case studies that demonstrated a link between past-life action (cause) and current circumstances (effect).

A woman came to Cayce trying to identify the cause of her loneliness in her current life. She had only experienced one love affair in her lifetime, but the attraction was only physical, so she was yet to experience the feeling of *real* love. According to the notes and paraphrasing used by Cerminara, this lady committed suicide in the Persian period, four lifetimes before the current one. In this past lifetime she was the daughter of the ruler but was taken hostage by Bedouin tribes. After the hostage-taking event she was controlled by the ruler of a new community and unwillingly had a child with him. She committed suicide and left her child alone at the mercy of strangers. During the reading, Cayce indicated that she committed suicide as she resented being subject to another's will and chose to destroy herself rather than make the choice to continue to care for and protect her child and endure the humility. Cayce suggested that this sin in her Persian life contributed to the barrier that was apparently blocking her ability to meet men in her present life. Specifically Cayce made the suggestion that her refusal to renounce self-determination may have deterred men from getting involved. The reading suggests that leaving her child alone in Persia was related to her current inability to have a child. She often felt like committing suicide—another feature from the Persian lifetime.

This reading demonstrates that despite the lady's initial victimization she was morally responsible for her actions after she was taken hostage. Her choices to avoid her life lessons (possibly the lesson of humility during the Persian lifetime) by committing suicide and abandoning her child seem to be reaping negative consequences in her current lifetime.

The mechanics of karma as demonstrated through Cayce's reading validate many important principles. There is continuity of life with the cyclical incarnation into various physical bodies. These alterations into various physical bodies are driven by soul contracts and the laws of karma. Cayce's readings also teach us that although the soul contracts have predetermined lessons, the laws of karma determine the parameters under which the agent has control. The agent still has the free will to make choices about how he or she will address or work through the karma. The analogy of the island may help illuminate this point. If you become stranded on a small island, you would still have free will to discover many solutions to escape your circumstances; however, because you are stranded on a *small* island, your free will is limited.

Karma seems to place the agent under circumstances that will ensure that karmic debts are repaid or assets are experienced in a future lifetime. Consider the female fashion model that was perhaps not generous in her past lifetimes. Karmic laws might create circumstances that would ensure this fashion model learns the consequences of greed in this lifetime. She might be endowed with infinite financial freedom and would have free reign to travel first-class all over the world. These circumstances would increase the model's chances of learning that greed does not buy happiness.

Karma is most definitely an important factor when one is assessing predictions. If Joe is in the process of clearing karmic debt related to past-life relationships and selflessness, Joe is not likely to experience his new partner until the energy is balanced and this debt is cleared. It is also possible that Joe's potential partner is also clearing a karmic debt, contributing to the delay in their meeting. There may be many possible partners for Joe that would actually help him learn his soul lessons, but his soul will not achieve its greater good until the karmic balance and the appropriate lesson can be learned.

Conclusions about Predictions

The discussion in this chapter indicates that there are a number of factors that need to be considered when one is assessing the probability of a prediction manifesting. I have used some of the case studies in the research of *Medium7* and the relevant literature on various doctrines to see how these teachings help us better understand the nature of predictions. While it was interesting to analyze what factors might contribute to Joe's failed prediction, the main purpose for conducting such a close examination was to obtain knowledge about the nature of the universe. To summarize the factors reviewed in this chapter, table 7 provides a summary of the factors and the level of evidence that is available to validate their claims.

Table 7 Summary of Factors that Clarify the Nature of Predictions

Grand Theory Element	What are the factors that clarify the nature of predictions?	Is the element based on scientific fact or theory based on levels of evidence?
Quantum Physics	• Uncertainty principle • Observer effect	**Scientific fact** • Uncertainty principle • Observer effect demonstrated by Thomas Young
Reincarnation	• Soul contracts (predetermined contracts created prior to entering a new physical body)	**Theory based on strong evidence** • Evidence based on centuries of oral and written literature found in various texts crossing several cultures and religions • Evidence provided by mediums
Karma	• Laws of karma that underlie the balance between past-life actions and future lifetimes	**Theory based on strong evidence** • Evidence based on centuries of oral and written literature found in various texts crossing several cultures and religions • Evidence provided by mediums (specifically those who can read the Akashic records)

Table 7 outlines that there are three elements of the theory and four separate factors that provide a better understanding regarding the nature of predictions. For the most part the levels of evidence supporting these theories are based on scientific fact, evidence from mediums, and oral/written testimony shared over many generations.

In Joe's example there were a number of factors to consider, and each of these factors is related to quantum physics, reincarnation, and karmic law. From the information shared in this chapter we cannot limit our understanding of predictions to mediumistic abilities. We most certainly cannot fully understand the nature of prediction without understanding quantum physics (subatomic particle behavior), reincarnation (soul contracts), and karma. What was the nature of Joe's thoughts about his future partner? Were Joe's worries, fears, and potential resentment about his last relationship, blocking his inability to manifest this new partner? Remember that the type of thoughts Joe produced would mirror his reality. Did Joe create loneliness for others in a past life, subsequently leading him to his current circumstances? Did Joe's inability to learn selflessness in his first relationship dictate the need for further preparation that would increase success in his second relationship?

These are all important questions that highlight the point that aspects of Joe's life are predetermined, but his ability to freely choose a variety of paths creates uncertainty and limited predictability about his life outcomes.

So what do I conclude? At the time a medium makes the prediction he or she is indeed viewing a probability. The outcome of the prediction can be heightened or diminished based on a variety of factors. A medium can successfully identify the nature of soul contracts and karmic relationships mainly because these experiences are based on a past lifetime (karmic law) or were predetermined at the preparation phase just prior to the soul's new incarnation. However, since the agent has free will to choose several paths, the medium may not be able to consistently predict the timing or the actual outcome of an event. The information about the behaviors of subatomic particles in the double-slit experiment described earlier in the chapter provided scientific evidence that outcomes are influenced by observation. Remember the world consists of a field of probabilities that are reshaped by our own thoughts and subsequent choice to pursue a particular path. When you produce a thought, this in turn controls emotions. These emotions create changes in your vibrational frequency, which in turn contributes to the realities you will experience. The mysterious changes in wave forms and subatomic particles in the double-split experiment provide proof that our thoughts and observations impact the universe—the infinite field of probabilities.

I realize that I have combined a great deal of abstract concepts in one chapter, so I have developed the following table to simplify these points.

Table 8 Grand Theory Elements: Levels of Prediction and Primary Technique Used

	Grand Theory Element		
	Quantum Physics • Uncertainty Principle • Observer effect	**Reincarnation**	**Karma**
Level of Prediction Possible	**Prediction is limited:** Agent plays a large role in the outcome through thought processes and free will.	**Prediction is possible:** The medium or practitioner can reliably identify past life information.	**Prediction is possible:** The medium or practitioner can reliably identify if the event or relationship is karmic.
Primary Technique Used	**Primary technique used:** Meditation (by the agent)	**Primary technique used:** Mediumship, past-life regression, near-death experiences	**Primary techniques used:** Mediumship, past-life regression, near-death experiences (life reviews)
Smith-Moncrieffe, 2013			

Most important is that mankind plays a larger role in manifesting the events that we experience in our lives to a greater extent than we once thought.

CHALLENGES OF SPIRIT COMMUNICATION

We are all on a journey to discover the truth about the nature of our existence. Some of us are born researchers who systematically calculate data to come up with plausible answers. Others are going through daily life, noticing specific trends and consciously asking questions. They read books and attend seminars in a quasi-conscious attempt to understand the purpose of our existence. Still, others go through their routine existence without asking any questions. They are looking for quick solutions to life's challenges, such as winning the lottery or consuming a drug that has the illusive power, to make life appear and feel rosy. Whatever the degree of intensity, most of us seek an existence that is meaningful, peaceful, and full of joy.

One of the ways humankind has been able to obtain answers to elusive questions is to meet with a medium who acts as a bridge to the spirit world.

People have been flocking to mediums since the official start of Spiritualism in 1848. In the twenty-first century, sitters meet with mediums to connect with spirit for a variety of reasons. The present study based on interviews with eighty-eight research participants and ten mediums provides a breakdown of reasons that motivate people to seek the services of a medium.

Table 9 What Was the Primary Reason for Seeing a Medium?

Primary Reason for Seeing a Medium	Percentage and Number
Grieving: Achieving contact with a loved one who has passed	55 percent n=48
Non-grieving: Achieving contact with a loved who has passed	15 percent n=13
Predictions about the following: • Relationships • Health • Finances • Career	22 percent n=19
Guidance about current and past experiences related to following: • Relationships • Health • Finances • Career	6 percent n=5
Curiosity about the spirit world	3 percent n=3
n=88	
Note: Various mediums in this study have different specialities. Some specialize in contacting past loved ones while some provide past, current, and future life readings.	

Table 9 identifies a variety of reasons for seeking the services of a medium. Just less than three quarters (70 percent) of the sitters (both grieving and non-grieving) wanted to hear from someone who had passed. In most cases the sitters were still grieving and were having a difficult time achieving closure. One fifth of the group was primarily interested in hearing predictions about their relationships, finances, careers, or health. It may appear surprising that the desire for knowledge about the future was relatively low amongst this study population. However, this finding may be related to who is consulted. Mediums are more likely to be associated with connecting with discarnates. Psychics are known for conducting life readings that provide explanations for past and current events and for making predictions about the future.

We saw in the previous chapters how individuals have benefited from receiving messages from a medium. In any objective investigation it is important to identify and explore potential challenges. For example, are there any unintended consequences that might occur as a result of obtaining a reading with a medium? Is meeting with someone to talk to the dead a socially acceptable activity, and if it isn't, what are the implications of participating in this controversial activity?

This chapter explores the potential challenges one might encounter if the sitter's use of mediumship is not balanced with personal responsibility and a greater understanding of how guidance from spirit should be used. This chapter will also examine prejudices and stereotypes about mediumship that make it difficult for people to feel guilt-free about exploring the nature of the universe outside of a traditional church setting. The purpose of discussing these challenges is not to dissuade the public from working with a medium. The purpose is to increase the public's awareness. Reducing confusion about expectations will allow serious knowledge seekers the opportunity to continue the journey for truth with an increased awareness that will reduce disappointment and enable more realistic expectations. During the *Medium7* study it became clear that the public was not informed about how to mitigate potential unintended consequences that may arise as a result of participating in spirit communication with a medium. These potential obstacles are explored throughout this chapter.

Dependency

If you have lost someone prematurely and have not found consolation from a traditional therapist, you may have found connecting with your loved one through a medium to be comforting. Hearing information that confirms that your loved one is still with you and is doing well can facilitate progress towards the final stages of grieving. The Kübler-Ross model[59] includes five stages of grief: denial, anger, bargaining, depression, and acceptance. For most sitters these stages of grief are experienced in no defined sequence. In phase one of the *Medium7* study sitters revealed that after they prematurely lost their spouses, partners, children, or parents, they seemed to be stuck in one of the stages of denial, anger, or depression. Sitters who met with a medium and received unequivocal evidence that their deceased loved ones were still *with them* in spirit stated that they felt a sense of peace and closure. In particular, if the sitter's child was missing or his or her loved one was killed in a catastrophic event, hearing that there was minimal suffering was extremely consoling. In fact, just learning that the soul usually leaves the body before any pain is registered in the physical body is an extremely consoling thought to those living with grief.

Where there is relief from pain, depression, and suffering, there is always the risk of dependency. Participants in the *Medium7* study were asked if they felt that dependence on a medium to resolve their life challenges could become a possibility. In the present study, dependency was measured by the amount of times the sitter visited a medium about the same subject. In some instances there were sitters who visited a medium three times in one week. While less than 10 percent of the sitters fell into this category, it is important that we highlight that certain personality types can become dependent on the source of information shared by the medium. A statistical relationship was found between potential dependency and purpose for seeking the services of a medium. Sitters who had a primary interest in receiving predictions or guidance on current and past issues were more likely to self-report being dependent on a medium compared to grieving sitters who sought the services of a medium to connect with loved ones in spirit. All of the sitters who went to see a medium primarily to abate their grief indicated that while the experience provided them with a sense of closure, they did not feel that they would be become dependent on a medium. They noted that just knowing that their loved ones were at peace was enough to help them keep going on with life. Some sitters who were dealing with the premature loss of a loved one did not feel that they were developing a dependence, although they did admit to having several readings with different mediums in attempts to validate the information.

One could argue that frequently seeing a psychologist might create a certain amount of dependency. Similar to mediums, psychologists analyze and provide advice on coping strategies and options to consider while one is moving forward on one's life path. The concern about dependency with mediums is that sitters often refer to the *divine nature* of the guidance, a quality that for them gives the advice greater credence than advice received from a psychologist. If the medium's advice is actually coming directly from a loved one, from a client's perspective, this can have greater impact than the advice provided by a psychologist.

In the present study, a majority of sitters in the post grieving period noted that they would never replace a medium with a psychologist. They saw the medium as a complementary resource to the psychologist to help process the pain, anger, and suffering. A number of sitters (30 percent) did note that closure did not occur until they connected with a medium who could bring them undeniable proof that their loved ones' spirits had survived death.

Two of the mediums in this study do work with organizations that help grieving parents. Faith Grant volunteers her time by working at a large hospital for sick children to help parents cope with their children's impending death. Faith provides proof of spirit by bringing detailed messages from spirit to parents that may or may not have previously experienced receiving communication from discarnates on the *other side*. For example, if a parent obtains proof from Faith about a deceased family member, his or her subsequent belief in life after death may reduce the fear and worry about the impending loss of his or her child. Although parents understand that they will no longer be able to experience their children the way they do on the earth plane, they are more at peace with the thought that their children's souls will live on, just in a different format.

Chris Stillar is another medium who participated in the present study. He has been endorsed by Mothers against Drunk Drivers in Canada (MADD). Mothers who are having challenges coping with the premature loss of their children find comfort in hearing validating messages that the child is still *with them* and did not experience pain during the passing. Chris notes that communication with loved ones provides strong validation and is enough to help parents begin or complete their healing so that they can continue with their own journeys.

Depending on a medium for continuous support did not appear to be a problem for grieving sitters relative to the findings related to those seeking prescient information. The sitters who were interested in learning about the future were often more likely to see the medium more frequently. The following testimony exemplifies this point:

> I wanted to know more about my future career. I found the experience of the medium consoling as there were always messages of hope. I heard comments like, "there are two opportunities occurring within six to twelve months. These opportunities are satisfying and financially fulfilling." Even if a small part of the message actually manifested in my life, this would create further reason to find out more. If none of the information became a reality, I found myself still returning to the medium as the hope generated from the reading provided me with motivation to continue doing the *daily grind*.

Caroline's testimony explains why dependency issues are more likely to occur with sitters seeking information about the future. Dependency was not a challenge for most of the research participants in this study population. However, the term *psychic junkie* was coined for a reason. To further understand the potential challenges of dependency, we need to discern how the *silver bullet syndrome* can keep sitters dependent on seeking external support to cope with daily life challenges.

The Silver Bullet Syndrome

In the present study, approximately 60 percent of sitters who visit mediums feel that the information provided is a silver bullet (also referred to as the magic bullet). This silver bullet would seemingly provide secret solutions for hard-to-solve problems. These sitters hold an underlying belief that messages about how to revive a stagnant career or how to manage a greedy family member who is threatening to mishandle the family estate will be the *absolute* remedy to resolve the issue. How many of us have searched for the solution to lose unwanted pounds in a week? How many of us as a result of this desire have tried silver bullet products that promise to help us lose thirty pounds in a week only to learn that even while we are taking *that* pill we actually have to avoid the tempting chocolate cake and do a few sit-ups to boot? Perhaps you have never had a weight problem, but you have tried to make money easily in a short space of time. You quickly learned that the make-me-some-money-fast guide included tips that entailed discipline, determination, focus, and persistence— concepts that take a bit of work and some time to manifest.

In this study, I learned that some sitters often viewed the messages from readings as a silver bullet. Somehow the information was a special way to obtain the answers from a credible source but circumvent the hard work. Many mediums suggest that after the reading the sitters review their notes, reflect, consider the advice, and actually do the work to address the issue that needs to be resolved.

The concern about the silver bullet syndrome became clear

after I listened to Thomas vent during a focus group with other sitters. Thomas shared his discontent with his reading from a medium. He indicated that he primarily sought to engage a medium after the recent passing of his mother. After the medium provided proof of his mother's continued existence, Thomas had hoped to gain a better understanding of how he could be more influential in his communication at work. Thomas considered himself to be of above-average intelligence but seemed unable to make key business partners buy or invest in his creative projects. After years of developing novel concepts that were repeatedly rejected at his workplace, Thomas hoped the spirit of his mother could provide some answers to help him make positive changes in his career. The silver bullet phenomenon is clearly illustrated in Thomas's discontent with the general advice provided. The challenge in this instance is to understand that there are no easy answers to life's challenges. Much of the thinking, the analysis, and the decision-making should be made by the individual.

Let's examine another case where the medium actually does provide specific advice to address the solution. In this case Darren is not satisfied with the advice provided by the medium, especially since that would mean that he would have to face his greatest fears.

Darren is a fifty-five-year-old male who has been divorced for twelve years but cannot seem to meet a new partner. He is not pleased with the medium's response as she encourages him to get out more and participate in social engagements. Darren knew that he had not been getting out enough. He went to church, to work, and to the grocery store and could not imagine why he was still not able to meet a partner. He was dissatisfied with the message as it was not the silver bullet response that he was expecting. He shares his dissatisfaction below:

> I would not expect spirit to encourage me to participate in more social networks to meet people. I am a church-going man and was discouraged by

the suggestion that I widen my networks and get out more. I have avoided this due to having great anxieties about meeting new people. This was not the answer I was hoping for.

Darren thought that by seeking advice from the medium, he would receive an answer that would solve his problems without his having to carry out activities that would force him to confront his anxieties. He did admit in his post-reading interview for this research study that he agreed that this advice was relevant and likely very necessary, but he had also hoped to meet someone without having to address his social anxiety. In this case, the guidance of the medium was simply reaffirming the need for Darren to examine his underlying fears. Darren like many others expected that the divine nature of the readings would reveal a fast, easy, and comfortable alternative. Mediums can share relevant advice, but they cannot provide silver bullet solutions. We need to recognize these parameters in spirit communication and adjust sitters' expectations by clearly communicating both the potential possibilities and limitations.

These vignettes illustrate that sitters were receiving potentially useful advice, but their actual consideration of the advice would mean making an effort. The mediums and spirit cannot actually take away fears and anxieties, but they can identify them as the source of difficulties and can further provide motivation to start the process of resolution. The actual soul-searching, facing fears, and growth of the soul still have to be achieved at an individual level.

The potential risk of dependency and the silver bullet myth, when combined, can result in the most damaging experience. The term *psychic junkie* is most appropriate when dependency and the hope for a silver bullet outweigh the benefits of seeing a medium. When the sitter sees a medium and realizes within a few weeks that the silver bullet did not present itself, he or she may go on to see either the same medium or a new one. This cycle continues as the sitter believes that the silver bullet will be discovered with the right reading and with the appropriate medium. Sitters need to be aware that simply receiving a message from a medium is not a *quick fix*. The work still needs to be done.

Just Give Me the Right Answer

The silver bullet myth is similar to the belief that spirit will just provide the answers and all will be well. Oftentimes the mediums will share the way they feel about a particular path that is more appropriate for the sitter. They might share a warning that a certain path is not for the greatest good. *Is that answer the only answer?* Sitters should not allow spirit or the medium to make *decisions* about their lives. The right answer can only come from *within* the sitter. Spirit provides loving messages that are shared to empower the sitter to see a larger picture or other perspectives. All of this guidance should be directed toward helping sitters make their own decisions about moving forward in their lives.

• • •

Personal responsibility is the most important consideration.

We should always make our own decisions and take full responsibility for this.

Religion of Spiritualism

• • •

My interview with Reverend Angela Morra, a member of the Spiritualist Church highlighted a point that addresses the *give-me-the-right-answer-challenge*. Rev. Morra participates in a church that honors the religion of Spiritualism, which asserts that "no one can save us from our wrong doing but ourselves. Man through his conscience knows the difference between right and wrong and is given free will to choose which road he will take." Rev. Morra further explained that although Spiritualism strongly supports the work of mediums, this doctrine also encourages sitters to take responsibility for their own decisions.

During interviews I have had research participants share their viewpoints about the potential divinity of the information shared with them. They ask good questions like, "If the guidance shared via a medium is coming from a godly source, doesn't that suggest that I should follow the advice? Why would I need to make any personal decisions if God is all-knowing?" These questions and the cognitive processes used by sitters are important to address, as many more individuals may make these erroneous presumptions and forget to consult their inner selves. In the chapter where we explored the factors that contribute to spirit communication we examined the infallibility of spirit. Most importantly we clarified that spirit communication was sometimes a bit like a broken telephone. In other cases *the answer* could not be revealed as this could possibly inhibit the necessary growth of the soul. For these reasons it is important for sitters visiting mediums to take the information and consider it using personal logic and experiential knowledge. The final decision must come from the sitter.

Unmet Expectations

All of us can relate to the experience of having certain expectations that have not been met. If we stayed at a wonderful vacation resort with all of the amenities and rebooked based on our past memories, we are certainly going to be disappointed if the hotel does not reach similar standards on subsequent vacations. We create various expectations based on our past experiences. When we attempt to communicate with spirit, however, we need to suspend any assumptions that what we desire will be fulfilled. Having an expectation that *Granny Lynn* will communicate via the medium will be disappointing if *Granny Lynn* either has not learned to communicate with a medium or actually does come through but does not answer questions posed by the sitter. The following example demonstrates the challenge when the sitter's expectations about the potential messages are not aligned with the reading provided. Kayla had been trying to get pregnant for three years. She was thrilled when the medium indicated that she would be pregnant within a short while. After a year Kayla was not pregnant and wondered if the disappointment was worse because she had heard she would soon become pregnant.

The challenge with unmet expectations is that sometimes the disappointment in the absence of the expected result is greater than the uncertainty the sitter experienced prior to hearing from the medium. This type of disappointment may deter sitters from further exploring the spirit world via the medium. The unrealistic standard of expectations might also create disappointments that overshadow the other beneficial advice shared by the medium. Unmet expectations can create confusion about the efficacy of Spiritualism and create false hopes.

At a personal level I find that unmet expectations are frequent when I have too many expectations of spirit. When I am following my meditation routine and accepting the present with all its good and bad experiences, my positive predisposition attracts experiences that bring me what I need but not necessarily what I want. A spiritual consultant shared with me that the constant barrage of expectations creates an internal turbulence that is similar to a choppy sea. When the sea is turbulent, the boat cannot come into shore. When we have internal turbulence, our needs cannot be easily met. I recommend that sitters and researchers not judge the success of an interaction with spirit on whether expectations were met or not. Mediums and psychics should make sitters aware that various factors contribute to effective spirit communication. This will help sitters understand the possible outcomes of a reading and make the necessary psychological adjustments prior to receiving spiritual messages from a medium.

Fraud

When a majority of the public does not have the ability to see or hear spirits, there is going to be cause for skepticism. There are many good reasons for rational people to question the validity of mediumship. Even if one was not acquainted with the history of mediumship and its associated religion (Spiritualism), one could imagine the potential for charlatans to take advantage of innocent sitters, especially those grieving the loss of loved ones. Just forty years after the advent of Spiritualism (1848), the same family who launched the philosophy and religion to fame also brought about its downfall. In 1888 the Fox sisters, who had toured the United States demonstrating their alleged gifts, eventually admitted to having manipulated the spirit rappings with their toes. Various versions of the story suggest that one of the Fox sisters was bribed. As a result of her need for financial compensation she deceptively shared with the public that the rappings were falsely generated.

Arthur Conan Doyle's work on the *History of Spiritualism*[60] provides important facts regarding the authenticity of the rappings the two sisters claimed to have heard from an unseen entity in their home. Margaret and Kate were age eleven and fourteen respectively when they discovered their ability to communicate with unseen forces. In fact they had little time to learn how and why they experienced psychic phenomenon. Due to the high level of public interest in Margaret's gifts and the pressure to perform, alcoholism began to plague Margaret's life. The alcoholism eventually made it difficult for her to support herself financially. Eventually, members of the religious community that were not supportive of the implications of mediumship bribed her to admit publicly that the initial rappings and her psychic abilities in general were unsubstantiated.

In 1898, one of the sisters recanted her confession about the trickery however the damage to the validity of mediumship had already become irrevocable. It was not until 1904 that evidence confirmed that the Fox sisters were indeed communicating with a real discarnate during their residence in what was known as the *spook* house. The *Boston Journal* (a non-spiritual journal) published that the skeleton of the man responsible for the rappings first heard by the Fox sisters in 1848 had been found in the walls of the house previously occupied by the sisters. The sisters had initially shared that the discarnate communicated that he had been murdered and buried in the cellar. Despite many failed excavations, the discovery was finally made by school children playing in the cellar. The peddler's tin box containing the bones is now preserved at the museum in Lily Dale, the headquarters of the Spiritualist church.

This discovery and the efforts of researchers in the nineteenth century served to diminish the claims of fraud by attempting to use scientific methods to assess the validity of mediumship. There were a few influential researchers in the nineteenth century who used sound research methods and published favorable findings about physical mediumship.

Trevor Hall's book titled *The Medium and the Scientist*[61] provided an account of an influential scientist's experience in studying physical mediumship in the nineteenth century. Sir William Crookes was a chemist and physicist who in 1870 decided that science had a duty to examine paranormal phenomena. Crookes conducted impartial inquiries into the phenomena of physical mediumship and described the study conditions as follows: "It must be at my own house ... and my own selection of friends and spectators ... under my own conditions, and I may do whatever I like regarding the apparatus." Among the phenomena he witnessed were movement of bodies at a distance, rappings, changes in the weights of bodies, levitation, appearance of luminous objects, appearance of phantom figures, writing without aid, and circumstances that pointed to the aid of an outside intelligence. His studies were published and supported by the Society for Psychical Research, and his report on this research was subsequently published in 1874, suggesting that these phenomena could not be explained as conjuring and that further research would be useful. Crookes was not alone in his views. Fellow scientists who came to believe in Spiritualism included Alfred Russel Wallace, Oliver Lodge, Lord Rayleigh, and William James. There were many scientists, however, who were not convinced and sometimes outraged at the possibility of considering parapsychology as a branch of science. Given the debate and chasm between scholars of the time, Kate Fox's admission to fraud and subsequent recantation served to solidify the extreme views held by the scientific community.

History suggests that in times of uncertainty humankind has an enhanced desire to want to believe in the metaphysical. This environment provides opportunities for charlatans to exploit unsuspecting sitters. During the era of physical mediumship[62] people were interested in viewing phenomenon like seeing tables move, hearing the direct voice of their loved ones, or seeing objects appear or disappear (also known as apportation). Making these physical phenomena occur on demand to a curious audience could be a challenging feat for even gifted mediums. The growing curiosity about the possibility of a spiritual world set the stage for magicians to create ways to produce similar effects and profit financially. Even gifted mediums could be tempted to produce these effects through trickery.

An interesting story about Harry Houdini is published in Dr. Todd Leonard's[63] comprehensive review of the history of modern Spiritualism in which the famous magician systematically tests the authenticity of mediums in the early twentieth century. In 1922 Houdini challenged mediums to demonstrate their gifts in a laboratory setting. He would award a prize of $5,000 to the medium who could demonstrate physical mediumship under controlled conditions. One medium, referred to as Crandon, claimed to be able to make objects appear and move during the séance. To control any fraudulent activity on Crandon's part, Houdini set up a number of traps that would prevent Crandon from moving objects herself. Apparently Walter, Crandon's deceased brother, was fond of ringing a bell as proof that the deceased were indeed immortal. Houdini had ensured that anything physical touching the bell would be exposed. During the controlled experiment just as the bell rang, Houdini felt the medium's leg pass his own to ring the bell. This convinced him that Crandon was using her own leg to ring the bell as proof that she was in contact with the *other side*. Houdini was able to recreate Crandon's alleged physical mediumship the next day, diminishing any validity she may have had. The medium was most certainly not awarded the $5,000.

Crandon's alleged abilities to make a hand appear were later discovered to be an act of magic and not of physical mediumship. Her reputation was further damaged when a member of the Boston Society for Psychical Research discovered that a fingerprint left on wax, as proof of her ability to summon the dead, was not from the spirit world but from her dentist. Apparently her dentist later divulged that he had taught her how to make these prints.

This type of fraud was common at the height of Spiritualism in the nineteenth century as both *real* mediums and not-so-talented wannabes recognized the profitable nature of the business. In today's society physical mediumship is rarely used to demonstrate proof of spirit. A more common practice is for mediums to use mental techniques to share detailed messages that resonate with sitters who are seeking a connection with their deceased loved ones. Fraudulent practices might involve sharing general messages that are not derived from spirit but are guesstimates made by the medium based on inadvertent verbal and physical cues from the sitter. As a metaphysics researcher I have not personally encountered these techniques as my studies only use gifted mediums who have demonstrated the validity of their talents.

The general public can also be concerned about the medium obtaining information based on the first and last name of the sitter as there is always the possibility that the medium could research his or her potential clients on the Internet. While this of course is a possibility, the information shared in a *true* reading will provide messages that could never be found on the Internet.

There is no question that fraudulent mediums and psychics exist in the twenty-first century just as charlatans existed during the height of Spiritualism. I do not find that there is a disproportionate rate of fraudulent behavior occurring in the parapsychology industry when compared to any other business industry.

Dishonorable behavior creates two major problems. The first and most important is that when someone has lost a loved one, he or she is already vulnerable. Capitalizing on his or her grief by using deception is criminal.

The second problem is if we lie to ourselves about the extent of a medium's powers, we will never understand the true nature of our universe. If we lie about the precise nature of spirit communication, we may prevent ourselves from learning about the true purpose of existence. This great disservice would be committed against ourselves.

The discovery of fraudulent mediumship in the early nineteenth century was damaging for the Spiritualism movement, but the controversy sparked great interest among scientific researchers who became motivated to systematically assess the validity of these alleged powers under controlled conditions.

Unfortunately the fraudulent activity that took place during the height of Spiritualism still persists among alleged psychic mediums in the twenty-first century. Mediums are no longer expected to make objects appear or move tables telepathically, but they are expected to provide information, such as names, dates, detailed information about deceased loved ones, and bestow evidence that loved ones who have passed on into the spiritual world are indeed immortal.

Fraud can be significantly diminished if the public knows how to identify an authentic medium. While this type of guidance goes beyond the scope of this book, I will share an obvious red flag. A medium who suggests that you need to pay any amount of money to have a curse removed is a fraud. In fact, any medium who provides information that is fear-based is likely more focused on reaping a financial profit than empowering their clients. Based on responses from eighty-eight research participants in the present study, the following activities in table 12 enhance or diminish the validity of spirit communication:

Table 12 What Enhances or Diminishes the Validity of Spirit Communication?

Enhances validity	Diminishes validity
• No information is known by the medium before the reading	• Information is leaked prior to the reading (i.e., the sitter's name or information about the sitter is shared during idle discussion prior to the reading).
• Details including names, dates, places, and cause of death are provided by the medium during the reading	• A disproportionate number of general messages are shared during the reading. These are so general they could apply to anyone.
• Successfully animating the deceased	• Frequent requests for validation by the medium during the reading.
• Successfully smelling the scent of the deceased	• Mediums ask leading questions.
• Successfully feeling the pains or sensations felt during the passing (validating cause of death)	• Providing frequent messages or information that is not relevant for the client or immediate family.
• Providing relevant and useful guidance	• Sharing fear-based messages that are not possible for the client to mitigate (i.e., sharing a future illness or death that is fatal).
• Discouraging frequent visitation	• Requesting additional funds to remove a curse.
• Requesting standard financial compensation	
• Providing information that empowers the client to take responsibility and action that is for a higher greater good	

If the activities that enhance validity are more frequently apparent during a reading, fraudulent mediums will not be able to thrive. They will not be able to thrive as the public will become more knowledgeable about the factors that enhance validity and will be better prepared to identify honest, gifted mediums.

Necromancy

The media will sometimes use the terms *mediumship* and *necromancy* interchangeably. The latter term is associated with more sinister activities, making it difficult for honest psychic mediums to have themselves regarded as channels for greater well-being.

In my research of the available literature I found two types of definitions. The first definition seems quite similar to mediumship in meaning. Necromancy is a claimed form of magic involving communication with the deceased either by summoning spirits, and imparting the means to foretell future events or discover hidden knowledge. This definition suggests that necromancy is the act of interrogating or making inquiry of the dead.

In other literature a more insidious definition is applied. This latter definition describes necromancy as black magic, an activity in which individuals use alchemy to raise the dead. This latter definition becomes even more sinister when it includes the intent of raising the dead to do *evil biddings*.

Religious sects have been conflicted about the term *necromancy* and its implied suggestion that human beings have the power to raise the dead. As a result of this ambiguity, the definitions acknowledging the possibility of raising the dead were modified. Some traditional religious groups have noticed the rise in Spiritualism and its association with mediumship and have often conflated the terms *necromancer* and *mediumship* to suggest that they are the same activity. Table 13 examines the similarities and differences between the concepts of mediumship and necromancy.

Table 13 Mediumship and Necromancy: Similarities and Differences[64]

Contemporary Mediumship	Necromancy	Similar/Different
In many instances today's mediums do not have to summon spirits. They claim that discarnates (those in the nonphysical world) summon *them* to communicate a message to their loved ones on the physical plane.	Summons dead spirits	Similar and different
Does not use rituals	Conducts esoteric rituals	Different
Provides sitters with messages	Receives or delivers messages May make requests for spirits to do one's bidding	Different
Does not attempt to raise the dead; assumes that the souls survive physical consciousness	Attempts to raise the dead	Different
Accepts spirit guidance "as is" (based on principles of Spiritualism)	May use manipulation, illusion, and sacrifices to alter the nature of the guidance	Different

The information in table 13 indicates that necromancy is very different from mediumship. Using the terms interchangeably is misleading and creates further confusion about the many ways our physical universe can interface with other planes in the nonphysical world.

Association with Evil

If a medium is given the power to heal, has clear seeing, or predicts the future, the idea is that this gift should be used to bring greater well-being to the world. If the gift is used to show off, hurt others, or bring further despair to the world, this is a complete misuse of the gift. Malevolent intent damages the credibility of the gifted mediums and limits the channelling of information that is for the client's greater good. A contributing factor to mediumship being associated with evil, relates to the events that erupted during the seventeenth and eighteenth centuries. Talking to the dead and making predictions were considered heretical. Some of these attitudes related to heresy have prevailed into the current century.

When the concept of mediumship is likened to concepts such as alchemy and necromancy, images of evil and the possibility of an infinite existence in hell interfere with the pursuit of knowledge. Many of today's religious fundamentalists have labeled the current new age movement, of which mediumship is a part, as an evil cult even though the movement includes health alternatives, such as Reiki, yoga, tai chi, acupuncture, meditation, astrology readings, the use of crystals to raise energy, and any innovative approach that may bring harmony to the mind, body, and soul. I can remember the day my massage therapist recommended that I try Reiki. After I watched a few YouTube videos describing the process, I happened upon a related video that suggested that Reiki was actually evil. The speaker in the video suggested that the energies transferred from the therapist to the client were generated by the devil. He warned potential clients that this alternative therapeutic approach was an abomination. Individuals seeking new alternative healing methods may be dissuaded after they hear theories that suggest such pursuits may attract evil into their lives. They may begin to fear all new age approaches that are possible doors to greater well-being. Associating these activities with fear creates a stagnation that leaves mankind in the dark about who we really are.

If we choose to engage in mediumship with the intent to learn more, help others, or heal, the intention would be considered positive. If we attempt to seek information to strengthen our egos, to hurt someone, or to achieve a goal that digresses from learning the lessons vital for the soul's growth, our purpose for engagement can be classified as a *negative intention*. As stated earlier in this book we are physical beings having a spiritual experience so if our intentions are contrary to the spiritual laws, we will not experience well-being in our lives. Let us keep this basic principle in mind as we assess the beliefs that have been linked to spirit communication.

Spirit communication has long been considered somewhat controversial as some aspects of this practice runs contrary to the tenets of dominant orthodox religions, such as Christianity or Judaism.

To fully understand how mediumship became associated with heresy, abomination, and evil, we need to examine a bit of religious history. Before I embark on a selected historical review, I would first want to point out that experiencing spirituality is not necessarily the same as abiding by a religion. While many people use religion as a route to find their spirituality, others discover inner truths and the purpose of their existence through other pathways. These other avenues are not necessarily evil.

The second point that I would make here is that any religious references to negative events, such as the Salem witch trials, should *not* be interpreted as a sign of disrespect. My view is that all religions that guide mankind to experience and create well-being for others should be respected. There may be variations within the sects and denominations, but if the core intent is for greater well-being and the tenets guide mankind to "do unto others as would be done unto thyself," then these should be respected. Events that are said to occur in the *name of religion* but have been hurtful to mankind (i.e., religious wars) are the acts of humankind and do not indicate that the religion itself is flawed. Given this understanding, let's begin the journey that will help us better understand how religious history has shaped the current perspective on spirit communication.

I start this exploration with my first recollection of feeling that there were some unanswered questions about life after death. This personal quest for knowledge starts when I was about fifteen years of age. After my choir practice at church, something prompted me to ask the priest where the soul goes after death. At this time, I was also reading a book on world religions as my inner self wanted to explore different beliefs. As a child growing up in the Anglican Church, while I enjoyed the stories about Jesus, Easter, and Christmas, I was also intrigued about what I learned from the Eastern religions. These doctrines seemed to clarify the pathways of the soul and the ultimate purpose for mankind's existence. The ideas of reincarnation, nirvana (Buddhist teaching), aspects of Jewish mysticism, and other stimulating concepts resonated within me, sending a clear message that these were important concepts to explore. I asked the priest at our church, "Where exactly does the soul go after we die?" I shared with the priest that I noticed that the Christian church clearly acknowledged the soul and its ascension but that there did not seem to be any mention of where it went after that. He replied tentatively, "It returned to God." I did not ask any more questions directly to the priest, but I continued to wonder why the Christian religion did not elaborate on what happened after the soul was reunited with God. Was that the end? Did the soul not have any further purpose or activity during its time with God? I had noticed that there was relatively little said about the afterlife in the Christian religion. I found the schism between the Eastern and Western world fascinating and wondered how mankind could have such divergent views about the soul's path. I laid these questions to rest for many years and decided to let the answers unfold naturally as I experienced life.

As I got older I noticed that a majority of the television

programs or movies about the spirit world were all fear-based. The horror genre consisted of movies like *The Exorcist, The Amityville Horror, The Haunting*, and *Paranormal Activity*. These movies conveyed to the public that there were entities that we could not see but these *beings* could drive us out of our homes, haunt us, and in some cases kill us. The horror genre has never died, and the sense of fear it seeks to arouse in us doesn't just persist during Halloween. It is commonplace for paranormal movies, talk shows, and documentaries to air fear-based content for general entertainment. Media associating the spirit world with well-being were quickly disappearing. I can recall my late grandmother's sadness when all of her religious television programs were removed from the air. The Public Broadcasting Service, a television network known for providing alternative programming, including spiritual shows that promoted connecting with spirit in positive ways, was canceled because of a lack of funding and perceived limited interest. Fear-based media in the genre of parapsychology continued to prevail, further demonstrating our interest in fear-based entertainment.

Fear regarding the spirit world has been further aggravated with the growing evidence of alleged evil associated with the Ouija board. The Ouija board, also known as a *spirit* or *talking board*, is a flat board marked with the letters of the alphabet, the numbers zero through nine, the words *yes, no, hello* (occasionally), and *good-bye*, along with various symbols and graphics. Individuals would wait for spirits to respond by moving the marker to various letters and symbols to communicate intelligent information. There are varying theories about the Ouija board, but in general the tool has been deemed to be associated with demons by orthodox religions. Many documentaries where individuals suffered frightening occurrences from entities have been tied to past Ouija board use. Anecdotal case studies that shared stories about hauntings were often directly linked to past Ouija board use. Apparently playing with this tool via inexperienced users could result in opening up portals, allowing both good and malevolent spirits to invade the physical world. My aim here is not to pass any type of judgment on the Ouija board tool. Instead, the goal here is to demonstrate how the consequences of using various tools related to mediumship have strengthened the public's negative perception about the paranormal.

It is not surprising, however, that our media and social discourse in the twenty-first century largely promotes fear-based communication about the paranormal. If we were to focus on one key historical phase that has shaped the way we view the paranormal, the Salem witch hunt trials[65] (1692) would be a useful one. During the seventeenth century the experience of the Salem witch trials marks a time where fear and ignorance created unnecessary executions of humans, limiting mankind's ability to discover and honor human potential. Throughout Europe in the seventeenth and eighteenth centuries there have been a number of related trials, but the Salem trial is the most famous so an abbreviated version will provide useful context for this discussion.

In 1641 English law made witchcraft a capital crime. Many people were accused of being witches, were put on trial, and subsequently punished. Those accused of witchcraft were portrayed as being worshippers of the devil who engaged in such acts as malevolent sorcery, magic, and rituals known as witches' Sabbaths. The term *sorcery* in modern times can be further understood by watching the well-known movie sequel about the school of Hogwarts attended by Harry Potter and his English classmates. In general the term *sorcery* applies to any magical act intended to cause harm or death to people or property. In the *Harry Potter* series, these acts of alchemy were used to defend against evil Lord Voldermort, although we have also watched a few sequels where Harry and his classmate had occasionally misused their powers to retaliate against an annoying classmate.

In the time of the Salem witch trials, using energy sources to create a perpetuated change in the unseen world was considered illegal and could warrant the punishment of hanging. Some of these alleged witches were hanged for practicing alternative healing methods, such as using strong intuition and/or harnessing nature and energy to create well-being.

The society's underlying preoccupation appeared to relate to an individual's involvement with unseen forces. In the eighteenth century the Christian sect, known as the Puritans, was preoccupied with hell and unseen forces, believing that these forces contributed to natural disasters, such as the bubonic plague and tuberculosis. This focus on unseen forces caused uncertainty, panic, and fear. However, the Puritans appeared to be selective about how to apply judgment in regards to these unseen forces. For example, the medical practice of bloodletting was common. Bloodletting required puncturing the afflicted area and draining the tainted blood. It may never have occurred to the judges and medical community at the time that this ritual also involved the manipulation of unseen energy. The doctors could not see the actual draining of toxins; they only *believed* that it was tainted. Yet this practice was considered legal as it was sanctioned by the church and could only be controlled by a few medical doctors.

A pivotal point in the Salem witch hunt was reached in mid-February 1692, when Dr. Griggs assessed four girls who claimed to be afflicted with fits. Their behaviors included throwing items, attempting suicide, and simulating possession. After he viewed these aberrant behaviors, Dr. Griggs declared witchcraft to be the source of the behavior as there were no physical causes for this medical condition. Further questions resulted in the identification of Tituba, a household slave who allegedly shared stories of voodoo with these Puritan children. The story goes that Tituba, who used an English folk remedy, baked a *witch cake* containing the urine of the afflicted and fed it to the dog as dogs were believed to be a familiar of the devil. As a result Tituba and other women involved were arrested. Tituba was aware that Puritanical law suggested that if a person confessed, the court should not be responsible for ending a life. That power would be already predetermined and managed by God. Having made her confession, Tituba thwarted a fatal punishment but also hinted that there could be many more possible *witches* in the Salem community. This confession aggravated an already simmering belief in the devil and propelled the trials into a witch hunt. At the height of the hysteria two hundred were accused, and of these, twenty-four were hanged, pressed on the rack, or died in prison. Once the governor's wife fell prey to the accusations, a more rational review for future accusations was initiated. Finally, in 1697 the general court ordered a day of fasting and soul-searching regarding the tragedy at Salem. Public confessions about the error and the guilt were made. The general court declared the 1692 trials unlawful. In 1706 Ann Putnam, Jr., one of the leading accusers, publicly apologized for her actions during the height of the hysteria. In 1957 Massachusetts formally apologized for the events of 1692.

Political, economic, and sociological factors have contributed to this chain of events. Historians and sociologists have identified a number of contributing factors, including the outbreak of the smallpox, attacks on the Puritan community by other residents who had different religious beliefs, and the conjecture that demons were waiting to prey upon man. Sociological conditions made courts receptive to allegations, further encouraging the use of charges as convenient weapons to unjustly resolve land disputes.

Credible historians suggest that the physical afflictions that were demonstrated by the accused were psychologically inflicted and perpetuated as evidence of witchcraft by landowners who stood to profit from the forced forfeiture of properties and deaths of those accused.

This abbreviated review of the Salem witch trials illustrates how various social, religious, and political conditions contributed to abhorrent events. Despite the public apologies and acknowledgment of error in murdering innocent people as a result of the implementation of the Witchcraft Act, the association of mediumship with the devil's work continues to underlie the social attitudes of many, even in the twenty-first century.

To fully understand the sources of contention related to life-after-death issues, the notion of unseen forces, and the existence of the spirit world, we need to further examine the fundamentalists' views on these issues. Prior to the nineteenth century, religious leaders and beliefs dominated the political, social, and financial spheres. Fundamentalist views mostly emanating from the Catholic and Protestant sects pervaded everyday life, and any individual or emerging movement that proclaimed ideas contrary to the accepted teachings of the Bible were considered heretical.[66] In some cases heresy was considered an attack on the political system warranting the death penalty.

In this section of the chapter I intend to identify some key pieces of scripture that have contributed to the fear-based spiritual paradigm we experience in contemporary society. This investigation into the relationship between mediumship, life-after-death issues and the religious sector started with a simple dialogue with my hairdresser.

My hairdresser, who is a devout Christian and is open to the research I am conducting, had some opinions about mediumship. During our first few conversations about life after death and the role of mediums, I was feeling rather confident in my research as I had carefully constructed controlled experiments and had been satisfied that the data was sound. Despite initially being adverse to any discussions about the paranormal, Antoinette was open to hearing about the results as my research unfolded. I shared how I had been convinced that there was unequivocal proof that life is immortal and that we survive physical death.

The conversation went something like this: Antoinette stated with conviction, "Well, of course the deceased live on. The Bible is very clear about this. I don't disbelieve that we survive physical death, but the deceased cannot speak to us as they are *sleeping.*

The dead sleep until Christ returns for the second judgement day." With continued conviction, she concluded that the dead could not possibly be communicating with anyone as they are not individual souls who maintain their characteristics, knowledge, and past experiences.

I was of course familiar with the biblical scriptures related to this topic and continued to ask, "So who would be providing unequivocal proof the soul is immortal? Who is providing detailed information, including names, cause of death, dates, and details about unique events via a medium?"

Antoinette firmly responded, "The information is likely coming from the devil. The fallen angels know everything about our families, and so indeed, this information is coming from a fraudulent source."

While I was initially disquieted by her firm conviction, I realized that this was not the first time I had been warned by my Christian friends about seeing a medium. There always seemed to be an underlying suggestion that associating with mediums meant you were consorting with evil. What would normally be an uneventful morning at the hairdresser turned into a meaningful experience that launched a journey to further investigate the validity of Antoinette's sentiments.

Ethics requires the objective researcher to consider different perspectives when one is examining an area of interest. With this intent in mind I began to research some of the key phrases that illuminate the biblical view on life after death. In a review of religious literature produced by the Catholic church[67], a section on the afterlife demonstrates the variation in beliefs depending on the religious perspective. At the beginning of the chapter on life after death, they share a quote as follows:

> In the village of Gazeley, England lies a graveyard on the grounds of the Church of England. On the Gravestone of a seventeenth-century tomb are these words, "He sleepeth until Jesus comes."

> No more than a few places from that grave
> is a nineteenth-century gravestone with the
> inscription, "At home with the Lord."

The example above of the inscriptions on the two gravestones signifies two conflicting concepts of life after death. As exemplified on the nineteenth-century gravestone, some Christian sects believe that our souls ascend into the afterlife, live eternally, and experience immediate life after death. This is consistent with many pagan traditions, a predecessor to most of the religions we are familiar with today.

As exemplified on the seventeenth-century gravestone's inscription, other Christian sects believe that only God has immortality. They believe that after death the soul sleeps until the return of Jesus Christ. The following quotes further elaborate on the belief that the soul sleeps after the death of the physical body.

> "During this sleep the dead know not anything,
> neither have they any more a reward; for the
> memory of them is forgotten. Also their love,
> and their hatred and their envy is now perished;
> neither have they any more a potion forever is
> anything that is done under the sun" (Ecclesiastes
> 9:5–6).

> "After this phase of sleep, when Christ returns he
> will render to every man according to his deeds"
> (Romans 2:6–7).

This latter belief would make communication with the dead quite improbable. Yet if this is improbable, then why do we have so many witnesses on this physical earth claiming to have evidence of communication with passed loved ones?

The Catholic Church has a response to this. Fundamentalists suggest that Satan and his angels impersonate dead loved ones or great people of the past claiming that they have come back from heaven to give a message to mankind. From a Catholic perspective these would be deceptive messages as the souls of our loved ones are still asleep.

These competing views create challenges for devout Christians who respect a literal interpretation of the Bible. As we move from the age of Pisces to the age of Aquarius, we are summoned to search for truth and knowledge, to ask questions, and to learn from new experiences. This means that to determine the truth, one would need to review history, obtain sound evidence concerning the possibility of life after death, and most importantly recognize knowledge and experiences that contribute to infinite well-being. Most people don't want to be associated with consorting with the devil and may stunt their spiritual growth by being hesitant about participating in conscious-raising strategies, such as meditation or self-development practices like yoga and tai chi.

If you are still perplexed at what to believe about life after death following these two conflicting views, I will share the story that put my own internal personal conflict to rest. During an interview with a medium, in the *Medium7* study, I shared my concerns about the varying perspectives regarding the authentic source of communication from spirit. I wanted to hear her reaction to the *evil impersonation theory*. The following story is shared by Karen in her own words.

> I have been a practicing medium for forty-five years. I was brought up in the Catholic Church, and I brought all my children to Catholic churches. I had many spiritual experiences as a teenager that made me question some of the dogma I was learning in the church. I continued to keep my spiritual gifts a secret. Except for my deceased grandmother, other family members did not seem to experience these spiritual gifts, which was a strong indication

that I might have to explore this path on my own. For many years I engaged in an internal struggle between my acquired beliefs (Catholicism) and my personal experiences (spirituality). By the age of twenty I could see deceased people all the time. I of course started to realize that this was not a common occurrence for most people so I did not openly discuss this phenomenon. I can recall the sermon where the priest spoke strongly against *summoning the dead*. I wanted to burst out in the church and scream, "What if you are not summoning them and they are coming to you?" I knew the church leaders would not be open to a discussion about seeing the deceased, and now after hearing that particular sermon, I was certain that a confession to the priest about talking to the dead would just not go over too well! I knew I was not crazy, and I knew that the guidance that was communicated via spirit was for the most part coming from a source of love. My struggle continued until the age of thirty-two. A special incident that occurred in the church relieved me of this internal struggle and shame about my gift. One evening I went to midnight mass and my spirit guide kept me focused on another lady in the church. She was a lady in her mid-forties. I had also noticed her young daughter running back and forth in and out of the pews, dropping her teddy bear so other members of the congregation could pick it up. As I sat in the church, the messages and feelings became stronger. I could clearly hear that this lady needed immediate help. My head said, "No, Karen, don't bother a lady at the end of the service about dead people!" My compassionate side said, "Yes, Karen, just go over to the woman as she needs you."

At that point I was not sure what I intended to tell this lady, but nonetheless, my legs were taking me toward her pew. She was startled when she saw me standing over her, so I quickly shared my reason for coming to her. I was quite disturbed at what came out of my mouth. I can recall me sternly telling her that it would not be a good idea for her to return home with her daughter. As I was sharing this message, I had seen visions of her husband brutally beating her to death. With no further delay I bid her a strong warning to find a safe shelter for battered women and children. The lady began to sob uncontrollably and with a forlorn voice asked me where she could find one of these shelters. This lady did not even question where I got this information. She was so fatigued and frightened about her family circumstances that she only wanted to be safe. After I helped her make the necessary contacts, she hugged me and thanked me for this guidance. I watched as this lady and her precious daughter drove away toward a new safe haven.

This story shared by the medium reminded me of all the loving advice that spirit, including discarnates can provide. It was not an evil force that sent the medium those visions of a potential fatal beating. It was a loving force that contributed to the continued existence of two precious lives. Karen shared in her interview that she would not deny that there could be *unfamiliar spirits* that, she learned during her career as a medium, were not sharing messages for the sitter's greater good. To further complement the heartfelt story she previously shared, she shares a final note about *wayward spirits*.

I am not going to lie to you and tell you that there are only *good* spirits in the spiritual world. I can honestly say that I am 100 percent sure that when I have protected myself with the white light[68] of God and have prayed that the messages be for the greater good, I am a channel for light and love. Having a pure heart opens me up to provide messages of well-being from those spirit guides, angels and discarnates who I believe to have once lived on the earth plane. I feel their pure energy and believe their messages help people find the path to greater joy and peace. These types of spirits are not demons.

During my career I have encountered *wayward spirits* who in their attempt to make contact with the living do so with selfish or harmful intent. In the early part of my career I had difficulty distinguishing between the pure and tainted spirits. As an experienced medium I am now able to identify and block the entrance of *wayward* spirits.

I would conclude that just as there is good and evil on earth, the same is true for the spirit world.

Final Thoughts

On the journey to finding yourself and discovering truths about the nature of your existence, it is important to examine all perspectives and come to your own conclusions. It is important to minimize the potential challenges of spirit communication by formulating realistic expectations, having positive intentions, and taking personal responsibility for final decisions.

We also need to be cautious and aware of potential fraud and harness the techniques used to stay protected from harmful unseen forces. Protecting yourself with the appropriate prayers and covering yourself with the *white light* are two key strategies that are useful just prior to participating in any type of interaction with the spirit world. Despite both historical and contemporary occurrences of fraudulent experiences with psychics and mediums, we need to recognize that there are honest, gifted mediums who have real capabilities that are intended for well-being. Revisit table 12 in this chapter as a reference for identifying authentic elements of mediumship.

By reviewing history (in this case, the Salem witch trials) and understanding diverse belief systems about the afterlife, this knowledge can help you come to terms with identifying a belief system that aligns with your understanding and personal goals.

My hope is that I have debunked prevailing myths that may have inhibited some of you from exploring your spirituality via mediumship and other related paths available for learning about the nature of the universe. We must recognize that light and dark forces are among us but must decide for ourselves what tools help to identify the enlightened path that is in our highest and greatest good.

9

SO WHAT?

The question "So what?" has been somewhat socially acceptable when children use it. You often hear them using the phrase when they are not quite sure how to respond. They whine, "So what, Mommy? I don't care!" Or the belligerent teenager might use this after you share a heartfelt story with them. They sarcastically reply, "So what? Whatever—" It surprised me, however, when I started to hear professional adults use it after they heard a comprehensive discussion about a specific topic. They would shamelessly critique a speaker by starting out by stating, "That information is interesting, but so what? What does this mean? What can I do with this?" My first reaction after I heard the question was something like, "What do you mean so what? Can't you see all of the hundreds of important points just discussed over this three-day conference?" It really was not apparent why presenters had to further explain the implications for what they just shared. My view was that conference delegates, readers, or whatever type of audience would make their own interpretations and use the information in a way that would best suit their individual needs.

In this chapter we review selected case studies that best highlight where mediumship can be beneficial. The selected case studies demonstrate how sitters have benefitted from receiving messages that validate the afterlife, provide guidance to address life's struggles, and contribute to healing and greater understanding in relationships.

Why Is the *So What* Question Significant?

I had two incidents that made me realize that even for adults, the "so what" phrase might be important to consider.

The first incident was an eye-opener. I started to realize that perhaps not everyone found the question and potential answer to life's purpose of considerable importance. I was interviewing a research participant named Melanie, who shared that during her reading the medium had revealed information about her husband's deceased father. She learned about the uncle's middle name and learned some new information about her father-in-law that she hoped to verify with her husband, Daniel. Melanie was thrilled with her reading on many levels but was particularly interested in attempting to validate this new bit of information with her skeptical husband. She thought to herself, if Daniel could validate this information while knowing that I never knew this information prior to seeing the medium, perhaps this would be additional proof that we live beyond death. Perhaps Daniel would take the afterlife hypothesis seriously after hearing this information.

Melanie found it particularly interesting that although she had been married to her husband for almost thirty-five years, she did not know that her father-in-law's middle name was Edward. She did not know that he had lifelong challenges with his left knee, and she had not been informed about the details of the car accident that resulted in his death. She excitedly asked Daniel if the three pieces of information shared by the medium were true. He replied, "yes" to all of them. Melanie, replied, "Why would the medium use the name *Edward* when I know him as *Burt*?"

Daniel answered, "While growing up, family and friends referred to him as Edward."

After Melanie's interview I asked if I could speak with her

husband, Daniel. Melanie was reticent about this request as she had not really shared the details about her participation in this research. Most of the interviews with participants took place by phone, but in this particular instance, because of the short distance from my home, I conducted this interview in person. My being in the home prompted me to encourage Daniel to participate in the final part of the interview. Fortunately Daniel did sit down at the table and respectfully tolerated my questions. I asked with great curiosity, "Who do you think provided Melanie with the information about your father?"

With a reserved disposition Daniel shared, "I think my deceased father, Edward, shared this through the medium."

I was quite astounded by the response and continued, "So you think that Edward is still alive in some form?"

Daniel quickly replied, "Yup."

At this point I realized that Melanie's perspective of her husband's belief system was quite in sync with hers but they did not seem to share the same enthusiasm. So I continued probing with the hope of further understanding Daniel's perspective. "So the information that Melanie shared about your father was correct? How does that make you feel?" I asked with increasing curiosity.

Daniel shared, "I believe that there is an afterlife but—" After a pregnant pause he finally blurted out, "But so what?"

I remember that being the first time I realized that perhaps not everyone felt the same way about the implications of an afterlife. I thought that this was a question that everyone was born asking. I thought it was as natural as needing to consume nutrients to survive. This incident made me realize that the implications of the afterlife issue might not be well understood by everyone, and it helped me realize that I needed to spend some time in this book making the implications of an afterlife more explicit.

The second incident occurred during a plane ride from Ottawa to Toronto. I was returning from a business meeting, and during this short forty-five-minute flight a gentleman sitting beside me could not help but notice the book I was reading about near-death experiences. I began to share a bit of my research. He was a businessman that had not had any former experiences that would lead him to question or consider the need to discuss the afterlife. After I explained that there is accumulating evidence that life exists after death, he said, "That's interesting, but so what can that do for me now? I am a businessman who sells multimillion-dollar products that aid agencies enhance communication systems. How can the spirit world help me land deals?" He went on to ask, "In other words, does all of this help me after I die, or can there be some benefits while I am here?"

I thought to myself, there was that *so what* question again. This time this *so what* came with a *what-can-they-do-for-me-now* question. Meeting Daniel and the businessman were necessary encounters as they opened my eyes to the fact that the implications of spirit communication were not self-evident to everyone.

These fortuitous meetings have helped me to see varying perspectives on this topic and have made me realize the importance of carefully documenting all of the ways this knowledge can help during our time on the earth plane. The following information is based on evidence shared during focus groups, key informant interviews, and one-on-one interviews with research participants. Interviewees were asked to share any strengths and challenges of information derived from spirit communication. The primary responses related to challenges were incorporated in chapter 8, and the responses related to strengths have been included in this final chapter.

Connecting with Loved Ones

During this research there were many participants who were grieving from prematurely losing a loved one. Many had shared that prior to seeing a medium they were still asking questions about the cause of death and status of their loved ones: Where are they exactly? I am wondering why dimes are showing up everywhere. Is that possibly Grandma? Are they at peace? All of these questions and feelings remain with many of us. I cannot say *all* of us. Some of the sitters indicated that they had limited need to connect with their loved ones in spirit as they felt the departed should be left alone to rest in peace. In some cases the sitters had no great need to communicate with loved ones in spirit as they were comforted by the belief that any suffering and ill-effects as a result of aging were no longer being experienced in the afterlife.

Connecting with loved ones who have prematurely died can be tremendously beneficial. In the research of *Medium7* I interviewed grieving widows, widowers, parents who prematurely lost their children, and children still grieving the loss of their parents. When these research participants heard evidence that substantiated the existence of their loved ones in spirit, they expressed relief that they were safe and comfortable. For some sitters after they heard these messages, the emotional pain was reduced just enough for them to continue on with their lives. Participants expressed renewed hope for a brighter future and seemed to have a greater understanding of why their loved ones needed to depart from the physical plane. Many parents are relieved to learn that there was nothing they could do to prevent the death of a loved one. They learned that it was simply time for their child to go. For those who had carried guilt about not giving unconditional love to the departed during their time on earth, they were usually relieved of their guilt when the medium conveyed messages that their loved ones no longer carried any grievances.

I can also remember witnessing an older man named Vincent break down after he learned that his mother in spirit admitted that she was abusive toward him all his life. This confession caused tears of joy. During the interview with Vincent he explained that he had been abused by his mother all of his life and had suffered low self-esteem and depression as a result of this abuse. Vincent shared that this revelation by his mother via the medium validated her malevolent behavior and allowed him to let go of the belief that he was the cause for her abusive behavior.

Knowing that loved ones who have passed on are still *with us* provides a comfort that cannot be experienced from any other source. Mediums are able to provide details about how discarnates directly communicate with loved ones on the earth plane. For example, Judy could never understand why small pieces of chips were randomly found in her home. They did not eat chips, but every now and then she would hear *crunch*, and when she would look to see what she stepped on, there would be crushed chips on the carpet or floor in her home. She never thought much of it until a medium shared that her father, who was now in spirit, would deliberately send crunchy food items for Judy to step on. Without this message Judy would not have linked the random crunchy food items with her father. After she had this knowledge, she felt a warm feeling, knowing that her father was with her every time she would step on a crunchy food item in her home.

Death Is Pain-Free

Mankind has been socialized to believe that death is a painful experience. It is not surprising that we have and maintain this perception as humans frequently experience emotional and physical pain. Messages conveyed via mediums suggest otherwise. There are countless stories shared in this research from sitters who heard that their family and friends did not feel pain when they transitioned between the physical (from death) and spiritual realms (to the afterlife). Discarnates who died from suicide, tragic accidents, or chronic illnesses felt no pain once they disrobed from their physical bodies. NDErs often report enjoying the freedom during their transition to the spiritual world. They feel light and almost weightless; they express relief from the ailments or pain they were experiencing when they were *living* in their physical forms. All souls have transitioned out of the physical body prior to feeling any mental or physical pain. Many of these souls share messages in the afterlife that the attraction to the white light is so natural, warm, and inviting. This is an encouraging thought for mankind that death, an event associated with much discomfort, could be the start of a journey back to a comforting place.

When people accumulate experiential knowledge that the afterlife truly exists, any fear of death is significantly reduced. Without this personal experience fear is a natural reaction to the unknown notion of death, especially if you believe in certain religious or philosophical perspectives that perpetuate the view that a person lives one life that ultimately results in an infinite existence in heaven or hell. This perspective would make anyone fearful, especially if the prerequisite behaviors regarding entrance to heaven and hell seem to be subjective and variable depending on the doctrine. If it is true that fear opens the door to negativity, greed, selfishness, despondency, and all sentiments that create feelings of lack, then endorsing a philosophy that brings hope would be of greater benefit to mankind.

To further explore the notion of being free of pain while still being in the physical body, attempt to meditate while you are experiencing any form of physical pain. If you are meditating appropriately by focusing on the breath and allowing your soul to vibrate at a higher level, you will eventually not feel any pain associated with the physical body during the height of the meditation. When your soul vibrates at relatively high levels, you are entering realms that extend beyond your physical body. This change of consciousness is responsible for your ability to liberate yourself from the pain, heavy weight, and limitations of the physical body.

As a result of having access to information shared by sitters, mediums, NDERs, and patients of hypnotherapy, we can confirm that we have limited perceptions of reality during our souls' presence in physical bodies. Once released from the physical form, experiences like pain are no longer perceivable. Many scholars studying oneirology (the formal word for the study of dreams) hypothesize that during the sleep state the soul releases itself from the body and travels in other planes of existence. One theory is that the soul needs to be released from the body to facilitate healing. The soul has infinite energy and can attain its lessons on a continuous basis, but the physical body needs downtime to heal and regenerate itself. You may have noticed that after a good night's sleep your mind and body feels refreshed.

They Lead Active Lives beyond the Death of their Physical Bodies

After reviewing results from the *Medium7* study and other literature validating the soul's immortality, although there are repeated references to death being pain-free, I must be honest. I am still somewhat uncertain about what immortality feels like. I think our collective investigations regarding the afterlife have reduced fear to a certain degree by demonstrating that our consciousness does continue; however, we need to do more work on describing what this transition feels like. I can remember the early days of my research when I would excitedly share my discoveries with my husband. He would politely assert, "Let's deal with the here and now and worry about the future or even death when it comes!" His philosophy actually sounds a lot like Eckhart Tolle's messages in his book, *The Power of Now*, which is a useful philosophy to live by. My husband would also ask, "But don't these mediums share any information about what the eternal life is like? Do they provide evidence regarding the physical experience during the transition period from death to the afterlife? What are these spirits doing up *there* exactly?" As I absorbed these comments, I must admit that while I was busy trying to determine if life after death truly did exist, I felt that these questions could not be seriously considered until there was more agreement amongst scholars and the public that the evidence accumulated was strong enough to substantiate the soul's immortality and its future destination.

Now that mankind has evolved and has enough lines of evidence that prove the soul is immortal, I do think that identifying the nature and activities of the soul during various states of consciousness beyond the physical plane would reduce any residual fear or anxieties about what the afterlife is like. Mediums do indeed provide a few insights into the nature of the afterlife during their readings with clients. Typical messages from discarnates suggest that our loved ones are busy both advancing their spiritual lessons and experiencing activities very similar to the ones we might engage in here on earth. Some are preparing for future lifetimes or preparing to help guide selected individuals on the earth plane.

In his book titled, *Destiny of Souls: New Case Studies of Life Between Lives*, Dr. Michael Newton[69] uses past-life regression techniques and records his patients' accounts of their activities in the spirit world. One of his patients shared an account of activities that took place in various geometric shapes; each of which represent a variety of energy systems. A partial list is shared as follows:

- Pyramids are for solitude, meditation and healing.
- Rectangular shapes are for past life reviews.
- Spheroids are used to examine future lives.
- Cylinder portals are for traveling to other worlds to gain perspective.

This account suggests that entities in the spirit world lead active lives. This is further evidence that can provide mankind with hope that life beyond death can be fulfilling and adventurous.

In the extraordinary book on the nature of reality titled *Seth*

Speaks, as shared earlier in this book, a discarnate or an evolved entity in the spirit world was responsible for the development and content of the concepts shared. He starts off his revolutionary book, by stating, "I do not have a physical body, and yet I will be writing a book." So indeed, we have evidence that Seth, an entity experiencing consciousness in another plane of existence, was actively co-creating with Roberts to write a book.

Areas of study that involve past-life regression therapy are most effective in learning about possible activities taking place in spiritual realms beyond the physical plane. When hypnotherapists ask their patients to describe the transition from death to the spiritual world, the patients have mentioned meeting masters (*groups of entities*) and other discarnates while under hypnosis and will make reference to participating in a variety of activities in spiritual realms.

Researchers have invested more time in proving the existence of an afterlife; however, once we have satisfied ourselves in this regard, the focus on describing the transition from death to the afterlife and details about the day-to-day activities should be further explored in a systematic manner to develop a more comprehensive picture of possible activities occurring in the various planes of existences.

Understanding Life Events: Why Do Bad Things Happen?

When we have an opportunity to examine spirit communication and the nature of predictions more closely, we realize that the universe encompasses many more elements that we simply cannot see. In chapter 7 we reviewed the concepts of reincarnation and karma and even touched on the nature of subatomic particles. Understanding these concepts helped us see that there was really more to this world than what we perceived through our five senses. Some of you may have experienced déjà vu (a French word that means *already seen*) or have had a deep sense that some of the experiences in your lives are orchestrated by unseen forces. Now that we have had some experience with Wi-Fi, many of you now understand that forces can indeed exist without them being seen or heard.

If the concepts of reincarnation, karma, and other aspects related to the *unseen* world make sense to you, it is possible that you might alter your mental disposition and general behaviors during your time on earth. For example, if you believe that you embody various bodies in different lifetimes to learn lessons, perhaps the difficult lessons that you are currently enduring may seem tolerable.

I attended a church service where the reverend preaching the sermon that day shared a story that explained how understanding the *larger picture* helps families cope with the premature death of children. She shared the story of a ten year old boy who was the most generous lad, sharing his time and heart with everyone at school and in his community. This young boy had prematurely died at the age of ten. The medium visiting the site of death said that there were angels still gathering around the spot and all she could feel in the area was love, warmth, and peace. The medium conducted a reading for the grieving parents where the young lad came through sharing information with the medium that he had only planned on staying on the earth plane for a short time. His mission on earth was to understand the feelings of pain, anger, and resentment so he could elaborate on these feelings with his fellow angels in the spirit world. He explained that he was able to tell his fellow angels about the growing sadness on the earth plane and that this would enable more angels to help mankind. After the medium shared this message, the parents began to cry. The medium thought the parents were crying as a result of being touched about learning that their son's consciousness was still present in the spirit world. To the medium's surprise, the parents left the room and returned with a picture of their deceased son taken the day before he passed away. When the medium looked closer, she saw the picture of the boy and noticed the angel wings protruding from his back. Apparently in this picture, the boy's angel wings were visible to everyone although they were not sure why these wings were present. The parents shared that the medium's messages about the purpose of their son's death combined with the picture validated the purpose of this premature death. Their son was an angel that had come forth for a short period to gain a better understanding of the challenges being experienced on the earth plane. This premature death was a painful sacrifice for a greater good.

Their understanding that there was a larger mission behind his birth and death made it possible for them to continue living their lives with hope and pride, especially now that they were sure that they had given birth to an angel who would be working with other angels to bring joy and peace to the earth plane.

As you consider this story, consider the challenges in your own life and trust that there is a greater purpose at hand.

Receiving Guidance

In addition to connecting with past loved ones, sitters visit mediums to obtain guidance on their current life. Sitters who have obtained evidence that the medium has contacted a deceased loved one will have confidence that the medium is adequately developed enough to obtain guidance from spirit guides, angels, and higher evolved entities. As shared in earlier chapters, once the medium has been able to validate facts beyond chance, there is a belief that subsequent information is also valid. Spirit guides, angels, and higher evolved entities, given their levels of evolution, have a greater perspective on the potential paths that might be considered by the sitter. This type of guidance is useful when the client is distressed or is too close to the problem, making it difficult to step back and make informed decisions. In fact, everyone has access to this information as well but may have difficulty seeing clearly because of the confusion of daily activities and the emphasis on looking to the external world for answers. Given what we learned in previous chapters about personal responsibility in decision making and the probability of predictions, guidance from evolved spirit entities should be considered, not necessarily acted on.

Remember that our deceased loved ones and spirit have a higher level view of the choices that you are considering. Their high-level view allows them to be more objective and rational, which is a perspective that is always useful when one is making decisions. We often make decisions based on finances and pleasure—elements that are transitory in nature and usually do not lead to long-term advancements of the soul. Deepak Chopra's book, *Life After Death: The Burden of Proof*[70] provides a useful analogy by using Hindu mythical characters to explain why mankind has challenges in seeing the soul and the pure path to peace and abundance. Chopra explains that when the mind is constantly active and creating confusion, it is like a muddy pond. If the pond is full of murky water, we cannot clearly see the reflection of the sunlight. If the pond is clear—reflecting a mind at peace and full of calm—the sun can be clearly seen shining within the pond. This analogy suggests that the sun (or our higher self) is always there. We are just not able to see it as a result of being distracted with the overload of daily activities.

This is also why those who meditate are also able to access their inner self and can obtain guidance directly from the *source*. For those of you who read John Edward's books, despite his notoriety as a talented medium, he transparently says, "People don't need me for a reading. They can actually look within themselves, which will subsequently create greater access to loved ones and other discarnates in the spirit world."

With that being said, using meditation and other techniques to access the soul and discarnates is easier said than done. It takes tremendous discipline to be still and focus on your breath for at least twenty minutes a day. For those of us living in the real world, even with meditation and strategies to help *silence* brain activity, we are still bombarded with social conditioning and external pressures that make it difficult to make informed decisions without seeking external support. Given the fact that most of us face the daily grind, I would conclude that seeing a medium to gain a different perspective can help validate or qualify thoughts and decisions you are considering. In answering the *so what* question, I would say that I have witnessed hundreds of people benefit from guidance from a medium in the areas of emotional and physical health, finances, careers, and relationships. Let's review a few examples of how these messages were beneficial.

Health

I provided cases in this book where the medium predicted the cancer which allowed the sitter to make the necessary medical arrangements to have the cancer removed. In one case the sitter saved time by seeing the doctor long before it began to spread. In the second case although she knew about the breast cancer, she was emotionally paralyzed and was not willing to move forward with the surgery. Her motivation to finally have the surgery occurred immediately after the medium assured her that the surgery would be successful. You will also recall the case of the medium in the church who saved a woman from returning home to her violent husband. In this case the medium saved this woman's life and guided her to a shelter where she and her child would be safe.

Another case that stands out for me is the case with mold in the house. One of the mediums in my research thought she was conducting a phone reading for a mother who was seeking consultation about a career choice. This had been the focus of the reading until the medium started to perceive unpleasant tastes in her mouth. While the medium attempted to continue with the reading, she became overwhelmed with a feeling of illness and began to see visions of unsightly mold in the lady's home. The medium politely interrupted and asked if she lived in a home that could have mold. When the sitter responded with a puzzled voice, she began to describe the colors and sections of the home. The medium also began to sense her son-in-law in the home and asked whether she had a son-in-law living in the home. Despite silence on the other end of the phone, the medium began to clearly hear from her spirit guide that there was danger in the home. Immediately the medium considered the staunch smell (via clairalience), visions of the mold (via clairvoyance), and the message from the spirit guide and strongly recommended that the house be checked for mold. The sitter would not have been inclined to check the house for mold; however, she knew the house was old and had always wondered if her son-in-law's frequent allergies and asthma attacks were related to *something* in the home.

This medium received a call several months later, letting her know that the sitter did follow through with the recommendation to have the house assessed for mold. Indeed, the house was full of a toxic mold that was triggering her son-in-law's excessive allergies and asthma attacks. The sitter thanked her profusely for this information mostly because her son-in-law's allergy and asthma problems had reduced significantly. More important, the newborn expected in the house may have suffered from the mold if it had not been removed.

Medical intuitives will always recommend that the sitter seek the advice of a professional medical practitioner. Mediumship is not a replacement for traditional medicine. In my case I had one reading with a medium I call the "human X-ray" as he is able to see current and potential ailments entering the body. I can recall one reading where he said that he had scanned all areas and indicated that I was healthy. I must admit that this information was reassuring. He went on to indicate that I should have my thyroid gland checked and suggested that my fluctuating energy levels may be related to my thyroid. He also shared that he could see some potential energy loss in the right shoulder and lower back areas. At the time of the reading I had no problems with any of these areas.

Given his success with reading others and his ability to validate other facts, I did ask my doctor during my annual visit to check my thyroid using a blood test. I also thought there was a possibility of this being an area of concern as another medium on a different occasion suggested that I should have my thyroid checked. The doctor added this *check mark* on the blood workup, and during a follow-up visit I found out that I had no problems with my thyroid. I have had another annual checkup, and according to the blood work this area still appeared to be functioning normally. I have provided this example as I want to emphasize that the messages are to be used in conjunction with medical advice and your own decisions. It is interesting to note that while the thyroid-related message did not *seem* to be accurate, the guiding message about my right shoulder and my back were absolutely correct. Approximately six months after I received these messages from the medium I began to experience lower back problems that would spontaneously spasm for two weeks and return to normal. Approximately a year after that reading I began to have a chronic shoulder problem—later diagnosed as calcification issues. I experienced these problems in the right shoulder—the same shoulder identified by the medical intuitive. One could say that my learning of this information from the medium contributed to the health problem; however, I never thought once about these health-related premonitions, so I cannot see how my thoughts might have contributed to the manifestation of these ailments. In my case two of the three ailments have materialized, and I continue to take the necessary precautions regarding thyroid testing at each annual doctor's checkup.

So what? The *so what* is that some people have experienced benefits from the diagnosis of health problems conveyed via mediumship. The lady who decided to take the surgery to remove her breast cancer or the medium's warning of the mold in the home produced benefits that might have been fatal if it were not for the timely messages shared by the mediums.

Finances

Responding to the *so what* question is difficult in relation to finances. The reason it is difficult is that the purpose of the soul advancing is a different goal from advancing one's bank account. This is not to suggest that accumulating wealth is an evil pursuit, although in my observations with readings from a medium, messages related to finances indicate that the pursuit of financial wealth is not really the priority. I have heard people frequently question, "If mediums are so good, why can't they just tell us the lottery numbers?" The question about the winning lottery numbers is a valid one if you are not fully apprised about the purpose of mediumship. When Faith, a medium in this research study, first started practising her mediumship, she was able to predict the winning racehorses. She and her husband were elated. They kept this a personal secret until her friend had other ideas of how to use her gift. He suggested that they share this special gift with the public. The first time Faith attempted to provide this information in exchange for financial compensation, she did not obtain the information at all. In fact, the very thought of using her psychic gifts for financial gain on a large scale shut the gift off. Faith has never been able to access that element of her gift again. This is not the first time I have heard of these types of consequences when financial gain was involved. If we refer back to the chapter about reincarnation, we saw how converging evidence suggests that the soul incarnates to learn various spiritual lessons and evolves with the hope of reaching a higher level of purity. A soul that has a focus on financial gain is not likely to achieve the its goals, especially if the life lessons relate to humility, patience, love, greed, and other typical soul lessons. In fact, a focus on financial gain can be contrary to learning this lesson. Any motivation that stints the soul's growth is not contributing to the greater good of humankind.

So how did I respond to the businessman that was sitting next to me on the plane who said, "So what can these spiritual experiences do for me when I am trying to land a deal in the boardroom?" I indicated that in my experience spirit does not help you *directly* augment your bank account. These spiritual messages from a medium, experiences during an NDE, or knowledge gained during hypnotherapy in a past-life regression therapy are devised to help you understand your soul (the self). Achieving this greater understanding allows you to achieve abundance, otherwise known as inner wealth in your life. This abundance far exceeds material wealth. I know that we live in a material world where it is very difficult to believe that financial wealth does not provide the optimal state of happiness. You only need to watch a few reality shows of the rich and famous to realize that these people are not exactly happy campers despite their exorbitant wealth. Some are in a vortex of relationship problems, spending addictions, and delusions about the appearance of excessive plastic surgery. True abundance is about feeling peace, achieving your desires with ease, and feeling joy and fulfillment with life. Maintaining this feeling cannot be permanently achieved by the accumulation of financial wealth, but it can be achieved by going within, learning life's lessons, and making peace with life's challenges. I cannot say if this response to my fellow travel mate was adequate as the short flight disrupted our conversation.

I can conclude, however, that the spiritual messages often conveyed via a medium are important for the soul's inner wealth, which is of greater importance than financial wealth.

Career Advice

The sitters in the present study provided many examples that helped address concerns they were experiencing regarding their careers. The following are messages shared by mediums to guide and help their clients cope in the workplace:

- The challenges you are learning in the workplace are helping you with your life lessons.

- The interactions you are having at the workplace are important. You are seeking a life of inner peace but cannot achieve this without appropriately managing the power dynamics and greed that permeates the work environment. You are needed in the workplace to teach integrity to people who are still focused on materialism, including goals related to acquiring posts with greater status or higher salaries.

- You need to be more grateful for what the workplace is teaching you. I see that your organization has provided you with technical skills. Did you go to Europe to learn a new type of technology? I see that this new skill will be of great value in the next few years.

In this latter excerpt, Craig was offered a short-term opportunity where his company paid for half of the educational opportunity to learn a new software program in Sweden. This validation about his career was encouraging.

Jason's story about his career was the most outstanding. He explained that he was doing everything possible to obtain a promotion at the workplace. He was the most outstanding on the team. He brought recognition to the team and often acted as the leader when the CEO was not present. In fact, he developed a patent that brought the company recognition. After he had worked five years in the company, he was not able to be promoted and began to feel resentment when other less qualified staff moved into higher positions. Jason shared that his strategy was to focus on getting another job where he could achieve his full capacity. In fact, although Jason enjoyed his job, every attempt to work in a position that would allow him to exercise his leadership skills was always thwarted. During a reading with a medium Jason was asked, "Are you involved with boats? I see you building boats and being really very talented with this craft." Jason was excited to hear this validation and nodded to confirm the medium's vision. She explained that Jason's sister, who had just recently passed in a car accident, shared a message that the doors were deliberately closing in his daytime job to help him be motivated about a future business that would be most fulfilling for him. Jason often dreamed of opening up a business building state-of-the-art boats. He had the skills and a bit of money that could help him launch this business. He put these thoughts to an abrupt halt as he was the primary breadwinner in the family with young sons and a third child on the way. He would have to do the responsible thing and stay in his stifling daytime job and delay owning and operating his dream business. How did this information shared by the medium help Jason? In Jason's interview, he explained that the reading validated that he could indeed have a business and that this was encouraging. Jason shared in his interview that he could tolerate working at his current job as long as he knew that he would one day own his own business. Jason has worked feverishly to build the foundation for his business and aims to make gradual plans to operate his boating business full-time within the next five years. Jason explained that he had more courage to build this new business and could endure the challenges at work now that he had hope and validation from his deceased sister via the medium.

Relationships

There were many research participants who shared messages about relationships. It turns out that although we think our careers, finances, and health are priorities, relationships are really the highest priority. When we go to work to attain goals and be productive, we are also working on managing our relationships with people. We are *always* trying to manage the dynamics with people at work. My theory is that we actually go to work to learn how to work collaboratively with others.

Unfortunately I have not heard many people share that they are *happy campers* in the workplace. For the most part, I hear many stories about people struggling to overpower each other, outwit one another, and undermine others. People are either the controllers or are being controlled. It seems to me that the workplace is the toughest environment for mankind—the university with tough graduate courses—where we learn strategies to cope, enhance resiliency, learn patience, gain humility, and learn respect.

I reviewed several statements during this research about parent-child relationships, adult relations, and romantic issues. I found a number of stories where sitters gained a new perspective about a challenging relationship via a medium's message. Gaining a new perspective allows people to see the true motivation of their alleged *enemy*. When one person has a better understanding of the true cause of the problem, he or she may see that there was never an intention to deliberately cause harm and pain. The following case studies provide a demonstration of how mediums were able to provide information that brought greater understanding, healing, and hope in their respective relationships.

The Estranged Mother and Daughter

Cindy was only attending the reading with a medium to provide her sister-in-law with support. She did not expect the medium to read her as well and was quite surprised when the medium shared that Cindy's grandmother Tessie was present. The medium asked, "Does anyone here have a grandmother in spirit named ... um, sounds like Tess ... um, with another syllable." The room was silent as the medium attempted to get clarification. "I am still hearing Tess. Is that someone's nickname?" Cindy hesitantly responded and said that her grandmother's formal name was Tessie but close family members called her Tess.

Once the medium was able to verify that the discarnate was indeed someone at least one of the sitters knew, he revealed that Tess had a message. Tess shared that it was clear that Cindy and her mother, Beth, had an estranged relationship for several years. Cindy and Beth enjoyed a tolerable relationship, but Beth felt that

Cindy had little time for her, and Cindy felt that her mother was too controlling and despondent. During the reading the medium shared that Cindy needed to be more tolerant of her mother. She explained that Beth had brain chemistry challenges that did not allow her to compute events normally. Unfortunately this seemed to make it challenging for Beth to perceive anything in a positive manner. The medium had suggested that Cindy be more tolerant of her mother and cover herself with the white light of God's love and protection to decrease the effects of the negative energy that was distilled from Beth during their interactions. This latter technique would decrease the negative impacts while it allowed Cindy to enjoy a respectful and loving relationship with her mother.

Cindy was quite moved by the information Tess shared through the medium. She was quite sure that the medium had described her mother's precise characteristics and was even more impressed that the medium was able to offer this plausible explanation. The insights provided about the brain structure allowed Cindy to have a better understanding of the possible reason for her mother's unhappy disposition. It made the insults and undermining behavior more tolerable. The guidance also prevented unnecessary arguments that usually erupted when Cindy could no longer tolerate Beth's undermining comments. Cindy would simply learn to ignore them. This practice became easier as the white light visualization strategy seemed to block the absorption of the toxic energies. All of the insights, strategies, and general guidance provided by the medium was important in helping Cindy and Beth maintain a positive relationship. This was a better option than enduring sorrow and experiencing the disintegration of a relationship that would impact the whole family, including Cindy's three children.

Brothers

Carry was groomed to be a medical doctor. His father was a general physician, and his mother was a prominent gynecologist.

Carry was interested in the medical field but was not able to grasp the concepts necessary to meet the technical requirements for entry into medical school. Carry often thought that it might have been his mental attitude that deterred him from being interested in becoming a doctor. He secretly worried about having the responsibility of others' lives and wondered if he unconsciously sabotaged his entrance into medical school. Carry turned out to be a great nurse. This position was suitable for Carry as he enjoyed working in the medical field but was comfortable knowing that the doctors would have the ultimate responsibility if there were unintended medical consequences. He was absolved of all responsibility.

Carry went to see a medium primarily to relieve his curiosity about the spirit world. He received a message from a contemporary friend he lost while he was at university. This friend, now in spirit, shared that his brother was no longer speaking with him as a result of the profession he chose. The medium had explained that the brother was ashamed that he in some way tarnished the family's reputation. The medium shared that the spirit world was proud of his choice as this is what he was comfortable with and also commended him on the accomplishments he had achieved by comforting the aged during their late years. Carry shared in his interview for this research that he was awestruck by this information. He had started working as a nurse four years ago, and one year later his brother, Darren, and his family had stopped attending family events where he would be present. Carry noticed that Darren failed to respond to phone calls or e-mails, which made it clear that Darren was no longer interested in maintaining any type of relationship. As a result of Carry's busy lifestyle he never stopped to analyze the problem but now had an important insight about his brother's absence in his life. The reason provided by Carry's friend in spirit made logical sense; however, Carry reflected on the medium's message and wondered why Darren could not be honest about his feelings toward Carry's profession. Carry did not have a great deal of experience with mediums and reflected carefully about the validity of the communication.

After several days of reflecting on this insight, Carry gathered the courage to have a family meeting with his brother, which unfortunately did not end well. Darren did not attempt to make any excuses for his absence. He explained that he felt Carry did not try hard enough to become a medical doctor. He felt Carry's choice to become a nurse diminished the family's reputation as esteemed physicians. Darren did not apologize for his viewpoint and was openly dismissive of anything Carry attempted to share during their meeting.

In this case the insights shared by the medium gave Carry the courage to face his family and share his reasons for becoming a nurse. At the time of the interview, in the *Medium7* study, Carry and Darren still had an estranged relationship. The guidance provided by the medium in Carry's estimation allowed him to have an understanding of what was bothering his brother. This understanding subsequently allowed Carry to share the truth with his family, which subsequently led to a greater understanding that Darren would have to come to terms with this problem in his own time.

While all did not seem to end well for Carry and Darren, Carry's enhanced understanding has allowed him to move forward on his journey without the emotional upheaval that resulted each time Darren rebuffed Carry's invitations to connect. Carry has moved forward temporarily without his brother.

Husband and Wife

Diana and Mark had been high school sweethearts. Diana had often felt that she had known Mark in *past* lifetimes but could not explain her feelings. After twenty-eight years of marriage their lives were filled with laughter, joy, and three wonderful children. Diana had sought the services of a medium mostly to find out about her career and to gain insights and potential guidance about her marriage. Diana was familiar with mediums, and despite already knowing about the favorable reputation of the medium she met with, she made every attempt not to share any personal information that could bias the reading. She wanted to be sure that the forthcoming information from the medium was coming from more evolved spirits or a specific loved one (discarnate).

In the research for *Medium7* Diana explained during her interview that her deceased grandmother came through during the reading and provided astounding reasons for some of the problems in her marriage. The medium was somewhat tentative and embarrassed before she shared the information. In fact, Diana remembers the medium reminding Diana, "These are not my words. I am just the channel for spirit to communicate the message." The medium went on to share the message that Mark had become sexually challenged over the past three years. The medium also encouraged Diana to focus on the relevant dream that she had right after Mark's problem started. This dream had been quite vivid and seemed to validate everything the medium shared about Mark's physical limitations.

Diana explained in the interview that at the time of hearing this message from the medium she would never have believed she would have the courage to share this story for research purposes. Diana returned home after the reading with the medium, and she hastily went through her dream journals as she did recall having a vivid dream about Mark. After several hours of searching she finally found the notes she wrote about the dream. She shared the following original dream journal notes below:

> I remember being so happy to finally find some quiet time to be with Mark. We were in our bedroom, kissing and caressing each other. The dream seemed very real as my emotions were heightened, and I could feel Mark's love and sexual excitement. I could see a visual of Mark's beautiful

body. I looked at his gorgeous face and his chest muscles—but when I saw the groin area—the dream turned from pure bliss to horror. Mark's genitals had been physically castrated. I was horrified and remembered feeling aghast. I woke up with a feeling of complete shock and dismay. I wondered why I would see Mark like this and was relieved that it was only a dream.

Diana shared that this reading provided insight into Mark's physical status. For the last three years Mark had stopped initiating any sexual activity. It was an abrupt change that made her wonder if Mark had been having a sexual affair with another woman. Diana had confronted Mark with this allegation a year ago, and this discussion further diminished any communication. By the time Diana had met with the medium Mark and Diana were in separate rooms and only spoke when it was necessary. The medium's insights about Mark's sexual limitations were also validated by Diana's dream. In fact, she had received the message very vividly in the dream but did not link the dream to Mark's aberrant behavior. She now realizes that the aghast feelings in her dreams were reflective of how she truly felt about Mark's shocking physical change.

Diana found it very difficult to confront Mark about what she had learned. She explained to Mark that she intuitively felt that he might be having some physical challenges, and after a few weeks of starting this discussion Mark shared that he had been secretly seeking medical advice over the past three years to address his sudden impotency. He explained how devastated he had been at his body's inability to respond adequately to the prescribed medications. He felt like a failure and was afraid of losing Diana and further explained that his only solution was to retreat.

In this case we see another benefit attained from the spirit world. A beautiful marriage was almost destroyed because a temporary physical limitation created a disruption in the relationship between Mark and Diana. The medium's insights about the cause of the problem and the validation about the dream's message resulted in Diana's courage to initiate a difficult discussion. Diana no longer felt rejected and was relieved to learn that Mark still loved her but could just not show his love physically. This discussion started the healing process, and Mark and Diana continue to work together to sustain their successful marriage.

So What?

In an effort to respond to the *so what* question, I have provided these testimonies about career, finance, health, relationships, and about the benefits of connecting with loved ones in the spirit world. In the cases shared in this chapter lives were saved, motivations reenergized, hope restored, grief diminished, positive emotions restored, relationships strengthened, and lessons for spiritual progress were learned. These experiences reinforce the importance of recognizing the spirit world's ability to guide and protect during our journey here on the earth plane.

In the final chapter it is important that we reflect and summarize how exactly mediums can provide answers about the nature of our universe. Utilizing messages from the spirit world to enhance our experience of the *here and now* is of great benefit, but it is also important to reflect on how these insights enhance our knowledge about the true nature of reality. We turn our focus to this subject in the final chapter.

WHAT HAVE WE LEARNED ABOUT THE NATURE OF REALITY?

*Y*ou will recall from the introductory chapter of this book that one of the key reasons for conducting an examination with psychic mediums was to gather further insights into the *real* nature of reality. If I were using a spaceship to go to the moon, it would be remiss of me to *just* examine and report on the spaceship (the vehicle used to reach the moon). If I were to go into detail about the furnishings inside the ship and discuss the experiences and mechanics of the spaceship but fail to elaborate on what I learned about the moon, an observer might conclude that the spaceship excursion was limited and somewhat anticlimactic. In this book we spent a good bit of time exploring the mechanics of mediumship, the nature of predictions, and afterlife evidence generated by mediums (*the vehicle*), but now it is important to review and clearly outline how mediumship has enhanced our understanding of what comprises the universe; our ultimate goal for this examination. Such an understanding creates important implications for our current and future existence.

Now I know there are some of you reading this book that fall into the group that just want to know what the medium can do for them right now. You are the camp that might be asking the question, "Mediums, what guidance can spirits provide to help me with the daily grind?" Then there is another camp that is saying, "So what?" For those of you sitting in those camps, I invite you to go beyond these parameters and even momentarily join the camp that says, "Well, what does that tell us about the world we live in?" Ask yourself, "Is our world limited to only the physical world we see? Is space and time just a perception experienced by mankind inhabiting the earth plane? Does the world emerge from a set of random events that place us in a limited reactive position?"

In this chapter I invite you to look beyond these limited perspectives and learn why an understanding of your *real* environment is important. The material in this final chapter summarizes how mediumship and other afterlife studies provide insights about the nature of our true environment. What emerged from the *Medium7* study were six lessons that we will explore. Some aspects of these lessons are new information, and other facets provide further confirmation of already existing beliefs about properties of the universe.

What Are the Consequences of Being Unaware?

Before we start this, I want to provide an analogy of what illusions we face when we are only aware of the physical realm of this universe. Imagine for a moment that you are a librarian and your universe consists of the library, the cataloging protocol for the library, and your staff. You are aware that your library exists within a university, but you rarely interact with members of the university, although you understand that the students who attend the educational institution are interested in your books to help them receive their certifications. In this universe you are not aware that other universities and libraries exist. You are also not aware that the public, including students attending your university, have access to books through other means. In your universe for some odd reason you are blind to the knowledge of the Internet. This system allows people to search for books, download information electronically, and purchase books online. In your reality you are only aware of books that are in a hard-print format. These can only be borrowed and returned to a library. As the person responsible for making decisions about the library's operations, your limited knowledge in *this* universe does not allow you to take advantage of all of the available materials online. Your purchasing, planning, and distribution activities are limited without the knowledge of these other systems.

Now I know it is hard for us to imagine anyone operating without knowledge regarding the existence of the World Wide Web; however, I use this analogy to exemplify how debilitating and misleading it can be to be unaware of these other systems and activities beyond our limited physical experience.

Now that we are convinced about the importance of being aware, let's turn to the six key lessons we learned from the mediums through their messages conveyed from the spirit world.

Lesson #1: Dead People Still Exist, and Mediums Can Talk to Them

Now that we have the results of eighty-eight participants who shared their experiences in the research for *Medium7*, the statement about *talking to the dead* may no longer seem so bizarre or controversial. Prior to reviewing the results of studies using mediums, we were like the librarian in the example noted above. We were only aware of our physical surroundings and thought that communication with only the *living* was possible. In fact, we also believed that once someone's heart stopped beating and the brain was no longer functioning, his or her soul, personality, memory, feelings, perceptions, and any lifelike characteristics would perish. Without the gifts of mediums we would have to rely on NDEs or past-life regression therapy to provide insights about the afterlife; however, due to the nature of these experiences, these are not readily accessible to everyone. Without the evidence obtained as a result of implementing rigorous afterlife studies, most of us would be like the librarian using antiquated and inefficient methods to purchase, catalogue, and distribute books. Such limited methods lead to a reduced opportunity for us to garner the resources needed to thrive in this physical plane of existence.

The nature of reality is no longer based on the belief that we live one life and die. It is not based on the belief that consciousness is conditional on the functioning of the brain and other parts of the physical body. We know from this study and other literature that consciousness or the ability to perceive reality is outside of the physical body. This fact is demonstrated repeatedly when mediums communicate with discarnates who were once living agents on the physical plane known as earth.

How might you live your life knowing that this really is not the last time you will be on the physical plane? What risks might you take knowing that beyond your physical death you will have opportunity to progress and experience all of the activities you have always dreamed about? Perhaps there will be less fear and less inhibition to take some risks. Now that you have an understanding that you have unlimited opportunities to address mistakes and take the risks required to live your dreams, you may live your life with less fear and less burden. There is hope in knowing that you will experience many opportunities to learn lessons in various lifetimes. Liberate yourself with this knowledge, embrace the learning, reconcile relationships, and live your dreams.

Lesson #2: Time Is a Three-Dimensional Concept.[71] It's Only Real for Us in the Physical Form

In the physical form we perceive time to be absolute. There is the notion that five minutes is experienced in the same manner by everyone. As we reviewed in this book, time is a perception limited to those of us in the physical form living in a world of three-dimensional concepts. Instead of reading about this in complicated metaphysical literature, we can learn more about this concept after we carefully review the messages shared by sitters after their readings with mediums and from the results in other afterlife studies.

In research with NDErs we read about how patients perceived space once their souls were released from their physical bodies. The past, present, and future all seemed to be simultaneously occurring and were not being experienced in a linear format. Patients participating in past-life regression therapy with the assistance of a hypnotherapist could experience various lifetimes within a short one-hour session. While undergoing this therapy, one could experience various lifetimes in different geographical locations and time periods further suggesting that the past, present, and future may be occurring simultaneously.

While you are in the physical form, it is very difficult to perceive a reality that could operate efficiently without the use of time. In our reality time helps maintain order, but it also augments anxiety as we seem to always be racing against time. Perhaps in the physical reality, the perception of time creates circumstances that increase our opportunities to learn lessons and advance our souls.

In the present study, mediums enhanced our understanding of how time *really* works. You will recall that in chapter 2 a few of the mediums shared how after they shifted consciousness, they were able to enter other states of consciousness where the notion of time no longer existed.

Results produced from the *Medium7* study demonstrated knowledge about *antemortem* facts. These are facts that took place prior to the discarnates passing. Most important, however, is that they were able to demonstrate *narrative knowledge* and *postmortem facts*. The former concept suggests that they can know and share information about what is happening from moment to moment on the earth plane. For example, we read in an earlier chapter where the medium was told that someone close to the sitter would pass at 3:15 p.m., and indeed, when the sitter checked, this was the exact time of passing of his brother-in-law.

What is remarkable about demystifying this aspect of the nature of reality is that there is a prevailing belief that time is different in the spirit world. Many mediums—not just limited to the ones who participated in this study—sometimes tell clients that they cannot place the time of the future occurrences as there is no concept of time in these other planes of existences. While it is true that time is not perceived on these other planes, we know that when spirit feels it is in the client's greater good to put a time on a specified event, they can communicate this if appropriate.

The other notion related to postmortem facts is also important. These types of facts relate to information known after the deceased passes. You will recall the examples shared where mediums convey knowledge about what they are still doing in the afterlife after they have passed. They share information about who they are in the spirit world with, what activities they partake in, and provide guidance based on their understanding of the sitter's current problems. If mediums can share narrative knowledge and postmortem facts, they are demonstrating that the physical and spiritual planes are not distanced by time or space. In fact, the discarnates are working in real time, which further demonstrates that although their existence is not bound by time, they can still perceive and provide guidance and facts using a time-bound paradigm.

Lesson #3: Space Is a Three-Dimensional Concept. It's Only Real for Us in the Physical Form

When you first begin to embark on learning about metaphysics and quantum theory, it is difficult to abandon the traditional teachings regarding space. The challenge is understandable especially when you constantly experience space in a three-dimensional format. You see rooms with walls. You perceive size, and you experience limitations based on what is within your immediate view. In the reports from sitters who met with mediums, many learned that their loved ones were not miles away or residing in the clouds. Mediums gifted with direct clairvoyance would say, "Uncle Bob is standing behind you or on your right side while he is speaking with you." Despite the medium's perception of Bob standing at the same level as the sitter, clients without extrasensory perceptive abilities would not be able to confirm the proximity of the discarnate. The suggestion that spirit guides, angels, and discarnates can exist *right here with us* and are not *over there somewhere far away* is an eye-opener to many.

You will recall that in earlier chapters I shared that the world is made of immaterial stuff. It is simply energy vibrating at different frequencies. The human brain only utilizes 10 percent of its potential to perceive the range of frequencies in the universe, which would explain why we cannot see other planes of existences or their inhabitants using our limited sensory powers. You will recall the example of the dog whistle. These examples demonstrate that some entities (in this case a dog) have different perceptive abilities that allow them to see and hear things that others cannot.

When your levels of vibrational frequencies change, you are able to perceive different realities. NDErs often note the feeling of being able to float freely. They do not perceive the existence of walls, floors, or ceilings. Generally no notion of space exists. During the transition from death the soul begins to vibrate at higher levels of frequency, and this is the reason why so many NDErs were able to report that they saw and sometimes communicated with family and friends who had previously experienced physical death. This change in vibrational frequency allows the soul to experience a sense of infinite space and liberation.

Lesson #4: Different Planes of Existence Are Associated with Different Levels of Spiritual Attainment

Sitters have taught us that there are many different planes of existence, and through their messages from the spirit world, we have also learned that these planes seem to be associated with the spiritual level of attainment reached by the soul. The latter point is most interesting as research participants during their interviews shared that they were surprised that some of their loved ones still demonstrated undesirable behaviors or characteristics. It seems to me that these research participants and others have a belief that upon transitioning to the spiritual world all souls become *saints* and *angels* who demonstrate superlative behaviors. This is not the case.

You often hear people referring to the *other side* as if there was this side (earth) and one other side known as the *spirit world*. In fact, I used this terminology at times throughout this book to achieve simplicity where possible. Sitters and mediums have taught us that there are more than just these two levels of existence. We know that humans and discarnates can vibrate at various different levels. Each vibratory level allows for varying levels of reality and perceptions. We have learned that angels and spirit guides vibrate at different vibratory levels based on their levels of spiritual attainment. We also learned from the *Medium7* study that discarnates also reside in various planes of existence. Again this is associated with their levels of spiritual attainment. You will recall in chapter 2 where some of the mediums and sitters explained that discarnates are still on a journey of continuous learning. Some of the discarnates' messages demonstrated that they learned some of their lessons during their time on the earth plane. For example, some sitters apologized for the pain they caused, some asked for forgiveness and shared that they now had a clearer perspective regarding their behavior during their time on the earth plane. On the other hand, some discarnates shared messages that demonstrated that their levels of understanding and spiritual attainment had not progressed. You will recall an extreme example where *Cousin Bob* in chapter 2, who despite passing on into the spirit world was still drinking heavily at the bar, not demonstrating any change in priorities or spiritual growth.

During the interview phase of *Medium7* many sitters expressed that they were surprised to learn during their readings that their loved ones in the spirit world were still taking courses, learning new activities, and reviewing the bank of information (also known as the Akashic records[72]). The latter activity is one of the tools allowing discarnates to review their activities on the earth plane and assess how they might have behaved in a manner that attained the highest good for all involved.

We learned that once you leave the physical form your soul is still learning lessons. Although it is believed that the earth plane is said to be the most difficult learning ground, discarnates continue to participate in activities that will help them reach higher levels of spiritual attainment. Although the spirit world provides an opportunity for continuous learning, as shared previously, the earth plane is considered to be the *grand* university of learning. We have ample physical restrictions of time, space, and limited knowledge or the lack of discipline required to make sense of the nature of existence beyond the surface. These limitations amplify the challenge of learning difficult lessons, including but not limited to unconditional love, patience, humility, and ego.

I know many of you reading this can relate to this concept of learning difficult lessons on the earth plane. Consider for a moment that you have just finished that great yoga class in the park on a gorgeous spring day. All of your troubles have melted away. You have been working on making a habit of maintaining a consistent schedule of physical workouts to feel good and strengthen your ability to be calm in the face of crisis. The yoga workout you just finished makes you feel that you can even manage to refrain from yelling at your next-door neighbor, who has been creating havoc in the community as a result of his yearlong messy and very noisy renovation. You even decide to jog home after your yoga workout, and despite feeling on top of the world, by the time you reach your home you notice that the garbage men have thrown several pounds of construction waste and debris on your lawn. You try to stay calm until suddenly you trip over several sharp roofing shingles. The *Zen-like* feeling you were having immediately vanishes. You race up to your neighbor's doorstep. Within moments you feel heat move from within the center of your stomach to the tip of your head. Without realizing what's happening you lose control and scream at your neighbor, unleashing hurtful language you had hoped to avoid ever using. What is most disturbing is that several neighbors who observed the event recount this incident repeatedly at the annual barbeque. After this fiasco, you wonder if you will ever learn how to manage life's tough lessons.

Unfortunately this example is typical and frequent. We are calm one moment and then distressed the next, demonstrating the level of challenge we face here on the earth plane.

On this plane of existence, when we don't seem to be communicating effectively with another party, we say, "You must be on a different planet," or, "We are not on the same wavelength." These phrases reflect an understanding that even on the earth plane people are all operating at various levels of spiritual attainment. This would explain why five people all experience the same event but these same five people may have different reactions, interpretations, and impacts because of their levels of perception. This notion of varying levels of consciousness exists in the spiritual world as well.

All of this information demonstrates that there are indeed several planes of existence and spiritual levels of attainment— these various vibratory levels seem to dictate the type of reality you will experience.

Lesson #5: The Concepts of Individual Consciousness and Group Consciousness Are Not Conflicting Concepts.[73]

You will often read debates about individual and group consciousness. The former concept revolves around the notion that after death the soul maintains its individual beliefs, memories, and personality. The notion of group consciousness supports the belief that individual souls merge into one, returning to the alleged original state where souls are all part of one larger entity. This latter concept of group consciousness is often used by scholars who support super-psi hypotheses that sometimes imply that psychic phenomenon, including messages from the spirit world, are derived from a type of *super* consciousness and not from discarnates who were previously residing on the earth plane. Super-psi theory propounds for the most part that information shared through a medium is derived from *living agents or the Akashic records (bank of recorded information)*; not from discarnates who were once residing on the earth plane.

Some scholars have developed elaborate tests to establish the validity of such phenomenon as extrasensory perception (ESP) independent of the involvement of discarnates. ESP may include, but is not limited to, some of the tools used by mediums, including clairvoyance, precognition, telepathy, and remote viewing. Some scholars hypothesize that mediums are using these techniques to extract information from this *group consciousness;* further suggesting that the source of the spiritual messages are not from the deceased.

Of course, this latter concept of group consciousness is not foreign to us. Dr. Carl Jung proposed the concept of a collective unconscious—a notion that would be different from the individual unconscious that allegedly collects personal experiences that remain *recorded* in the soul. The collective unconscious in simplified terms would be the reservoir of all activities and memories experienced by mankind as a whole. Perhaps Jung was referring to the Akashic records, which seems to have a similar function and purpose.

If we return to Dr. Quantum's helpful teaching lessons for those of us who are not quantum physicists, Dr. Quantum explains the theory of entanglement where researchers found some innovative ways to test the reactions of separate subatomic particles. They found that despite these particles being located at great distances from one another, when one moved, the other responded instantly. The experiments support the hypothesis that at a subatomic level everything is connected, including mankind. This notion also supports the concept of a group consciousness.

Scholars more heavily involved in super-psi investigations sometimes claim that if a group consciousness exists and we are all connected, this fact somehow diminishes the validity of survival of death—that is, after we die, our soul transitions to the spirit world.

While the group consciousness theory has been supported by scientific experiments, it is also important to remember that we have observed messages from mediums that provide strong evidence that the medium was *not* obtaining the information from a group consciousness derived from living agents. In many cases the information received was coming from an individual discarnate who was the only one who knew this information.

You may recall the example in chapter 2 where Kelly learned from her deceased father, Arthur, that there was a box with money in her mother's home. Neither Kelly nor her mother knew about this box until they learned the information from Arthur via the medium. This provided further proof that the medium was not reading the minds of anyone on the earth plane. We also heard from sitters who spoke about the awe they felt when the medium shared very specific individual unique characteristics during the reading that mirrored the behaviors of the discarnates. Again this type of evidence does not support the hypothesis that the source of information is derived solely from a group consciousness derived from living agents.

These experiences from mediums and their sitters have taught us that although group consciousness and entanglement does indeed exist, this does not diminish the fact that individual discarnate's memories, beliefs, perceptions, and characteristics *still* survive as well. This fact has been demonstrated through the various types of messages shared in the *Medium7* study.

I have often experienced readings where a medium obtains messages from discarnates and then from a *group entity* (similar to the notion of group consciousness). I can recall my earlier experiences with this. I would ask, "What happened to Grandma Beryl? She was just providing guidance. Is she still providing this guidance, or is someone else?" I would hear the medium express that the group of discarnates in the room were now communicating as one. This made it challenging for me to match the information with a particular discarnate.

After I observed several readings over the years, I have surmised that depending on the vibratory level, the discarnates can communicate as individual discarnates but they can also merge into a group consciousness. Some of the mediums in this study shared that the group consciousness could occur if many discarnates are vibrating on the same level. A more popular hypothesis among the mediums in this study, however, is that when individual discarnates are highly evolved they merge with the higher source. Some refer to this highest source as God.

If we accept the possibility of this *merge-disband* effect, then we can abandon the view that survival of consciousness and super-psi theories are mutually exclusive. Indeed, both concepts can exist simultaneously.

Given the information obtained through the *Medium7* study, I conclude that information garnered from the spirit world is derived from discarnates (supports the survival of consciousness theory) and at other times may be derived from other sources, including spirit guides, angels, Akashic records and group entities (also known as group consciousness). Given this information, it is logical to suggest that both survival of consciousness theory and elements underlying the super-psi phenomenon can indeed coexist. Given the case studies shared in this book, these theories do not conflict or cancel out one another.

Lessons #6: You Create Your Own Reality.[74]

At the dawn of the new age movement we began to learn about a new way of thinking. We learned that it might be possible to use our own inner power to feel a certain way, partake in various opportunities, or create new opportunities. Prior to the new age movement, we felt that other people or events exterior to us were barriers to our ability to live the lives we dreamed of. Most of the time we felt reactive or victimized by circumstances.

Perhaps some readers still feel locked in the third dimension, where there is a predominant belief that reality is shaped and determined by people and things that cannot be controlled.

I realize that it is difficult for many to embrace the belief that we create our own reality. After all, most of us experience quite a lag between our ultimate desires and their materialization. Some feel they never experience their dreams at all. After one experiences a pattern of absent dreams, negative experiences, despondency, and continuous failure, depression may become prevalent. If we consider the logic of probabilities, when we focus too much on what sometimes appears to be an overwhelming ambush of negative experiences, this reduces our ability to focus on new dreams or nurture old dreams. Remember that space is a field of probabilities, so what you focus on becomes your reality.

The work with mediums in this study has demonstrated some support for the claim that you create your own reality. During readings with mediums, discarnates often shared the encouraging words you must *believe to receive*. If you take this phrase literally, it suggests that if you desire something but don't believe it will occur, it will not materialize. Let's break that down even further. If you believe in something, you have likely visualized it, studied it, and spent some time focusing on it. Perhaps you have even seen others experience this dream, and this has reinforced your belief about your desired outcome. It seems then that there are some necessary actions that need to occur prior to reaching the belief. The act of visualizing and focusing seem to be key ingredients required to create the reality you desire.

You will recall the examination of eighteen participants who received predictions by mediums in the *Medium7* study. The results demonstrated that mediums can indeed make accurate predictions; however, the probability of making accurate predictions about the sitter's future is conditional on other factors.

Quantum physics provides us with an understanding that we cannot predict the space and time of the subatomic particles. Given particles' relationship to thoughts, we cannot predict exactly when the thoughts will eventually manifest. This uncertainty coupled with the notion of free will to produce various thoughts suggests that the outcome is partially controlled from within the individual person.

We reviewed the observer effect, where it was clear that subatomic particles that form the basis of matter change each time they are observed. This scientific experiment helped us link the findings related to predictions with the claim that our thoughts do create our reality. You will also recall that we reviewed how our thoughts, visions, and focus on a subject could enhance the probability to a point where the desire actually is experienced in the physical realm. When sitters' predictions did not materialize within the time predicted, it was hypothesized that free will and its complementary scientific concept, the observer effect, helps substantiate the claim that we have the power to shape our reality. We did of course review how reincarnation and karma also played a role in the probability of a prediction materializing, but the examination of subatomic particles, free will, and quantum physics in general helped substantiate the claims that we have some control over our experience and the people we encounter in our daily lives.

If you are still living in the old paradigm of thinking, one that supports the view that exterior events create your experiences, it is at least useful to be aware of the various lines of evidence that continue to point to the possibility that humans are not just reacting to random events that are happening to them. It is useful to be open-minded about the possibility that you may be very much in control of the reality you experience.

Final Note

The study, *Medium7*, and complementary afterlife studies have taught us these six key lessons about the *real* nature of our reality. Some aspects of these lessons are new information, and other aspects provide support and further confirmation of already existing beliefs about properties of the universe. Mediums provide insights and confirmation about the infinity of the soul. This wisdom has helped sitters find comfort during their time in the physical world. The insight that consciousness resides outside of the parameters of the brain suggests that our personalities and memories go beyond the parameters of the physical body. Such a notion alters the way we perceive individuality. Such notions make the claims of a parallel universe more probable.

The concept of space-time is an abstract one that is difficult to measure and confirm, but the messages shared via the mediums have helped us understand that although the notion of time is absent in the spiritual world, or the various planes of existence beyond the physical, when appropriate, discarnates, angels, or spirit guides can provide specific *times* that correspond with our understanding. In other words we may have difficulty conceptualizing a reality without time, but in the spirit world *they* are able to translate time-related information accurately when it is appropriate to do so.

Through their messages, mediums have confirmed the existence of different planes of realities and provided evidence to substantiate the hypothesis that discarnates are still learning in the spirit world. This learning process is associated with spiritual levels of attainment and varying levels of consciousness.

Most important, we learned that every individual plays a key role in creating their own reality. This understanding produces hope and courage to set positive intentions, create desirable visions, and ultimately paint a life of joy and well-being.

It is important for humankind to embrace the insights shared through scientific research with mediums, NDErs, OBErs, past-life regression participants, and patients experiencing deathbed visions. The lines of evidence from these studies converge and subsequently strengthen the evidence about the existence of an afterlife.

It is most important for you to review the chapter on the challenges of spirit communication and mediumship so you will be better able to distinguish between myth and fact. By reviewing these chapters, you now have a greater comprehension of how to be discerning when you are attempting to interact with the spirit world. When you are using the right intentions, meeting with an authentic medium, and understanding the limitations of spirit communication, you will be on your way to learning more about your purpose of life. You will have a greater understanding of how to address life challenges, and most important, you will be enlightened and more confident about your final destination, also known as the afterlife.

NOTES

Details about the *Medium7* study can be found on <u>www.medium7.com</u>. The following provides key literature referred to in the book and shares additional explanations to qualify points raised in each of the chapters. At the end of the notes section you will also find information about institutions that support the development and examination of metaphysics, mediumship and parapsychology.

Introduction

1. The term *metaphysics* is broad, and in every different article and book I have read to date, the definition varies somewhat. In this book I have narrowed the focus of metaphysics to areas related to *existence*, *space*, *time*, properties of the *universe*, and *consciousness*. These are abstract concepts that are better understood after I elaborate on how the medium's messages help us further understand properties of our universe. A comprehensive definition that describes more concepts that this book does not cover can be found on <u>www.wikipedia.com</u>.

2. Karma-glin-pa, translated into English by Lāma Kazi Dawa-Samdup, *The Tibetan Book of the Dead: The Great Liberation* (London: Oxford University, 1927). This book is the first English translation. There are many different versions available; however, all of the versions focus on the experience of each stage after the physical life has ended. The original work was initiated to guide those who have died in their new environment. I mention this book in this chapter to help readers understand that the focus of my research is more about providing evidence of an afterlife but does not provide a comprehensive understanding of the experience of death and the afterlife.

Chapter 1

3. See the endnote in chapter 7 for further references and notes on reincarnation.

4. James Redfield's, *The Celestine Prophecy: An Adventure* (New York: Bantam Books, 1995) was one of the first books to highlight and popularize the concept of spirituality in an adventure format. In this book the discussion about humans competing for energy is an eye-opener for readers who are not familiar with the notion that humans are composed of energy.

5. In the event that there is any doubt that we are energy, Kirlian photography provides useful visual evidence that everything is indeed energy. Dr. Harry Oldsfield conducts a lecture at the Glastonbury Symposium that provides many visual examples of how Kirlian photography works. This lecture is available on YouTube. Jane & Grant Soloman's, *Harry Oldsfield's Invisible Universe* (Toronto: HarperCollins Canada, 1998) provides a deeper understanding of how such technology can be used to diagnose illness.

6. Dr. Bruce Taino's work has been referenced in books that discuss how understanding vibrational energy enhances our opportunity to heal ourselves. With the advent of holistic healings, such products like essential oils have been studied to better understand how the oils' frequencies can heal the body. Richard Gerber's book, *A Practical Guide to Vibrational Medicine* (New York: HarperCollins Canada, 2001) provides a better understanding of how vibrational energies enhance our understanding of how homeopathy, acupuncture, color/light healing, and other therapies are effective at healing the human body.

7. See detailed references and notes for Danielle MacKinnon under chapter 7.

Chapter 2

8. Two of the five mediums who were willing to share their case studies and real names joined the *Medium7* study after the analysis of "life after death" and "predictions" data was complete. They were still able to provide insights and data that could be used to respond to other research questions in the present study.

9. During my examination of the afterlife, I have not come across a standard definition to describe a medium and psychic. There are some variations in the definition; however, the definition I have provided is a product of the similar responses I received from the ten mediums participating in the *Medium7* study. The literature provides various typologies; as a

result of this variation, I have combined the literature with information provided by the mediums participating in the *Medium7* study.

10. Swami Bhakta Vishita published *Genuine Mediumship or the Invisible Powers* in 1919. Some of the writing on mediumship in the twentieth century provides comprehensive information on both physical and mental mediumship. It is interesting to note that many masters in meditation, such as Swami Bhakta Vishita, who have experienced very high levels of consciousness during meditation, have many mediumistic experiences. Their primary goal is not to conduct or participate in mediumship. In this context clairvoyance and other extrasensory experiences are often an unintended result of frequent meditation and mental work related to strengthening the spirit, body, and mind.

Todd Jay Leonard, *Talking to the Other Side: A History of Modern Spiritualism and Mediumship: A Study of the Religion, Science, and Philosophy* (Lincoln: iUniverse, 2005). Leonard's book provides some rare and useful information regarding physical mediumship.

Chapter 3

11. The term *survival of consciousness* is used interchangeably with the term *life after death* throughout this book. Scholars attempting to be definitive in their studies refer to *survival of consciousness* when they are referring to the survival of a past living agent's memories, personality, perceptions, and experiences. Consciousness is really everything that comprises a human being—that is, everything except for the physical body. Practitioners in the medical field are particularly interested in this discussion. If consciousness can survive the physical death of the brain, this would change the traditional medical perspective that consciousness relies on the functioning of the brain.

Alan Gauld, *Mediumship & Survival: A Century of Investigations* (London: Granada Publishing Ltd, 1982). Gauld's book provides some discussions that reflect the early period of scientific research regarding survival of consciousness theory.

12. In the *Medium7* study I used a variety of research methods to gather the information. These are noted as follows:

1. *Prospective design (A)*: Set up controlled individual experiments where the sitters are recruited by an independent party. Using an independent recruiter would ensure that the medium and the researcher did not know the sitter prior to the experiment.

2. *Prospective design (B)*: Set up controlled group experiments where a group of sitters are recruited by an independent party. Using an independent recruiter would ensure that the medium and the researcher did not know the sitter prior to the experiment. This design would involve the researcher observing the medium conduct a reading with a group of four to six sitters in each group.
3. *Retrospective design(C)*: Obtain a list of sitter's names for each medium. This list formed the basis of a sampling frame. Names of sitters were selected using systematic random sampling to reduce selection bias.
4. *Retrospective design (D)*: Mediums who were not comfortable providing their list of contacts referred or encouraged all of their sitters to contact the researcher for an interview. This design is the least desirable as it enhances opportunities for selection bias. The prospective controlled experiments were used as comparison studies to ensure the results in the more stringent designs were similar.
5. *Focus groups*: Groups of sitters were contacted for a group session to provide comments on the quantitative data that required clarification. Focus groups conducted in the early stages of the study were used to help build the constructs used in the *Medium7* scoring tool.
6. *Key informant interviews:* Interviews with members of the Spiritualist Church, researchers, sitters, and mediums (outside of the study) were contacted to provide comments on various aspects of the study.

13. The website www.medium7.com provides a comprehensive list of all of the research questions posed for the *Medium7* study. The three questions noted in this section specifically relate to questions about the existence of an afterlife. There were other research questions posed to explore the nature of mediumship, predictions, the utility of spirit messages and the nature of reality.

14. In this study, the term *spirit* is used frequently as mediums often refer to *spirit* as a source of knowledge. In some cases mediums receive relevant information from spirit and not from a specific individual discarnate. It is for that reason that a separate question relating to *spirit* was posed.

15. *Medium7's* assessment tool was based on the common themes emerging from focus groups and by an assessment of sitters' comments after a reading with mediums both within and outside of this study. In general, most sitters view the same types of evidence to be worthy of the label

high level of evidence. Constructs relating to *specificity* and *relevance* formed the basis for the statements developed in the tool. If a comment shared by a medium is highly specific and relevant to the sitter, it was categorized as high level of evidence. If a comment is generalizable to many people and not relevant to the sitter, it would be categorized as having low levels of evidence. Sitters have various scores to choose from and can review the criteria prior to scoring their statements.

Scores for relevant and specific statements can be classified as no evidence (0), low (1), moderate (2), and high (3). Scoring a three in this study permits the reading to be included as evidence for life after death. Statements that were not relevant and not specific were classified as no evidence and would receive a score of zero. Hence the scoring tool is based on a four level model ranging from 0-4. Details regarding the criteria used to guide the classification of statements can be found on the www.medium7.com website.

Statements shared in a reading with a medium were scored, and where necessary or applicable, sitters were contacted to confirm scores.

16. The *Medium7* study was not conducted to assess the individual medium's abilities. Given the eligibility requirements for the study, the working assumption was that the study included authentic mediums with *real* psychic abilities so assessing individual capacity was not a study objective. The goal was to pool the results from the ten mediums and learn about the maximum results possible. Mediums have a variety of unique skills; pooling these skills together demonstrates the range of diversity but most important, it establishes confidence about the conclusions drawn from the findings related to the afterlife and predictions.

17. Although not all of the eighty-eight participants were observed under controlled conditions, questions posed to the research participants during their initial interview clarified the arrangements made between the medium and the sitter prior to the reading. In the retrospective designs where the controlled conditions were relatively less stringent, the sitters had no motivation to provide misleading information during the interviews. The type of data admitted to the high-level-evidence category could not have been obtained through fraudulent means.

Conducting fully controlled laboratory experiments with mediums and their sitters is challenging. Although the study design used in *Medium7* was pragmatic and still controlled for the necessary areas, the design offers an opportunity to obtain information directly from sitters who have the best knowledge about their own lives and the discarnates they may hear from during a reading.

18. The actual video of Chad's reading can be seen on YouTube: *Life after Death: A medium conducts a reading with a Nonbeliever.* A prerequisite for the nonbeliever's experiment was that all sitters consent to being videotaped. The idea was to ensure that these experiments would be transparent.

19. To protect Chad's privacy, the specific meaning of this word has been omitted from the book. The specificity of the term and the relevance of what this meant for Chad and his deceased friend was very strong. In this case although donkey-dick is not the name of the person, it is a rare name used to describe an item they would frequently refer to. This is the reason why naming this would be categorized as high-level-evidence.

20. There are a few websites that provide data on the number of names in the world and provide probability calculations for different types of events. After I reviewed these sites, the mode (or the most frequently reported calculation) was used as the reference data used in the book. It should be noted that although I have used the 1:20,000.00 ratio as a general reference point, it is indeed true that some names like John and Bob are more commonly used names that would warrant a lower probability ratio. This reduced ratio should be considered in future studies; however, it should be noted that although the probability would be lower, it would still be a high enough probability that would suggest that the medium could not guess the name *by chance.* In the *Medium7* study, to be rated in the high-level-of-evidence category, the medium would have to achieve at least three high-level-evidence messages. This stringent criteria suggests that the medium would have to demonstrate probabilities that were well beyond the criteria suggesting that the messages provided could not be a result of *chance.*

21. The misses discussed in the context of this statistical model relates to whether all statements provided by a medium during a reading should be calculated. It should be noted that in the *Medium7* study when names were provided, mediums were able to identify the name correctly the first time so the *misses* generally don't relate to the provision of names. Providing names as evidence of survival of consciousness is usually an all or nothing phenomenon.

The probability ratio should be altered if the medium shares other names prior to sharing the correct one. In the *Medium7* study, when the correct name was provided, it was always provided first; in other words the medium was not providing several names prior to sharing the correct one. There were instances where the nickname or mispronunciation occurred but if the elements of the name were similar enough to the correct name, this was still scored accordingly. For example, we had one case where the medium persisted that the name she was hearing was Catrina, but the family pronounced it Catarina (with four syllables and not three as communicated by the medium). After further discussions it was clear that the medium did bring through a discarnate who the sitters could relate to but the medium did not have an Italian accent so the name sounded slightly different. There were several other identifying factors that confirmed that the medium did bring through information from the family's daughter in the spirit world. The information in this reading was included as high-level-evidence.

22. Stanley Krippner and Harris Friedman, *Debating Psychic Experience: Human Potential or Human Illusion?* (California: Praeger Publishing, 2010).

23. Gary Schwartz, *The Afterlife Experiments: Breakthrough Scientific Evidence of Life After Death*. (New York: Atria Books, 2002), 120-121. In this book Dr. Schwartz conducts a number of scientifically rigorous studies. I have selected this study of Patricia Price in particular to demonstrate how an evaluation research design of spiritual phenomenon attempts to reach the scientific standard of validity and reliability. I have also included it as it demonstrates the significant results achieved by a medium when compared to a group of individuals who function with the *normal* five senses. It should be noted that this table has been reconstructed based on the written material in the book. I have also provided examples for the categories, including a name, initials, descriptions, historical facts, and temperament, only to demonstrate what these categories mean; however, these were not examples used in the book. See page 120 to 121 for the original charts and narrative related to this particular experiment.

24. Julie Beischel, "Contemporary Methods Used in Laboratory-Based Mediumship Research," *Journal of Parapsychology*, no.71, Issue: Spring-Fall (2007):37–68.

25. This experiment can be viewed on YouTube by searching the terms Dr. Oz and Dr. Amen Psychic Experiment. There are other emerging studies using brain scans and mediumship. Dr. Andrew Newberg's latest research, published in *PLOS ONE*, involved high-tech brain scans of ten Brazilian mediums, while they dictated messages from the deceased during a trance state.

26. This review of the research should not be considered an exhaustive review; it was also not intended to be a literature review or systematic review. Selected cases and studies were identified to provide the reader with an understanding of how diverse contexts, different professionals (i.e. psychiatrists, doctors), and varying research methods still produce similar findings regarding the afterlife.

27. In Dr. Jeffrey Long's book *Evidence of the Afterlife: The Science of Near-Death Experiences* (New York: Harper Collins, 2010) he provides a comprehensive discussion and review of the nine lines of evidence. These lines of evidence demonstrate how each area contributes to the evidence of an afterlife and refute competing theories that attempt to attribute the NDEr's afterlife experience to other explanations (i.e., insufficient amount of anesthesia, effects of a dying brain, and other explanations).

28. Kenneth Ring and Sharon Cooper, *Mindsight: Near-Death and Out-of-Body Experiences in the Blind* (Nebraska: Morris Publishing, 1999).

29. This surgery is complex, so to understand the details of the surgery and the timelines, this information can be found in Dr. Sabom's book *Light & Death: One Doctor's Fascinating Account of Near-Death Experiences,* (Michigan: Zondervan Publishing, 1998).

30. Brian Bethune, Maclean's Magazine: *What if Heaven is Real?* May, 2013

31. Eben Alexander, *Proof of Heaven, A Neurosurgeon's Journey into the Afterlife,* (New York: Simon & Schuster Paperbacks, 2012)

32. Bob Olson hosts a TV program with many scholars studying various aspects of the afterlife. A one-hour interview with Bob Olson and Dr. Brian Weiss on January 19, 2012, involved a discussion about what past-life regression therapy teaches us about the afterlife. I have paraphrased some of the points expressed in the video.

33. A horoscope reading might include prophetic information about finances, health, relationships, and career.

34. Many books written about Edgar Cayce recount the story of when he revealed that his patient had a past life as a monk. This story is important as it highlights the first recorded incident of a medium sharing information alluding to a past life. It is most important as Cayce was not influenced to investigate past lives; this came naturally after reading recorded messages regarding past lives.

Thomas Sugrue, *The Story of Edgar Cayce: There is a River,* (Virginia: ARE Press, 1997).

35. *Journal of the Society for Psychical Research*, Volume XI, 1903–4, 187 provides a full account of this example of deathbed visions. There is an abundance of literature on deathbed visions in early twentieth century. In 1903 W. H. Myers included several accounts of deathbed visions in his book on *Human Personality and Its Survival of Bodily Death*. James H. Hyslop wrote *Visions of the Dying* in the first issue of the *Journal of the American Society for Psychical Research*. Sir William Barrett, a British physicist, published *Deathbed visions* in various parapsychology journals in the early twentieth century.

36. It should be noted that this grandmother referred to in this chapter is not grandmother Beryl referred to in other chapters. Grandma Beryl's name was conveyed by a medium during a reading but Grandma Henlin (2nd grandparent) experienced the deathbed visions.

37. Details of this remote viewing experiment can be viewed on YouTube: Joe McMoneagle, *Remote viewer No. 1 in the US Army's psychic intelligence unit*, May 2, 2010.

Chapter 5

38. Hudson Tuttle, *Mediumship and Its Laws: Conditions and Cultivations*, (Pomeroy: Health Research Books, 1990).

39. The original quote can be found in the e-book version. See the Project Gutenberg e-book, *Bhakta Vishita Genuine Mediumship or The Invisible Powers*, (Chicago: Advanced Thought Publishing Co., 1919), 105-153.

40. Lisa Williams, a famous and talented medium, has her television program titled *Life among the Dead.* Some of these episodes can be viewed online.

41. Jane Roberts, *Seth Speaks: The Eternal Validity of the Soul*, (New York, Amber-Allen Publishing and New World Library, 1963). This book is also available in audio book format on YouTube.

42. During a reading you will occasionally hear a medium identify a spirit unknown to the sitter; however, the information being communicated is accurate and relevant. If the medium is a strong clairvoyant, he or she will note that the entity communicating is only there to *bring* in the discarnate that is unable to directly communicate to the sitter.

43. Hicks, J., and E. Hicks, *The Astonishing Power of Emotions: Let Your Feelings Be Your Guide*, Hay House Publishers, 2007.

44. Brough Perkins, a medium who participated in this research, used this quote with a research participant. The quote provided was shorter;

however, the author expanded it to further exemplify how our vibrational energy contributes to the type and timing of events that we experience in our reality.

Chapter 6

45. Various journalists have conducted their own polls to gather data about the number of people interested in seeking the services of a medium. After I reviewed various polls, I found 70 percent is the average number since 1990. A research colleague and I also conducted an analysis of online data to assess the growing interest in mediumship in relation to other areas of interest. It was noted that the interest in psychics and mediumship has been growing steadily over the last decade. This type of analysis of online data was conducted using a number of various search terms in Google AdWords.

46. Jerome Groopman, *The Anatomy of Hope: How People Prevail in the Face of Illness*, (New York: Random House Publishing Group, 2005).

47. Esther Hicks and Jerry Hicks, *Ask and It Is Given: Learning to Manifest Your Desires* (Carlsbad: Hay House Publishing, 2008).

48. Paul Halpern, *The Pursuit of Destiny: A History of Prediction* (Massachusetts: Perseus Publishing, 2000). Halpern's book discusses the key scholars in the early twentieth century who helped shape our early and current thinking regarding predictions. Halpern also demonstrates how emerging knowledge demonstrates that because of the uncertainty principle and free will, notions of determinism, that dominated the early nineteenth century, are diminished. Halpern's theories and discussions provide validation for the prediction-related findings produced in the *Medium7* study.

49. Concepts of quantum physics can be challenging for laypersons without a background in physics. To learn more about quantum physics, the movie *What the Bleep Do We Know* is a film released in 2004 that uses nontechnical language and an engaging storyline to introduce viewers to the notion that there is a spiritual connection between quantum physics and consciousness. The movie uses computer-animated graphics and a fictitious character known as Dr. Quantum to explain concepts like the uncertainty principle and the observer's effect. The movie or various related educational videos of Dr. Quantum can be viewed on YouTube.

50. Edgar Cayce's work makes reference to the principle that the soul's purpose was predetermined prior to birth. The uncertainty, he notes,

revolves around the choices that living agents make to achieve their predetermined life goals and soul lessons. In Robert Smith's book, *No Soul Left Behind* (New York: Kensington Publishing, 2005), Edgar Cayce provides answers to a series of questions, related to the theory of determinism and free will.

51. A client's prediction needed to be precise enough to be included in the longitudinal aspect of the *Medium7* study. Not all of the eighteen clients' predictions included in this sub-study had specific dates. The prediction may have included precise information, but without a specific date it was not always possible to confidently measure the result at the follow-up periods.

Chapter 7

52. The areas of quantum theory, reincarnation, and karma are not new doctrines or theories; however, putting them together and applying them to predictions made by mediums is new. Each of these theories should be considered when one is assessing the probability of a medium's prediction manifesting.

53. If you are not a physicist by training, I do recommend that you watch some of the YouTube videos where Dr. Quantum illustrates various quantum physics concepts, such as the uncertainty principle, the observer effect, wave-particle duality, entanglement theory, and the double-slit theory. In addition to my review of many YouTube videos regarding Newtonian physics and quantum physics, I also reviewed the following books to confirm the information being shared on the YouTube videos. I have found for the most part the YouTube videos, while easier to comprehend, provide accurate definitions and explanations to those found in the following two books:

Gregg, Jaeger, *Quantum Information: An Overview* (New York: Springer Science + Business Media. LLC, 2010).

Cannavo Salvator, *Quantum Theory: A Philosopher's Overview*, (New York: State University of New York Press, 2009).

54. Dr. Masaru Emoto's water experiments are highlighted in the movie *What the Bleep Do We Know?* His work with water and their subsequent formations provide strong evidence that thought creates reality. For people who find it difficult to comprehend this notion, the water experiments are useful as they produce visual results that can be critically reviewed and assessed. To view the water patterns that

result from positive thought compared to those resulting from negative thoughts, Google "Masaru Emoto's experiment" under the images section. Dr. Emoto has demonstrated his experiments and has interviews about this subject on YouTube.

55. William Atkinson, *Reincarnation and the Law of Karma: A Study of the Old-New World, Doctrine of Rebirth, and Spiritual Cause and Effect* (Chicago: Yogi Publication Society, Chicago, 1908). This book has been republished in an e-book format available on the Project Gutenberg e-book website. This article provides rich historical information that substantiates the belief in reincarnation amongst various cultures in both ancient and contemporary society.

56. Elaborating on the concept of soul group systems is beyond the scope of this book. However, more information can be found in Dr. Newton's book. Newton's work as a psychologist and master hypnotherapist provides compelling evidence of reincarnation using case studies to substantiate his findings. Michael Newton, Destiny of Souls, *New Case Studies of Life Between Lives*(Woodbury: Llewellyn Publications,2000), 125-190.

57. William Atkinson, *Reincarnation and the Law of Karma: A Study of the Old-New World, Doctrine of Rebirth, and Spiritual Cause and Effect* (Chicago: Yogi Publication Society, Chicago, 1908). This book provides rich historical information about the definition and beliefs regarding karma.

58. Gina Cerminara, *Many Mansions: The Edgar Cayce Story on Reincarnation* (New York: The New American Library, division of the Penguin Group, 1999). This book makes the important link between mediumship, reincarnation, and karma. There are many people who believe in mediumship and the afterlife but are not sure about reincarnation and karma. Dr. Cerminara documents many of Cayce's case studies that demonstrate how information conveyed through mediums can confirm the existence of reincarnation and karma.

Chapter 8

59. Elisabeth Kübler-Ross and David Kessler, *On Grief and Grieving: Finding the Meaning of Grief through the Five Stages of Loss* (Great Britain: Simon & Schuster, 2005).

60. Arthur Conan Doyle, *The History of Spiritualism* (London: Cassell and Company Ltd.,1926), 81-105.

61. Trevor Hall, *The Medium and the Scientist: The Story of Florence Cook and William Crookes* (New York: Prometheus Books, 1984).

62. Roy Stemman, *A Comprehensive Guide to the Extraordinary World of Mediums, Psychics, and the Afterlife: Spirit Communication* (London, Piatkus Books Ltd, 2005).

63. Todd, Leonard, *Talking to The Other Side: A History of Modern Spiritualism and Mediumship* (Nebraska, iUniverse, 2005).

64. Table 13 has been compiled from a number of different pieces of literature. The term necromancy is used in the Bible and in various religious literature. Each religious denominator or sect describes necromancy differently. In most contexts the term has a negative connotation and implies an association with evil. Wikipedia has a comprehensive definition of necromancy and provides a historical review beginning in the early and high middle ages to the modern period.

65. Frances Hill and Karen Armstrong, *A Delusion of Satan: The Full Story of the Salem Witch Trials* (Massachusetts, DA CAPO Press, 2002).

66. Irene McGarvie, *Pious Fraud: How Religion Has Evolved throughout History* (Toronto: Ancient Wisdom Publishing, 2010).

67. This Catholic booklet titled, *Be Careful of Protestant Teachings* can be found online. There are a few reviews online that can be found by entering the title of the booklet in the Google search engine.

68. There are a number of "white light meditation" videos on YouTube. These resources provide a more comprehensive understanding of how this visualization technique can protect your energy fields, limiting the absorption of negative energy from other beings (both spiritual and human beings).

Chapter 9

69. Michael Newton, Destiny of Souls, *New Case Studies of Life Between Lives* (Woodbury: Llewellyn Publications, 2000).

70. Deepak Chopra, *Life after Death: The Burden of Proof* (New York: Three Rivers Press, Random House, 2006). The analogy referred to in this section can be found in Chopra's book. The analogy is paraphrased in the *Medium7* book to respect the copyright requirements.

Chapter 10

71. Many of the mediums in the *Medium7* study referred to the third-dimension concept. This was usually compared to the fourth or fifth

dimensions, which are states of reality that are said to be associated with varying levels of consciousness. The third dimension is the reality that a majority of the population currently experiences. This includes limitations related to space, time, and levels of cognition related to one's abilities. You will not find a concrete definition (in a systematic form at least) for the fourth and fifth dimensions as a majority of mankind has not evolved to these levels and have not experienced these realities while in the physical body. Monks and others who have mastered meditation and other techniques are able to experience these higher dimensions.

72. Kevin Todeschi, *Edgar Cayce on the Akashic Records: The Book of Life* (Virginia: Association for Research Enlightenment Press, 1998).

73. There are a few scholars, including myself, who do not feel that the existence of Super-psi or the Akashic records diminish the claims of survival of consciousness. There is a growing understanding that different sources of information from the spirit world can exist and it is possible that these various sources do co-exist. To have a better understanding of the two theories, the article by Michael Sudduth referred to in this book is accessible online.

Michael Sudduth, "Super-Psi and the Survivalist Interpretation of Mediumship" *Journal of Scientific Exploration,* no.23 (2009): 167–193

74. There are a number of books that have emerged out of the new age movement that shares insights about the power of intent and the ability to create your own reality. In particular, Louise Hay and Hay House Publishing have produced many books that explain and promote this concept. Dr. Wayne Dyer's book is a useful one for those learning the concepts related to this notion.

Wayne Dyer, *The Power of Intention: Learning to Co-create Your World Your Way* (Carlsbad: Hay House, 2004).

RESOURCES

Afterlife TV
www.afterlifetv.com

After-Death Communication (ADC)
www.after-death.com

American Society for Psychical Research
www.aspr.com

ARE Association for Research and Enlightenment
www.edgarcayce.org

Arthur Findlay College
www.arthurfindlaycollege.org

Hay House Radio
www.HayHouseRadio.com

I Can Do It! Conference
www.icandoit.net

Infinite Quest
www.InfiniteQuest.com

Lily Dale Assembly
www.lilydaleassembly.com

Metaphysics Research
www.medium7.com

Near Death Research Foundation
www.nderf.org

Society for Psychical Research
www.spr.ac.uk

Spiritualist Church of Canada
www.spirittualistchurchofcanada.com

Spiritualist Association of Great Britain
www.spiritualistassociation.org.uk

ABOUT THE AUTHOR

Donna Smith-Moncrieffe, director and founder of Metaphysics Research, has been involved in conducting and reviewing scientific evaluation research for the past twenty years. Donna's research interests include mediumship, the survival of consciousness, predictions science and reincarnation—all areas of study that enhance the validity of life after death and augment humankind's understanding of the purpose of existence.

Donna earned her honors Bachelors of Science degree in psychology, sociology, and philosophy from the University of Toronto. She went on to complete a postgraduate diploma in criminology at the University of Toronto. She completed her Masters of Science degree in sociology and social policy at the University of the West Indies.